CRYSTAL
BLADE

KATHRYN PURDIE

KATHERINE TEGEN BOOKS
An Imprint of HarperCollins Publishers

Katherine Tegen Books is an imprint of HarperCollins Publishers.

Crystal Blade

ISBN 978-0-06-241239-3

Typography by Carla Weise
17 18 19 20 21   PC/LSCH   10 9 8 7 6 5 4 3 2 1
❖
First Edition

FOR MY BELOVED
FATHER,
a profound writer, teacher, and an
incredible man. For the strength and faith
he gave me to finish this daunting story.
Rest in peace, Daddy.

Ilvinov Ocean

Isker

Torchev

Ormina

Orelchelm

Montpanon

Bayac Mountains

Illola

Alaise

ESTENGARDE

Artagnon Sea

Sanbriel

Grishina

RIAZNIN

Gensi

Dubrov

Bovallen

ABDARA

SHENGLI

Kamran

Xikeng

CHAPTER ONE

BANNERS RIPPLED WITH THE RED AND GOLD OF RIAZNIN, along with blue, a new color to symbolize the open sky of a free nation. Colorful tents dotted the palace lawns around reviving hedgerows. And between ribbon-wrapped posts, garlands hung with every variety of blossoms.

Only a few weeks ago, these same grounds were tilled by gunpowder and soaked in blood.

I sat at the grandest table at the Kivratide celebration. Moonlight glinted off two bottles before me, red wine and amber kvass. I poured the kvass, averting my gaze from the sleeve of my sarafan. The traditional peasant dress I'd worn for the holiday was also red. Even when I glanced away, my vision swam in the color.

"So you're the one who's been hoarding the candied cherries." Tosya approached me from the side and leaned against the table. I sensed him before I saw his lanky legs and patched trousers. His laid-back aura eased away my momentary gloom. I glanced up to take in his narrow face, tawny skin, long nose, and kind eyes. He plucked a cherry off a small dish, tossed it in the air, and caught it in his mouth.

"I've been hiding them from *you*." I smirked, snatching the dish closer. But Tosya nabbed a second cherry with familiar disrespect.

"What's all this?" He gestured to my flower crown and makeshift throne. "Are you the royal fairy of auras now? Finally found a role in the new world?"

His jab pricked, but I quickly recovered. I could still be useful to Riaznin without being sovereign Auraseer. "I'm the summer queen of Kivratide," I said proudly. "Poets such as you should be kneeling before me."

He burst out laughing and flourished a bow before he grabbed an entire handful of cherries.

"Hey!" I covered the dish with my plate. "I haven't even had one yet."

He continued to chuckle and popped two more cherries in his mouth, which made mine water.

"What's so funny?" I narrowed my eyes and tried not to indulge Tosya. He knew humor was the quickest way to make me lose my composure. The Romska had rebuked me more than once when Tosya worked me into a state of wheezing hysterics, and often when he got me to laugh at myself.

"Summer *king* and *queen*?" His shoulders shook at the irony. "I can't believe Anton agreed to go along with this, especially for a silly holiday to honor the goddess of love."

"I shouldn't have," came Anton's grumbled reply.

I turned in my chair to see the newly elected governor of Torchev approaching. Anton had *attempted* to appear common for the celebration. He sported a green kaftan cut from homespun cloth and set aside his signature polished boots for a simple brown pair. But no amount of plain clothing could mask his regal posture and air of decorum, remnants of his royal upbringing. His aura, however, fell flat with fatigue, and my chest wilted with it. He sank onto his throne beside me.

"What happened with Feliks?" I asked. Anton's old revolutionary ally had been lecturing him for the last several minutes across the gardens.

"He thinks we're not presenting a united front to the people." Anton nudged a leaf from his wreath crown out of his eye. "Feliks says having mock royalty at Kivratide confuses them, even though it's tradition and the people chose us to rule over the festivities."

I rolled my eyes. "We only passed royal decrees that outlaw freedom of speech and the right to bear arms. That's hardly abusing our one day of power."

Tosya snorted and cherry juice dribbled to his chin. Anton cracked a smile and brushed a strand of my dark-blond hair off my face. "Have I told you, you look beautiful today?"

"Six times." I beamed. "I'm hoping you'll make it to ten."

He kissed my hand. "I accept the challenge."

"Challenge?" Tosya scoffed. "He'll make it to twenty without

thinking twice. He practically wrote an ode to your hazel eyes this afternoon."

I ignored Tosya and bumped my knee against Anton's. "Ready for your big speech?"

He took a sharp breath and straightened his knife and fork. My stomach quivered, responding to his simmering anxiety. "I am," he replied.

I lifted an unconvinced brow.

"What speech?" Tosya choked on another mouthful of cherries. He grabbed my goblet of apricot kvass to wash them down.

"Anton is dedicating a monument he's commissioned to honor those who died in the One Day War—the peasants *and* the imperial soldiers." I rubbed Anton's arm. "Things you would know"—I threw Tosya a sharp look—"if you hadn't spent the last few weeks flirting with every servant girl in the palace."

He held up his hands. "I'm writing again. I need inspiration!"

I poked a tattered patch on his vest. "Maybe if you kiss enough seamstresses, they'll sew you proper clothes. Doesn't the 'Voice of Freedom' deserve better than this?"

Tosya's book of poetry had spurred the revolution, but he still dressed like a peasant at all times, not a "reformed gypsy," as some of the people liked to call him. But Tosya still considered himself Romska, even though he'd stopped traveling with the caravans years ago.

He shrugged and nibbled another candied cherry. "That's just the sort of entitled thinking I'd like to avoid, thanks. Why should people have everything they deserve?"

"Well spoken," Anton said. "Write that into your new book."

Tosya nodded absently like he might consider it. His hand snaked out for the rest of my fruit, but I swatted it away. "Besides," he continued, "I think the starving poet look is working for me." He preened, combing sugar-dusted fingers through his hair. "I can't keep the ladies away."

I was on the verge of snorting when Anton's aura shifted, pricking pins and needles under my feet. That was all the warning I received before he drew me in for a kiss that warmed my blood and turned the heads of our nearby guests.

Lightheadedness stole through me as Anton pulled away. I blinked with a stunned grin. "What was that for?"

"For good luck." With a steadying breath, he let go of me, rose from his makeshift throne, and tapped his fork against his crystal goblet.

The gathered people, seated at an eclectic assortment of tables and picnic blankets, hushed and murmured for their neighbors to be quiet. Within moments, five hundred pairs of eyes fastened upon the former prince. Their anticipation skipped along my nerves.

My palms tingled as Anton's nervousness gripped me. The people's energy faded to the periphery of my awareness, as so often happened when my aura latched on to Anton's. I felt the pluck of the cord stringing our auras together, the reverberation.

He withdrew a piece of parchment from his pocket. Its worn creases attested to the many times he'd read it.

Anton bit his lip. A breeze sent his dark hair tumbling across his brow. The candles flickered, bringing out the gold in his brown eyes that were still locked on the paper.

The people were silent. My heart beat in time to the pulse in Anton's wrist. The parchment trembled in his grip, and my knees responded with a shiver. He wanted to console the people and give them hope for the future, not just one day of forgetting as they lost their troubles in Kivratide.

He folded the parchment, set it down, and turned to me, extending his hand. I stood and laced our fingers together. Courage surged through him and broadened his chest. When he looked back to the people, he appeared as the emperor he could have been, the more meaningful leader he now was. Eyes full of sympathy but sure vision. He didn't let go of my hand.

"People of Riaznin, partakers in liberty, Kivratide has brought us together for a day of celebration. It has long since been a day of professing admiration and making promises, of planning a dependable future with someone." His thumb brushed over mine. "Sonya and I wish to carry on this tradition."

My body flushed with warmth. I felt both shy and honored that Anton acknowledged my role in front of everyone. As I turned to smile, ice tore through my chest. I drew in a tight breath and looked out to see where the threatening sensation radiated from. Across a grouping of tables, Feliks's unsettling blue eyes bored into mine. The revolutionary ally who went against Anton's orders by marching on the palace in the One

Day War had been elected governor of Isker, therefore winning himself a seat on the Duma, the forming council of governors who would jointly rule Riaznin.

As Anton continued speaking, I worked to match myself to the steady beat of his aura and pushed away Feliks's cold energy. I did more—I lifted my chin and met his intimidating gaze with a lofty stare of my own.

Feliks wouldn't bully me like he did to gain power among the revolutionaries—like he'd surely attempt with the new Duma.

"We will not attain an ideal government just because we desire it," Anton said, his voice echoing into the far reaches of the palace grounds. "Change is a bitter friend. It remembers the old ways with frustrated fondness and expects perfection in the new transformation overnight." My muscles cramped as some of people the shifted uncomfortably. A nobleman in a velvet kaftan stared in disdain at a ragtag peasant man sharing his same table. "Let us choose a better path. Let us be slow to judge. Tolerant. Forgiving of each other. Let the memories of those we loved be our reminder to remain stalwart in our continued fight for equality."

Anton motioned to a group of men standing in a nearby clearing. Four of them held torches and surrounded a tall structure covered with a great red cloth. Two women walked forward, one a fine lady in a pearl-scalloped headdress, the other a peasant woman in a blue sarafan and floral headscarf. They reached together for the cloth, and with a nod to time it perfectly, they pulled it to the ground, revealing the monument Anton had commissioned.

A small gasp escaped my mouth. I'd known a monument was being built, but Anton hadn't shared any details. He'd wanted it to be a surprise.

As I gazed over the sculpture, I felt the people's auras shower my own admiration with a blanket of awe. The monument was a bronze obelisk covered with nicks and scratches. A marble dove was perched on top, its wings unfurled. In Tosya's book of poetry, a dove in flight symbolized a free Riaznin. Glowing with pride for my friend, I twisted around to find him. He'd remained back near a tree. His gaze was lifted at the monument, his mouth slowly spreading in a smile.

Anton laced his fingers through mine and led me away from our table to the grassy clearing. The people rose up and followed after us, walking to the base of the monument. Their auras were reverent. Even the children were quiet.

What had first appeared to be flaws in the sculpture were in actuality engraved names, scrawled in all directions and around every space on the four tapered sides. They were the names of the people who had died in the One Day War.

Anton caught my eye, then touched the side of the obelisk that faced northward. There, in a prominent place, was the name, *Pia Lisova*.

I took a startled breath, my throat growing thick with emotion. I saw more than those two words scratched in bronze. I saw Pia's heart-shaped face. Her radiant smile. I felt her echoes imprinted inside me, the light and loving dance of her aura.

My dear friend hadn't died in the battle. She'd been unaware of any brewing revolution. She'd died because she came too close to the crossfire between Emperor Valko and me. But Anton honored her, just the same.

I looked up at him. He'd been watching my reaction in earnest. My eyes burned and blurred in the torchlight, in the haze of my gathering tears. "Thank you." My voice was a soft croak.

His smile revealed the vulnerability he knew I felt within him. *"The mighty isn't one, but many,"* he said, his voice raised for the people as he read the inscription at the base of the monument—words from Tosya's book of poetry—but his eyes never left mine. "Riaznin is free because of you."

I heard the rush of everyone's trembling breaths. Some crept closer and touched the monument themselves, their fingers running along the groove of a name I didn't know.

As I watched each moment of recognition, each private memorial, I leaned my head against Anton's chest. His arm circled my waist. Peace flowed between us all, pulsing solidarity through my veins. Despite all of our differences, the people shared one thing in common—the loss of someone we had known or loved. I rubbed the frayed end of the black ribbon of mourning around my wrist.

The quiet wore on as the people took turns at the foot of the monument. Several long minutes passed, and then the children grew restless. The teenaged boys and girls also fidgeted and started chatting on the fringes of the gathering. A girl near my age of seventeen approached me, biting her lip. "Might we announce the last game now . . . or should we not celebrate any more tonight?"

"Um." I glanced at Anton, and he gave a small nod. "I think that would be all right."

The girl's face lit up. "It's time to seek out the fern flower," she called to everyone. "Our queen will lead the way!"

As the people turned their attention to me, my pulse raced with a thrill of purpose. Until today, I'd never been a leader of anything—anyone—and the feeling it incited was more intoxicating than barley wine.

Murmurs of excitement rippled through the crowd. My chest filled with a sustaining breath. Giving a mischievous smile, I said, "Come with me, girls. Now is our chance to gain an advantage on the boys." My invitation gave everyone permission to set aside their mourning—at least long enough to give the favorite tradition of Kivratide justice, the moment every young, hopeful lover had been waiting for.

The girls began to gather on the path, and I stepped forward to lead them, letting go of Anton's hand. My fingers curled, wanting his touch back. "You *will* come to find me, won't you?" I gave him a threatening look that said he'd better join me in this game.

He lowered his voice, but it still rumbled in its deep octave, his endearing difficulty to whisper. "I think you should know—before you get too carried away in that orchard—ferns do not flower."

"That's the point." This impossible quest was merely an excuse to play hide-and-seek with one's beau, and if a girl were lucky, have a few minutes alone with him before the trumpets sounded, ending the game. "Makes the quest all the more drawn out." With a suggestive lift of my brows, I said, "Hurry and find me before some other boy does."

Anton frowned, not amused. I laughed and spun away, dashing down the path to join the other girls. They moved aside to grant me the lead. Together, we headed into the palace orchard, no candles in our hands. Darkness was half the game.

As soon as we broke the tree line, the girls darted off in various directions. Their giddiness danced inside me. I rushed deeper into the orchard, leaping over tree roots and narrow streams. I'd left my shoes beneath the banquet table, but it didn't matter. Being barefoot heightened all the sensations of life around me, the night birds, the small creatures, the growing things of the earth, the rising energy of a hundred hiding girls.

Faraway, the strum of balalaikas and beating drums played the lovers' song of Kivratide.

Boys entered the orchard. They plowed through the grass in their urgent searching. There was only so much time while those outside "Kivra's forest" turned a blind eye.

This was the first time I'd played this game. The Romska didn't worship Kivra or any of the seven gods, while the sestras at the convent demanded we save our devotion for Feya, goddess of prophecy and Auraseers. But I'd lain awake at night while my best friend, Yuliya, had told me stories of Kivratide and the culminating game of the fern flower. That was how Yuliya's mother and father had met.

Since Yuliya first told me of Kivratide, my head swam with romantic fantasies and fiercer dreams. Living freely outside the convent walls, no need to hide among the Romska, no forced servitude under the emperor.

One of the boys came near and reached for my hand before he saw who I was. I shifted away, and he fled past.

I ran into the darker stretches of the orchard, ducking under branches and skirting around trees. There was no more empire to own me. My possibilities were limitless. I could do anything I pleased. I clutched my crown of blossoms and ran faster. My breaths came quickly, my smile broad and unrestrained.

Girls' shrieks of laughter rang out. My heart pounded as more and more lovers paired together. I ran a couple more minutes, then stopped to catch my breath. I looked around me. Anton should have caught up by now.

I wrapped my arms around myself and kept walking—slower this time, taking care with my footing. A twig crunched beneath my toes, and I winced, though I wasn't sure why I felt the need to be silent. Dread trickled icy water through my chest. I couldn't say why. I glanced into the shadows, half expecting to see Feliks's cold eyes staring back at me.

The ominous feeling magnified. My muscles tensed, ready to spring. The night wasn't terribly dark, but it felt weighted, thick. The heaviness seeped inside my blood and coiled around my brain.

Somehow, without feeling another person's aura nearby, I knew I wasn't alone.

Foreboding swept through me like fire. Something rustled behind me. I jerked around.

Several feet away, in the perfect center between two trees, stood a figure swathed in black. Her cape fell to her narrow hips where the outline of her skirt stood out faintly against the dark orchard. The hood of her cape cast her face in shadow.

I startled, my heart caught in my throat. I couldn't grasp her feelings, her intentions.

She faced me squarely and statuesque. "Do you really think you deserve this, Sonya?" Her voice sounded shredded, like it raked past a gravel-lined throat. "Did you honestly believe it would last?"

I stepped backward. "What do you—?"

I never got the chance to finish. From the opposite end of the orchard came a high-pitched scream.

CHAPTER TWO

"Stop, Sergei, you'll kill him!" a faraway girl cried.

I whipped around just as a crack of gunpowder split the air. Gasping, I grabbed the folds of my skirt and broke into a run. Then I remembered the hooded girl.

I spun back around and froze. The space where she'd stood between the two trees was empty.

More shouts sprang up in the distance. I took off running again, racing back through the orchard. Another scream. Boys and girls popped out from behind the trees like field mice from burrows. "What's going on?" a boy with mussed hair and flushed cheeks asked as I flew by.

I shook my head and called backward between gasps of air, "Anton . . . have you seen Prince Anton?"

"He isn't a prince, miss," the boy replied.

His insolence splashed oil on the fire of my panic. I flung

around, eyes sharp and intimidating. "Have. You. Seen. Prince. Anton?"

The boy gave a hard swallow. "No, I haven't."

I dashed away, sprinting faster toward the shouts and crazed, violent energy that throbbed madly through my body. I tunneled my awareness on the path ahead. If I wanted to help, I couldn't let myself be overcome by anyone else's aura. Last time I'd failed to do that, half of the convent had burned, along with most of my sister Auraseers.

I tore around a tree just as a dark figure converged onto the same path. We nearly collided. For a moment I thought it was the hooded girl come back to haunt me. Then the moonlight caught the slant of Anton's aristocratic nose and the thin sculpt of his upper lip. I threw myself at him, practically wringing him with my embrace.

"Sonya!" His arms squeezed back with equal force. He kissed my head twice.

"Where were you?"

"I couldn't find you."

We spoke over each other.

A third voice shouted above us, "Sergei, no!" Another blast of gunpowder fired. This time from much closer.

Anton and I stilled. I searched the auras within my awareness. "No one's dead," I said at last. "At least not yet."

He released me, and we launched in the direction of the gunshot. "Stay back," he said, voice tight. "This will be dangerous."

I pushed a branch aside from my face. "You have me."

Anton flinched. His shock of fear chased through my limbs. "You're not getting involved."

More shouts rose up. We didn't stop running. Not even as angry auras clawed through my body.

Anton and I emerged from the orchard into a rose garden on its west side. The night brightened without a leafy canopy above us. A large marble fountain rested at its center, pouring water from tiered bowls.

A few couples from the fern flower quest gathered at the edges of the garden, and more trampled in by the moment. Their auras pinched my breath and locked my muscles. They clung to the tree line, observing what was happening with terrible fascination, as one observes a ship sinking when both feet are on the shore.

Two boys, a noble and a peasant, crouched at opposite sides of the fountain, taking cover from each other. The peasant held a musket, the noble a flintlock pistol. A girl huddled beside each boy. One held her hands protectively over her head, while the other, a baron's daughter I recognized, gripped the noble boy's sleeve, crying, "Sergei, please." My nose burned from her tears. Chunks of the fountain had been blasted off, but no blood stained the stones around it.

Anton leaned to the ebony-skinned girl beside us. "What's happening here? Why are these boys armed?"

The girl's eyes widened when she saw who addressed her. "Your Imperial High—" She caught herself mid-bow and bit down on her lip. "Rurik, that peasant boy"—she pointed at him— "insulted Sergei's fiancée, Helene, during the Blind Man's Kiss game this afternoon. It turned into a fight, and the boys planned this duel. But it got out of hand before it even started."

We glanced back to the fountain, about twenty feet away. The noble boy, Sergei, held his pistol tightly drawn, its barrel pointed upward, his thumb on the hammer. He called out to Rurik, his words a muddled slur, "You think you're above us because your filthy lot conquered *one* battle?" His injured pride made me feel both larger and smaller than myself. My head prickled, and my limbs grew slack. He was drunk. "The emperor may have removed his crown, but the nobility still bear our lands and titles. You peasants are nothing without us!"

Rurik burst out in laughter, but his cockiness wasn't genuine. My stomach quivered with his nausea, my brow flashed with perspiration. "It's only a matter of time before your lands are partitioned and your precious titles are stripped away. Let's see how well you like sweating for your bread then, like the rest of us." He scoffed. "You'd blanch at the sight of dirt under your nails."

A blaze of anger swept my body. My hand fisted. The pistol fired. The bystanders gasped. Their panic ricocheted through my chest. My ears rang as I tried to comprehend what had happened. Sergei's pistol smoked, but it still pointed upward. He'd shot into the air.

Rurik couldn't see that from his crouched position on the

other side of the fountain. With a cry of fear and desperation, he sprang to his feet and whirled around to charge the noble, his musket eye level. Sergei scrambled to reload his pistol. Helene screamed and dashed out from her hiding spot and into the cover of the orchard. At the same time a new influx of people flooded the garden.

Anton ran toward Rurik. "Nobody move!" His voice rumbled with authority. "Lay down your weapons!"

Rurik's eyes rounded. "It's the prince!" Frightened, he whirled to face Anton, his pointed musket swinging around with him.

My heart flared with dread. I rushed forward. Everyone's frenzied emotions begged to manifest through my body. But my own feelings rose above them all. "Don't shoot him!"

Rurik recoiled, jerking the musket toward me.

"Lower your gun!" Anton shouted.

With a start, Rurik returned his aim to him.

"No!" My voice cracked.

A spasm sliced through Rurik's brow. The musket barrel shook. Beads of sweat dripped from his hairline. His shoulders slumped as his panicked intent drained out of him. He lowered his arm, and the gun clattered to the ground. I started breathing again. Sergei gave a drunken chuckle from the opposite side of the fountain. Rurik growled and grabbed his musket. Anton was still in his line of fire.

"No, turn away!" My terror slashed through Rurik's aura.

He spun left and blindly shot into the orchard.

The blast echoed in my ears. Hot pain seized me, and I sucked in a cry.

A gurgled whimper rose from a few feet behind me. The baron's daughter stepped out from the trees and held a clenched hand to her upper arm. Rose-red blood spilled through her fingers. Her head nodded incoherently, and she collapsed to her knees.

"Helene!" Sergei dropped his unloaded pistol and ran over to her.

Rurik gaped, stumbling backward. "I—I didn't mean to . . ."

A few heads twitched toward me. I lifted a trembling hand to my throat. My mouth opened, but I couldn't think to speak. I looked to Anton and shook my head wildly. His gaze cut into me, his shock and rage coloring my shame even darker. Tears flowered behind my eyes.

"It was an accident," I told him. My tongue loosened to spill the words. A ripple of murmurs spun around the garden.

I glanced at the others and clapped eyes on Feliks. His hatred made my gut twist. He looked winded, like he'd just arrived on the scene. He paused near the fountain, his cunning eyes sliding from Rurik to Helene to me. My chest caved with anxiety.

Anton had insisted that, for my protection, the extent of my abilities remain a secret. No other Auraseer had manifested the unheard-of gift to manipulate another person's emotions. If the people found out, I wouldn't be trusted. They would surely fear me and threaten my life. Anton never told Feliks what I truly did to make Valko abdicate. And even then, it was only when Valko held a dagger to my throat that I managed to open a channel between us and use it to curb his will.

Anton's mouth formed a hard line as he caught sight of the man who'd betrayed him in the revolution. "Yes, it was an accident," he said to everyone, his voice strong and edged in determination. He strode over to Rurik and took the musket from his stunned hands. "These boys were only try to bully each other with a little gunpowder. You all saw that." Crossing to the other side of the fountain, he collected Sergei's pistol from the ground. "Unfortunately, someone got hurt." He tossed both weapons into the water, rendering them useless.

My body still throbbed with the echoes of Helene's pain. She moaned and rolled onto her back. I hurried over to her side, where Sergei knelt and ripped open her sleeve to expose the wound. Around the shot, her skin was folded back, raw and bloody.

Tamping down my revulsion, I tore off a length of my slip and began wrapping her arm. Sergei's nostrils flared. I felt his violent burst the moment before he sprang to his feet.

"Anton!" I shouted in warning.

Sergei launched toward Rurik. Anton raced between them and fought to hold Sergei back. While they struggled, another noble boy darted out from the hedges. He bolted for Rurik and clocked him hard in the jaw. Rurik blinked with pain, then growled and struck back, slugging the noble in the gut.

The entire garden broke into chaos. Everyone's pain and

anger battered through me. I gasped for breath and dragged Helene back a few feet so she wouldn't be trampled, clinging to her aura so the others wouldn't pummel me.

Someone was thrown into the fountain with a loud splash. In front of me, two boys shuffled back and forth in a double headlock. To my right, a girl dug up stones from the ground and prepared to hurl them. Anton was lost in the madness.

I had to do something. Calm everyone's emotions, bend their impulses.

I winced and let their pain overtake me. I opened myself to all the sensations around me.

As I clenched my jaw, bracing myself against the torture, a pair of piercing blue eyes met mine across the dust-choked air of the scuffle. Feliks's aura lit inside me, a dark flame curling with curiosity and challenge.

He wasn't watching the fight; he was watching me.

Caught unaware, I was thrust back into myself, my growing connection to the people broken.

More people spilled into the garden, among them soldiers. They wore the red and gold regimentals of the imperial guard, but with a sash of blue tied over their jackets, denoting them as soldiers of the new regime. They took aim with their muskets.

"Hold your fire!" Anton's voice shouted above the chaos.

At the warning of firearms, the boys and girls drew to a shuffled halt. A few grunts came from those pinned and half beaten on the ground.

Anton staggered forward, raking a hand through his

disheveled hair. His wreath crown was missing. "Everyone will leave the palace grounds at once!" he announced resolutely, though his voice came on a labored breath of air. "I suggest on your way out you pass the monument and think a bit harder about those who died to buy you the liberties you so ungratefully abuse."

His gaze found its way to me, and he glanced over my body, as if to assess that I hadn't been hurt. Once he saw I was fine, his anger slammed my heart against my ribcage. My guilt made it pound harder. I'd lost control, used my power in public, almost killed someone.

"Guards, escort everyone off the premises," Anton said. "The Kivratide celebration is officially over."

CHAPTER THREE

"WHAT BROUGHT YOU TO THE GARDEN SO QUICKLY?" ANTON asked Feliks once the three of us were alone. A seam was torn at Anton's shoulder, but no significant pain radiated from him— at least no physical pain. His body shifted, angling slightly away from me as I approached him and Feliks by the fountain. "Searching for the fern flower, too?"

Feliks wasn't amused. "I was searching for *you*."

Anton's mouth gave a wry twist. "I'm flattered, but you should know I'm taken." Feliks's eyes narrowed. It wasn't like Anton to be so sardonic, but having to deal with Feliks right now, on top of everything that had just happened, taxed the last of his patience and energy.

"I came to tell you the Shenglin have raided two more border towns." Feliks's energy whirred quickly in calculation, fanning through me like a deck of shuffling cards. "We just received the news. The Shenglin are headed toward Gensi.

They may try to take the city."

"The Shenglin have never broken our defenses at Gensi," Anton replied.

"The Shenglin have also never attacked while we were so vulnerable."

Anton exhaled with mounting worry. "What can be done to help? We can't afford to send any more regiments." Between the One Day War and those who had withdrawn from Riaznin's military, defiant to the democracy, Torchev had lost half its soldiers. "Once the Duma forms, we can rally more support and recruit soldiers from all quarters of the nation."

"We cannot delay any longer," Feliks said. "The Duma must take the government now."

"But it will take weeks for the rest of the governors to complete the journey to Torchev."

I stepped closer, in defense of Anton. "How can Riaznin be represented fairly until they do?" I asked Feliks. Only four governors were here, including him and Anton. But the Duma was designed to be a council of twenty.

Feliks cocked his head, as if mildly affronted I'd spoken. "Times are desperate," he replied. "Would a father and mother wait to give their starving children bread if two were missing from the table?"

"*Sixteen* are missing from the table," I quipped.

His brows lifted slightly. "And you are not one of them." Feliks's tone was matter-of-fact, but the ice in his aura was cold enough to freeze kvass. He turned to Anton. "Governors Trusov and Dernova are meeting at the Swallowtail Inn tonight. As provisional ruler of Riaznin, I hope you'll come to discuss it with us."

Anton took a deep breath and held it. My chest tightened with his inner struggle. "Very well," he said at last.

Feliks gave him a curt nod. "I'll arrange for a carriage. Come directly to the stables."

"I'll walk Sonya back to the palace, then meet you there."

Feliks nodded again and his gaze slid to me, traveling up to my flower crown before returning to my eyes. "Good evening, Sonya."

I stiffened, saying nothing in return.

He exited the garden the way he came, his pace steady, his steps surefooted. "I don't trust him," I whispered to Anton. "He's trying to seize control of the government while it's susceptible."

"I have no doubt about that," Anton replied wearily without meeting my gaze. He looked around at the chipped fountain, the stones dug up from the ground, the blood spatter from where Helene had been lying. "Still, what Feliks has suggested may be the best course of action." He crossed a few feet away and picked up his flattened wreath crown, then tossed it into the fountain with the drowned guns.

I bit my lip, sensing the angry pulse of his aura, which hadn't let up after Feliks left us. "I doubt anyone caught on that I have hidden power."

Anton gave me an incredulous look. "You think *that's* my largest concern? That boy almost shot you. And that girl, Helene, could have died."

"*You* could have died. That was all I could think about."

"You shouldn't have come into the garden in the first place. How did you think you could help, Sonya?"

"I stopped the One Day War, didn't I?"

"You stopped *one* man who you knew far too well. *Valko* called off the battle."

Except for Anton and Tosya, none of the revolutionaries knew I'd used a secret power to compel Valko to relinquish his throne. They were told I persuaded him by taking advantage of his fondness for me—if sadistic ownership could be defined as fondness. Now Valko was in the dungeons awaiting his trial, another undertaking delayed until the full Duma arrived.

I balled my hands, biting my tongue. I didn't want to argue; I wanted to find out what was happening with Shengli and what Feliks proposed Anton should do about it. "Let me come with you to the meeting tonight," I said, as we began walking out of the garden.

Anton turned apologetic eyes on me. "They won't admit you. You don't hold any leadership position."

"Then let me come as your Auraseer. I'll warn you if anyone seeks to do you harm. I did the same for Valko. I've attended dozens of council meetings."

"That was different," he replied. "You went as Valko's *guardian*. If I bring you with me, what message of trust will that convey to the new governors?" At nineteen, Anton was the youngest governor elected across Riaznin, but I feared his age wouldn't make him any less of a threat to the Duma. He was the last member of a tyrannical royal family, and now he held a powerful position in the new government.

"But I want to be helpful."

"You *are* helpful, Sonya. You organized this celebration. It was a major step forward in uniting Torchev." His gaze drifted back to the rubble we left behind us in the garden.

We walked through the orchard in silence. Anton's anger lifted, but deep concern still hung about him. I wished I could carry some of his burdens, but more than wanting to help Anton, I wanted to help Riaznin. I'd felt a legion of auras when I'd persuaded Valko to abdicate his throne; I'd felt the people's rampant desire for liberty. Triggering the fall of the monarchy wasn't enough. The people needed more than that.

As we passed onward through the trees, I turned my head, vainly searching for a fern flower.

CHAPTER FOUR

ANTON HAD BEEN GONE FOR THREE HOURS. AS I WAITED FOR him to return and bring me word of the meeting, I paced the main level of the palace. I was barefoot, wearing only a linen nightdress and thin robe against the stifling heat of the night. But I didn't have to fear anyone seeing me. The interior and exterior guard were outside bellowing songs, drunk on the last of the Kivratide wine.

I moved through the great lobby and tiptoed over what remained of the blasted amber-inlaid floors. They'd been patched with common cement and unvarnished oak planks. The rest of the room looked equally scarred, having taken the brunt of the damage from the One Day War. Marble banisters were pocked from musket fire, and moonlight filtered in through the gaps of boarded-up windows. Far above me, chunks were missing from the fresco of the seven gods of Riaznin, riding their seven steeds around a seven-beamed sun.

I rubbed anxious palms on my nightdress and ventured eastward down the main corridor. Everything inside me felt constricted. I ached for the open road I'd traveled with the Romska. Riaznin was free now, but it didn't feel that way.

Veering down a branching hallway, I gave myself over to instinct and turned my course on any sudden whim. Nightmarish feelings flitted in and out of me. The sleeping auras of the palace. But they couldn't do me any real harm.

Eager for an escape, I fell into an old game I used to play with Yuliya: guessing what scandalous dreams our sister Auraseers had when they were asleep and couldn't bully us anymore.

Auras snatched at me like nipping kittens, excited to play.

The first one danced across my awareness, and a woozy smile lifted the corners of my mouth. As the feeling intensified, I gave a snort of laughter and glanced down to make sure my robe was cinched closed around my nightgown.

This dream was easy to solve. Someone in the palace believed they were naked.

I tripped forward, hardly able to walk in my half-awake state. I scratched an itch beneath the black ribbon on my wrist and sought another dream to lose myself in.

A dark mist of sensation seemed to collect in the air. I trudged through it and extended the reach of my awareness, tasting it deeper. The writhing feelings of dreamers sent my imagination spinning. I pictured vampires from old Romska myths. Scaled monsters in the fathomless sea. Demons in human skin who ate runaway children. Fitting nightmares for the dark auras I felt.

Shivering in fear, my thoughts turned to more rational terrors. Thieves in masks. Murderers in black clothing. Criminals who crept through easy entrances in ramshackle palaces.

A cold breath slid down my spine. I quavered and felt the bite of my wet and frozen feet. I stared at my toes and frowned. Not wet, though the dampness felt real.

A prickle of familiarity made goosebumps rise on my arms. I could almost pinpoint the source of the dream. Almost. My head was too muddy. I stumbled onward, nearly sleepwalking. Sliding against the walls, the halls closed in around me. Narrow. Stone-lined. I blinked and scratched my wrist. No, these walls were plaster. Wood.

Something sharp struck my back. The stab of a knife. I cried out and whirled around. The pain let up. "Hello?"

I couldn't see into the patches of surrounding darkness. It didn't matter. No one could be here with me. No auras pulsed nearby. The pain I'd just felt, vivid though it was, seemed to radiate from farther away.

"Hello?" I called again, my voice shaky as I remembered the hooded girl from the orchard.

The piercing pain of a blade ripped across my throat. I gasped and doubled over. Frantically, I glanced around me and clamped my neck to stop the flow of blood from the new wound.

But I felt no blood. No cut. No wound.

I labored to steady my breathing. Since the One Day War, I experienced other people's sensations more acutely. I recognized their sources more readily. I just needed to force logic into my tired mind. Whose murderous dream was I feeling?

The pain vanished, replaced by a terrible thrill of satisfaction. It pumped through my veins with energy, urgency, desire. Then, just as quickly, the satisfaction withered. The pain wasn't enough. The dreamer wanted something more, something darker, something endlessly gratifying.

Realization hit my sleep-addled mind like a brick to the head. I gasped again. I'd been wrong. This madness wasn't the aura of some dreamer. It incited a level of violence that felt more lucid, more tangible.

Like snakeskin, I shed the dark aura holding me in its clutches. My mind jolted wide awake and pieced the puzzle together. Moments ago, I'd felt a damp coldness. *The dungeons.* I'd sensed its distinct atmosphere before. But the person's aura emanating from within it now wasn't one I recognized. This wasn't the emperor; this was someone else—an intruder with murderous impulses. At least two people were dead already, probably guards. I'd felt their deathblows. Worse, I'd felt the lust for more blood, a craving for one final, satisfying slaughter.

The last piece of the puzzle locked into place. My hands went clammy. The floor seemed to fall out from beneath me. Spinning around, I bolted down the narrow corridor and around the first corner.

An assassin was loose in the palace. An assassin who'd already killed. Who meant to kill again.

Only one target made sense. The palace dungeons held only one prisoner.

Valko.

CHAPTER FIVE

I FLED DOWN THE STONE STAIRS AND THROUGH THE MAZELIKE corridors of the dungeons. My heart crashed and seized in a violent rhythm. I climbed over the rubble in the passageways, fallen debris from cannon blasts of the One Day War. Repairs to the dungeons had gone neglected, what with the work needed aboveground. I skidded through crumbled stones and slipped on spots where the ground was wet with condensation. I took no care to be quiet. Stealth wasn't an option, and time was a luxury I did not have. As my robe caught on a jagged, broken beam, I didn't bother untangling it. I yanked it off and raced farther into the darkness.

Only a few torches glowed between the long intervals of pitch black. I groped the walls like a blind girl. Twice I tripped and fell. I scarcely felt the pain. I scrambled back to my feet and kept running, running.

Horrible emotions slashed into my aura. The assassin's

seething hatred. His bloated sense of supremacy. Just as his impulses raged to a soaring height, making me feel unconquerable, more deaths assaulted me. They ripped through my belly. Strangled me for air. Knocked hard blows to my head. They sucked me of energy. I gasped, panic flaring, each time they struck. They sent me stumbling to the stones. I dragged myself up and fled onward.

Crumpled bodies littered the ground. Fallen guards. I passed at least six, then stopped counting. I was too late to help them. I couldn't let my guilt consume me. I fought to detach myself from the lingering pain of their deaths and attuned to Valko's distinctive energy. I would know if he died.

I couldn't let him die.

That thought was as terrifying as the blood and carnage all around me.

At last I came to the long gallery of cells and dashed across it to the solitary prison that once held Anton and Tosya. The heavy door was shut and hung crooked on its hinges. More damage from the war. I pried it open and a cloud of dust and pebbles showered down over me. Coughing, I waved them away and peered within. Enough torchlight from the outer corridor bled inside so I could see into the room. It lay in ruins. This wasn't Valko's prison.

I grabbed the nearest torch from its sconce and raced around the corner into the gallery.

I heard a scuffing noise behind me, like feet skidding on gravel. I glanced over my shoulder. Narrow corridors branched off the foot of the gallery, but I couldn't see past the bright ring of light from my torch. My heart pounded. For the third time today, I had the eerie sense that someone was watching me, though I didn't feel the close pulse of another aura nearby.

The scuffing sounded again, this time from the gallery. The dungeons' stonewalls reverberated the noise. There was no way to tell where it had originated.

It didn't matter. I ground my teeth and rushed on through the darkness. The noise was probably a rat. Or if it *was* the hooded girl, she could very well *be* the assassin. I should have guessed her intent. I had to find Valko before she did.

The number of cells overwhelmed me. The length of the gallery rivaled the great corridor on the main floor of the palace. Its width measured at least thirty feet and held cells on both sides. I raced forward, shining my torchlight into each barred prison. I searched for Valko. Prayed I wasn't too late. Ignored the tug in my mind that asked why I cared if he died.

I neared the middle of the gallery. Up ahead on the left was an open cell door. I bolted for it with renewed speed and strength.

Inside, Valko lay slumbering on a bed of straw. He looked peaceful. Unaware of the person crouched beside him like a panther.

The assassin wasn't the hooded girl. He was a man dressed in black with a shock of red, greasy hair. His beady eyes turned on me. My heart jumped with his desperate aura. He lunged for Valko, hand raised, his grip on the hilt of a gleaming dagger.

I shouted Valko's name. Hurtled my torch at the assassin. The flame streaked. Pinwheeled through the air. It gouged the man in the shoulder. Seared me with his pain.

He hissed and dropped his dagger. The torch fizzled out. The gallery's firelight kept the space dimly illuminated.

Valko's eyes shot open the same time I leapt for the blade. "Sonya?" he asked. His voice rang hoarse from disuse.

I ran inside the cell. My fingers wrapped around the dagger's hilt. I spun on my knees to face the assassin. He was too quick for me. With a practiced move, he hit my wrist, and the blade flew behind Valko. "Fetch that!" I yelled at him.

He didn't have time to react. The assassin lunged for him where he lay. The man's large hands circled Valko's throat. I sprang on the assassin and pounded my fists on his back. With little trouble, he jerked me off of him. I landed hard on my side.

The man's focus never tore from Valko, his grip never eased. My head throbbed with Valko's pain and my own. For a moment, it overtook me and I writhed on the cell floor, blackness prickling my vision.

Valko's arm stretched out. His fingers reached for the snuffed-out torch. I nudged it into his grasp. His face mottled a darker shade as he hefted it. My muscles flexed with his exertion. He swung the torch at the assassin's head.

Upon impact, the man pitched over, his chokehold broken. Together, Valko and I inhaled a ragged breath.

The assassin was still alive, still conscious. He and Valko clambered to their feet and curled their fists. My gaze swept over the assassin's full and intimidating stature. I was no match for him, blow for blow. I needed his dagger. I crouched low and crept around him.

The two men circled each other. The assassin spit out a mouthful of blood. His pain faded as my awareness gravitated to the dominant call of Valko's aura. Its heavy pulsing felt familiar, welcoming. Our energy melded. Gained strength. I gave myself over to his instincts. We could save one another.

The men started throwing punches. I crawled backward and raked the straw for the dagger. My breaths grew hot, labored, as Valko's burning desire to kill consumed me.

He grunted as the assassin's fist connected with his jaw. My own jaw burst in pain. The man followed the blow with a thrust to Valko's stomach, which sent me wheezing. Valko staggered over, his hand on his gut. "You're next," the assassin said to me, his eyes like flint, his teeth red with blood.

My lips curled back. A rush of craving flooded my veins. The pain I felt was nothing. It wouldn't stand in the way of my purpose. "I dare you to try."

With the assassin distracted, Valko slugged him hard on the shoulder where he'd been burned by the torch. The man buckled at the waist, and Valko kneed him in the face. I didn't feel the man's suffering, only Valko's dark elation. It coursed through me. I wanted more.

I searched in earnest for the dagger.

The assassin recovered, backed up a step, and sent a sharp kick into Valko's chest. Valko slammed backward against the wall of bars. I grunted and fell forward on my elbows with searing pain.

My vision spun as Valko unhitched himself from the bars and shook his dizzy head. The assassin paced the cell, growing nearer to Valko, a cat playing with a caught mouse before eating it. I panted for breath. Balled my hands. Squared my jaw. Valko and I wouldn't die down here.

The assassin's body tensed, like an arrow pulling back on a bow. He sprang at his target.

Valko was ready for him. He dodged sideways an instant before impact. The assassin was thrown off balance. Valko swiftly rotated behind him and wrapped an around the man's neck. I flashed a grin. My arm muscles contracted. With his air cut off, the man's struggling slowed. As Valko hung on him, the assassin rammed himself backward into the opposite wall of bars.

The air knocked out of me. My body went limp. I toppled over, straining to focus my blurred vision. Three feet away in the straw, a sliver of iron swam into view. My pulse quickened. My bloodlust thrummed. I dragged myself within reach of the blade.

Valko smashed into the wall again on the back of the assassin. His pain tore through me, but my body overflowed with deadly surety, one entity with Valko. His heart struck an urgent drumroll with mine.

The cool press of metal slid into my palm. My fist closed

around the hilt. I drew up the dagger. Met Valko's wild and violent gaze.

"Now!" he shouted, his voice breathy but commanding.

My legs trembled as I stood and faced the assassin. A vibrant need to kill pumped through me. Intoxicating. Driving. The assassin's beady eyes looked larger with all the air pressing out of him. They widened another fraction when he saw his weapon in my hands.

A cry of fury and raw desire rose up my throat. I never released it. I hesitated. Felt a spark of my own feelings. I couldn't kill this man. Not with my own hands. Still, I wanted him dead.

"Sonya!" Valko shouted again.

The assassin stumbled backward in one last attempt to knock him off.

I adjusted my grip on the dagger. "Get off him!" I said to Valko.

He gave me an incredulous look.

"Trust me!"

He released the assassin's neck just before the man barreled back into the bars. Valko landed in an agile crouch. He extended his hand to me, anticipating my next move. My bloodlust multiplied. I tossed him the dagger.

Without hesitating, Valko leapt up and plunged the dagger into the man's chest, his aim straight at his heart.

The blade didn't strike deep. The assassin caught Valko's wrist and wrestled to pull it away. *No!* I ran across the cell.

Wrapped my hands around Valko's grip on the hilt. Together, we shoved the dagger fully in with a vicious grunt.

The assassin's eyes bulged and watered. He dropped to his knees.

Lightheadedness buzzed through my head. A rush of euphoria. Shocked laughter spilled from my lips. I took a step back, tripping in my dazed gratification.

The assassin crashed to the ground. His aura flickered out like a breath on a candle, but his eyes remained open. Staring at me.

My heartbeat slowed. Each throb brought me back to myself and out of sync with Valko. I couldn't look away from the man's beady eyes.

A startled breath hiccupped in my throat. My stomach threatened to lurch out from my mouth. I fell to my hands and knees and spun away from the man's accusing gaze.

I felt the stain of death over every inch of my body. This was nothing like barricading my sister Auraseers inside a convent that later burned to the ground while I lay unconscious in the snow. This was deliberate, no accident, no excuse. And I did it to save someone I hated.

I glanced up to see Valko, but he was gone. Panic seized me. Horror flooded my thoughts. *I let him escape.*

"Sonya," Valko said. I froze. He hadn't left. The sound of my name caught between comfort and censure.

I couldn't speak to him, couldn't look at him, couldn't admit we'd been accomplices. I pinched my eyes shut and fought to pull inside myself to hide from what we'd done. Tentatively, Valko's hand touched my back, his pressure brittle, cool, and quavering, like a falling autumn leaf. He offered a small measure of calmness. Rightness. Even a trace of tender feeling.

I gave a shaky exhale and turned to meet his gray eyes. He'd grown thinner in the last month, paler. A short and matted beard concealed the noble structure of his face.

Our gazes searched one other, trying to find understanding. The last time I'd seen Valko, he'd held *me* by the point of a dagger. Then I'd convinced him to step down from his throne, and, as I'd left his room, he'd sworn his vengeance upon me. I'd rid my heart of any lingering compassion for him. Yet I'd saved him tonight. I'd played into his intentions and helped him kill another person. And now he remained beside me while his jail cell was open.

"Why . . ." My voice faltered. "Why are you still here?" As the question fell from my lips, it unwittingly rang with intimacy, as if instead I'd asked, *Why have you stayed with* me?

Valko tilted his head, and a sliver of humor and curiosity shone in his eyes. "Because I am awaiting the fair justice of my trial."

I couldn't utter another word, couldn't believe I was ably breathing, let alone speaking to him in such a casual manner. It felt too casual, with a dead man lying behind us. Whoever hired the assassin must not have wanted Valko to live to see his day in court. Perhaps they feared he would be acquitted. I snuck a glance at the assassin, then bent over with a sharp inhale, my body fluctuating between hot and cold. Tears clouded my vision.

"Sonya, stop." Valko brought his head down to force me to focus on his face. "Look at me." His eyes held mine with a power I loathed but craved. A power of understanding. And I hated him for it. Hated the thrill that raced through me when we'd stabbed the assassin. Hated how much I enjoyed the recklessness that still trembled through my limbs.

"What we did was necessary," he said, clear of remorse. "What *you* did was necessary." His voice dropped to a whisper, and it shivered over me. "Ever my sovereign Auraseer."

I yanked away and jolted to my feet, running to the cell door and throwing it shut with a loud clang. "I am not yours," I said, then turned the key the assassin had left in the lock, my fingers curled tight around it. "Not in any way."

Valko remained crouched. He watched me with the eyes of a patient lion. I knew that look. Even while imprisoned, the former emperor sought to use me somehow, though for what purpose I couldn't say. "Are you going to leave me in here with a dead man?" he asked, his tone wry and unaffected.

"Yes," I replied without wavering. "When has another person's death bothered you?"

He had the audacity to smile. "It was a pleasure to see you, Sonya."

CHAPTER SIX

ANTON'S AURA FELL STUNNED, LIKE A GLASS TOPPLED OVER, its water frozen before it splashed the floor. "What did you say?"

I let myself breathe a few moments. I'd run straight from the dungeons to the third floor of the palace. Anton had finally returned from his meeting with the Duma. "I went downstairs— I was waiting for you—and I started to drift through the auras of bad dreams. But then it wasn't a dream; it was real. I felt a slit throat—the life leave a man. A dungeons' guard. Others died after him. Then I felt more—I felt the assassin's feelings, and I understood his intentions. His aura radiated from below ground. It was simple to guess whom he was pursuing."

Anton's eyes widened, revealing more fear and concern than I'd ever sensed in him. It made my body shake harder. "And you followed this man? Alone? Unarmed?"

I nodded weakly.

"Sonya." He briefly closed his eyes. His anger tightened my

chest and locked my trembling knees.

"I had no time to search for help," I explained. "The great corridor was deserted. The guards on duty were outside drinking."

Anton's jaw muscle contracted. He'd had a difficult time keeping the guards on task after the empire had fallen.

My tongue twitched with everything he wanted to say. From his rage and panic, I could almost form the words. *How could you be so reckless, Sonya? What made you think you could take on an assassin? Why did you risk your life to save Valko?* Instead, he asked, "Why are you bleeding? What did he do to you?" His eyes, shadowed by fatigue, rapidly assessed my body, my bloody wrist, the straw clinging to my nightgown, and my matted braid.

"I'm fine. The assassin is dead. I . . . I helped Valko kill him." I could no longer look at Anton, and so I lowered my gaze, tears collecting in my lashes.

"Where is Valko?" Anton asked, his mind flashing to the next terrible conclusion. I felt him tense up, ready to spring for the dungeons.

"He's locked back inside his cell." The tears rolled down my cheeks.

Anton's grip on my face softened. "Sonya," he murmured, smoothing wisps of hair off my brow and kissing my temple. I ducked my head into the curve between his neck and shoulder and let myself sob. His arms came around me, and he rubbed my back. "Shhh. You're safe now."

"I lost control. I should have used my power to bend the assassin's desires." I curled my hand in frustration against Anton's chest. My mind spun, caught in a loop, making me relive every moment in Valko's cell. "I didn't even think to try. It all happened so fast and . . ." *I let myself be consumed by Valko's aura instead.* I thought I'd moved beyond succumbing to his impulses.

My teeth chattered from all my quavering. "The assassin said he'd come for me next, so I—I took his dagger and threw it to Valko. He tried to stab the assassin, but the man wrestled him for the weapon." Bile burned up my throat. "So I helped Valko drive the blade in through the assassin's heart." *And I enjoyed it.*

"You defended yourself."

I also defended your brother.

Anton's hand slowed to a careful circle around my shoulder blade, as though he'd read my last thought. I pushed his aura to the edges of mine. I didn't want to know what he felt about my saving Valko. My own shame was enough of a hardship. "And Valko didn't even try to escape?"

I shook my head, my stomach twisting as I pictured the last look Valko gave me, his unnerving, patient stare. I withdrew from Anton's embrace, wiped under my eyes, and opened my hand, offering him the key.

Lines of resolve formed on his noble brow. He pocketed the

key, then took my hand in both of his, his thumbs brushing the angry red marks on my palm, evidence of where I'd gripped the key too hard. We stood with our heads bent together, our gazes lowered at our joined hands. I couldn't stop shaking. The cold and horrors of the dungeons cleaved to my bones. "And the assassin is still there," Anton asked, "in Valko's cell?"

"Yes."

"And you're sure you're all right." His lifted his eyes to mine. "I could wake the physician."

"I'm all right."

He assessed me, unconvinced but finally relenting. "Will you stay here and rest?"

My panic flared. "You're leaving?"

"I have to take care of this," he answered solemnly.

I struggled to calm my breathing. "Yes, of course." I imagined what he must do. Assign more guards to the dungeons, dispose of the body, question Valko about what had transpired. Still, selfishly, I didn't want him to go. "When will you be back?"

"Morning."

My shoulders fell.

Anton kissed my cheek. "It's nearly morning now. I won't be long. Get some rest while you can." He kissed me again, this time on my mouth. I clung to him, lengthening the kiss for as long as possible. It wasn't enough to ease my troubled heart or make me believe his affection was unaltered.

As he pulled away, he kept my face close, his gaze fierce.

"Promise me you'll never endanger yourself like this again."

"I didn't mean to—"

"Promise, Sonya."

I swallowed. "I promise."

He drew back with a sigh, tugging a hand through his hair. I felt him growing distant, distracted by all he must take care of before the palace awoke.

He blew out the candles and made his way to the door. "Don't go anywhere until I return." Turning the latch, he added, "If anyone comes here asking questions, say nothing."

I bit my lip and gave another nod.

He looked over me one last time, his face lost in shadow with the light from the corridor behind him. I didn't need to see him to know what he was feeling. His worry and pain fed my guilt. At length, he left and shut the door.

I pulled the blanket to my chin and fought not to think about the dead man's face, the way his eyes watered when Valko and I drove the dagger into his chest. I vividly recalled the force we had to use, the burn in our muscles, the tight grip of our hands. Once the man's aura had silenced in death, I'd laughed with shock and triumph. Anton wouldn't have recognized me.

My fingers stretched out under the blanket, seeking the black ribbon I wore as a visible reminder of my guilt and mourning.

But my wrist was bare.

I sat up, looking around me. The black ribbon I'd worn

since Yuliya and the Auraseers of the convent died was missing. Without it, I felt uprooted, drifting, with nothing to hold onto. At length, I sank back in the pillows and breathed in Anton's lingering scent in the bed sheets.

His fragrance of musk and pine was already fading.

CHAPTER SEVEN

AFTER WAITING ALL MORNING, LIKE A CHILD SENT TO HER room after breaking a mirror, kept at a safe distance while an adult cleaned up the broken glass, the latch of the door turned. I looked up to see Anton on the threshold, as regal as the princes of old whose portraits used to line the great corridor of the palace. This was how I always saw him in my mind, full of vision and greatness, ushering in a new age for Riaznin. I would never be as noble as him.

"Did you discover who the assassin was?" I tried to keep my voice casual, my emotions controlled, as if we were chatting about Tosya and his new book of poetry and not the identity of a man I'd helped kill.

He averted his gaze, shut the door, and dropped his cape on a chair. Worry and fatigue weighted his aura, though urgency still buzzed at its undercurrent. "The man's dagger had a crudely fashioned hilt, and his clothes were rough and over-worn. He wasn't a man of means, though that tells us nothing. Anyone—noble or peasant—could have hired him."

Anton's unease seeped inside my stomach, and I gripped the bedpost. I noted his distance from me and his air of hesitation. "Surely it was a peasant," I replied. "Why would the nobles want Valko dead?"

Anton shrugged and walked over to a small table, where a breakfast tray resided. "I doubt it was the nobles, but the possibility shouldn't be disregarded." He turned the bread over with a frown, then pushed it aside and picked up the fruit.

"I suppose if Valko died, it would stir up sympathizers for the old empire, the way killing Tosya would have made him a martyr for the revolutionaries." Perhaps if I kept talking, kept striving for normalcy amid unrest, Anton would see I was still the same Sonya. I had to be. I wasn't myself in the dungeons.

He didn't comment. Instead, he grabbed a small knife and cut off a section of the apricot, spearing it on the tip of his blade.

"But if there were a second rebellion," I went on, "this time instigated by loyalists—and if Valko were dead—the nobles would want another emperor." *Look at me, Anton.*

He twirled the knife around, staring without seeing it. "Either way I'm the victor," he said, his voice low and bitter.

"Pardon?"

"Valko's accusation." Anton dropped the knife. "He thinks

the assassin *was* working for the nobility. He believes I'm still after his crown."

I tentatively crossed the room. "Did you tell Valko the idea for a Duma was yours?" Anton had relinquished any wish to solely rule Riaznin. One seat among twenty governors was all he had campaigned for and won.

"Valko is deaf to anything rational I wish to say to him, whether it's about me . . . or you." He pushed the tray away.

My chest collapsed. "What did Valko tell you?"

"What I saw in the dungeons was worse than anything my brother said."

I felt the pain lodged behind his troubled aura. I reached out to touch his shoulder, but he jerked and spun around to me, the careful shell around his emotions cracking.

"Can't you sense when a man is twice your size and ten times your muscle? What made you think you could overtake him, Sonya? And why would you endanger yourself to save *Valko*?" He briefly closed his eyes, trying to compose himself. "I saw the assassin, his dead body in the bloody straw of my brother's cell, and all I could think was that could have been *you*." His voice broke with emotion, with the vulnerability he rarely allowed anyone to witness.

A terrible ache flowered in the back of my throat. "Anton . . ." I shook my head, struggling to find a reason that would satisfy him. "When I feel someone's suffering, *I* suffer. It's instinct that I want to stop it." *Or inflict it.*

"At the risk of your own life?" Bewilderment lifted his voice. "*Twice* you could have been killed yesterday. You had your moment of triumph during the war, but you're not invincible. Just because you feel things other people can, doesn't mean you're stronger than them."

My eyes narrowed. "Don't be cross with me because I saved your brother when *you* asked me to do the same in a moment when my survival was just as impossible. In case you've forgotten, more than one of your revolutionary friends wished Valko dead by assassination, but *you* wanted justice. And I risked my life for that justice, too."

The cut of Anton's grief opened wider and split through my heart. He knew I was right. Still, he held himself back and kept to the edge of the table.

I crossed my arms, trying to get to the core of his mood. "What happened at your meeting with Feliks and the other governors?"

Guilt dimmed his aura.

"Has the Duma taken the government?"

He gave a heavy exhale. "Yes . . . all things considered, it was the best move for Riaznin." His misery multiplied, cutting down the length of me. My jaw clamped with his resistance to say anything more. "And the Duma has an assignment for you."

"Oh?" My hand slid across my stomach. Curiosity replaced my disappointment that Feliks had gotten his way.

"This wasn't my decision." Anton held up his hands and

bristled with anger again. "I had nothing to do with it. I think it's a terrible idea, especially in light of what occurred last night."

"Aren't you going to tell me?"

He looked down, his boot scuffing the floor. "It's in regard to Valko."

"Valko?" I repeated. Anton glanced up to study my surprised reaction. "Do they wish me to be his guardian again?" The former emperor *did* need better protection. The assassination attempt had proved that much.

Before I could decipher how I truly felt, Anton spoke again. "The Duma, they want you to . . . *assist* in Valko's trial."

My mouth parted in bewilderment. "How?" I had no training in the law; law for the new Riaznin hadn't even been settled upon.

He dragged a hand through his hair.

"Anton, what exactly does the Duma need me to do?"

He lifted his gaze to the ceiling. After a long breath, he said, "They want you to judge Valko's trial."

I stiffened. "I—I don't understand." My heart gave a hard pound of warning. "They wish me to decide his verdict?" *And declare his death sentence?*

"No, no, you would be another kind of judge. A judge of Valko's intentions, a kind of barometer for the truth. The Duma wants to know if his answers to the court are genuine."

My emotions tripped over themselves like snagging gears of a clock.

Anton finally pulled away from the table. He crossed over to me slowly, carefully assessing my face. "Please tell me how you're feeling, Sonya." He touched my arm. "I don't have your gift."

The gears turned harder, faster, whirring and spinning and assaulting me with panic. How could I judge Valko when my aura had a terrible tendency to blend with his? How could I be that unbiased if I couldn't separate my own feelings from his intentions? And how could I be in his presence in front of a court of the Duma—and at a public trial—without revealing my role in his abdication?

The former emperor was a master of manipulation, and for too long I'd been his favorite puppet. I thought I'd cut the strings when he removed his crown, but what happened with the assassin had proved otherwise. Valko would use me at his trial to his advantage. He'd seek to humiliate me in front of everyone. But I couldn't refuse the Duma. I'd wished for some new and important occupation, some precedence for the way Auraseers could be respected in Riaznin, and now I must seize my opportunity.

When several moments passed and I still hadn't spoken, Anton nodded with grim acceptance. "I'll tell them no." My muscles tightened as his aura firmed with resolve. "They can't ask you to do this."

"You said they weren't asking."

"This is a democracy!" He threw up his hands from the

injustice of it all. "The Duma is required to give people a choice. I'll *make* them ask you."

I managed a grin. "That's a lot of forcing in the name of free will."

"You shouldn't be put into a position of filtering out my brother's intentions—or speaking for him in any way. He tried to *kill* you, Sonya." Anton took hold of my arm and pushed back my sleeve to expose my dagger wound from the One Day War. Fierce protectiveness lined his brow and plated the shell of his aura. "You're lucky this is the only injury you sustained."

I felt the blood rise in my cheeks. Anton hadn't mentioned my wound since the night I'd received it, nor did his gaze ever linger on that part of my arm, not even to ask how it was healing. Years ago, an old Romska fortune-teller told him he'd find a girl who would change his life forever. Their souls would be fitted for one another, and she'd have a lynx-shaped mark to match his own. Mine did not.

I pulled down my sleeve. "I don't see what the trouble is." I smoothed my features into a mask of indifference. "Of course I'll help the Duma. They don't know that Valko hurt me, and they have no need to. He can't do me any harm if he's surrounded by guards." *Besides, he didn't hurt me in the dungeons when he'd had the perfect opportunity.* My fingers clenched. "Will the Duma investigate what I did last night?"

"No one will ever know you were in Valko's cell," Anton said solemnly.

"No one but Valko, you mean."

"He's agreed to back the story—he defeated the assassin himself."

"And you trust him to keep his word?"

Anton's energy rippled with anxiety, which made me fall deeper into the current of my own. "It's a chance I must take so the Duma trusts you. They won't if they still believe you're acting as sovereign Auraseer."

"Then there's nothing to worry about," I replied with as much confidence as I could muster. "My job is simple compared to your new role of ruling with the Duma. I'll probably fall asleep during the trial for lack of a challenge."

Anton studied me, the late morning light revealing golden flecks in his irises. "Are you sure you're prepared to do this?"

"If I can hold the auras of the dead and the gods and all living souls in Riaznin, I can surely tell a court of governors what a dethroned boy's intentions are. Valko has no lasting hold over me."

"There is a dead man buried six feet below the earth who would say otherwise—another man who almost killed you."

"This time will be different. I'll be prepared, and my life won't be threatened." I lifted a hand to cradle Anton's cheek. "This time *you* will be with me."

His mouth quirked, a failed attempt to smile. "But do I have as much sway as my brother?"

I rose up on my toes, my calf muscles tensing as I kissed him. My lips against his were a promise stronger than words. I said them anyway. "You have my heart."

He caught my hand and kept it pressed against his face. "Forgive me." He leaned into my palm. "I won't have any peace until this is over."

"Do you fear the verdict?" No matter what the former emperor had done, he was Anton's brother, his last living relation.

Anton gave a hard swallow. "My goal all along has been to see justice served to Valko. I can't save him from the repercussions of his crimes; all I can ask for is an impartial trial. It will take place in two days. Three more elected governors should reach Torchev by then and will be able to take part. So long as the proceeding is fair, I want this trial smooth and done with."

"So I'm not subjected to Valko for long?" I asked, getting to the meat of the matter.

Anton gazed at me, his aura tentative. Dread crept in at the base of his emotions, like a rolling fog. "I can't shake the feeling that something bad is going to take place, no matter how much I reason with myself."

"What's the worst that could happen?"

"Valko could win over the Duma with his impeccable charm and make you forget all the ways he's wronged you," he answered without hesitation.

I lifted my brows.

"You said the worst." He shrugged.

I pressed closer. "I can do this. Trust me."

Anton bowed his head in defeat and kissed me, his mouth

soft and pliant with his surrender. His forehead against mine, he whispered, "You win, summer queen. I trust you."

"We won't let this change us," I promised.

His fingers slid down to mine. "We won't let *anything* change us."

His mouth met mine again, and just as we were getting lost in another kiss, an onslaught of impatience and frustration hammered into me. The sentiment didn't radiate from Anton.

The outer door to his room swung open. Feliks strode inside, unannounced.

CHAPTER EIGHT

FELIKS'S PIERCING BLUE EYES MADE QUICK WORK OF THE SCENE before him, Anton and I caught up in one another's embrace. "I didn't realize you'd have company," he said to Anton, though his cool gaze lingered on me. I smoothed my mussed braid.

Anton stood up taller. "Do you need something?"

"Yes, as a matter of fact, the other governors and I are trying to settle the matter of our apartments."

"There are several vacancies on the second floor. Any of the servants can point them out to you." Anton's irritation itched my back in a spot I couldn't scratch. He couldn't stand to be in Feliks's presence, that much was clear, but he held an air of nonchalance, which he'd mastered when he'd been both a prince and a secret revolutionary.

Feliks walked to a bookshelf in the corner of the room and ran his finger along the spines of a set of matching volumes. "Surely it's better to lodge the Duma on the third floor. After all, that is how this palace was designed, to fortify its rulers from the highest level."

"The rooms are full," I blurted. The thought of sleeping so near Feliks made my skin crawl.

The governor's threatening stare slowly turned to me, his aura pulsing with sharp interest. My heart beat like a kettle-drum. I may as well have announced that I wished him gone to the cold and barren wastelands of Riaznin.

Anton cleared his throat. "What Sonya means to say is that it will take some time to prepare the rooms for you."

"Yes, it's quite the treasury up here," Feliks said, after a tense moment. "What a wealth you're hoarding for the Ozerov dynasty."

Anton had employed a curator to store heirlooms of the empire in the vacant guest rooms. Encouraging peaceful remembrances of the old regime, though they'd often left dark smudges in the pages of Riaznin's history, was a classic move of his pacifist heart. To Anton, they were part of the mortar that built this nation.

"Our portraits and family histories aren't of any value to the democracy," he replied, the tendons of his neck cording.

Feliks arched a refuting brow. "They are when the frames are gold and the journals are locked in silver chests." He bent closer to the bookshelf and examined a small cedar dish on top. "In truth, I don't see the merit of preserving relics that might further confuse the people's allegiance—not at such a critical hour for our nation." He lifted a gold locket from the dish and turned it over in his hand. I'd never seen the necklace before.

Anton's enraged aura made my skin burn. He forced a steady pace as he strode over to Feliks and removed the locket from his grasp. "This was my mother's," he said. His tone conveyed that Feliks had crossed a dangerous line by touching it. Shortly before the revolution, the dowager empress had been poisoned in an assassin's failed attempt to kill Valko.

The governor nodded placidly, though his aura sparked with cunning. "I see."

Anton took a measured breath and placed the locket back in the dish. "I'll have the rooms cleared as soon as possible—which will be, at best, a few weeks. I'll strip the canvases from the frames and give you what you find valuable. Until then, you may search out apartments elsewhere in the palace." Nostrils flared, he turned away from Feliks and grabbed his cape. "Come, Sonya," he said. I moved to his side, took his hand, and felt his aura forge together like a shield, as if I were one of the treasures Feliks desired.

The governor revolved to watch us as we made our way past him to exit the room. "There's also the pressing matter of Shengli, Anton," he said, timing his words just as we reached the door. "I've received news of more"—he glanced at me—"developments."

Feliks's declaration came with a distinctive punch to Anton's aura, and his energy plummeted. He halted, muttering something that sounded Esten in the way he rolled his "r."

"What's happened?" I asked. "Have the Shenglin raided

another border town?" I looked back and forth between Feliks and Anton. The land was rich along the Jinshan River between Shengli and Riaznin, and border wars had been a problem for centuries. But after the fall of the empire, they were growing more rampant.

"That information is privileged." Feliks lifted his chin.

"I can be trusted. I sat in on countless council meetings as sovereign Auraseer and never breathed a word about them."

He nodded with understanding, though the sentiment felt false. "I'm sure it must be hard to adapt to all the sudden changes, Sonya. You've been in the confidence of the emperor, as well as his brother. But the Duma is enforcing a closed-door policy on our intelligence. In light of a recent break-in last night, we've realized we can't be too careful."

My heart seized. "You know about the assassin?"

Feliks angled his head at me, his eyes narrowing. "*You* know about the assassin?"

My mouth parted, both in shock and horrible realization of my slip. I blinked and stole a glance at Anton, whose expression matched the stampeding panic inside him.

The apple in his throat bobbed. "She—"

"I felt the attack." My words spilled out with a slight note of desperation. I closed my hands into fists and strived to sound stronger, less apologetic, less guilty. "The death blow awoke me in bed. I told Anton what I'd felt as soon as he'd returned from your meeting at the inn. I assumed Valko was dead, but . . . but Anton told me otherwise." My cheeks flamed with heat. I was holding my breath. I released it in a staggered exhale.

"Ah," Feliks said with a small grin of discovery, though it didn't spread to his eyes. His gaze never wavered from mine during my clumsy recounting. "I'd wondered how Anton came upon the scene so swiftly."

My muscles burned from shock and anger. *Anton told Feliks about the assassin?* I pressed my lips together and turned to Anton, trying my best to withhold my accusatory stare. I shouldn't be so upset. Of course Anton told the other governors. The attempt on Valko's life was a matter of national security and probably the reason the Duma was now rushing Valko's trial. Still, I'd foolishly hoped the Duma wouldn't have found out about the assassination attempt at all.

Feliks clasped his hands behind his back and walked deeper into Anton's room. He paused near the open midnight-blue door and peered past it into the room of tapestries, the dowager empress's old bedchamber. "Is this where you sleep, Sonya?"

"Yes." I hated how small my voice sounded.

He assessed the space and nodded with appreciation. "For your sake, I hope the third floor provides enough rooms so the Duma won't need it. But if it comes to that, you can always move elsewhere in the palace, given we can continue to find some occupation for you."

"I won't be leaving," I snapped, then steadied my voice. "I'm devoted to Riaznin; I'll make myself useful to her."

Feliks clapped his hands together. "Then I'm sure you'll

understand why I need to speak to Anton privately now."

My fingernails dug into my palms. I bobbed my head in a little bow. "Of course." I brushed away from Anton, and he grabbed my sleeve.

"Sonya." My name formed his apology.

I managed a smile. None of this was his fault. But I couldn't help feeling like I was back in the convent and excluded from sitting at the dining table where Nadia and her ring of friends reigned. "It's all right. I'll see you soon."

Once I'd left the room and was alone in the corridor, a chill swept into me, damp with the weight of the dungeons' air. With a shiver, I wrapped my arms around myself and fought to push out the spider crawl of Valko's aura.

CHAPTER NINE

MY HANDS CURLED AND FLEXED AS I STRODE INTO THE PALACE stables. The sweltering day made the scent of horses, saddle leather, and hay pungent and inviting. I was glad for the heat. The more I fretted over Valko's impending trial, the more the dungeons' cold clung to my bones.

"Hello, girl," I said to Raina as I reached her pen. She nickered and walked over to me, sniffing at my hand. "I don't have any apples today. But here"—I crossed to a barrel and scooped up a handful of oats—"this is better than nothing."

Raina lowered her mouth to my hand, and I stroked her neck. Valko had given me the mare as a gift, a cruel one in many ways because I wasn't free to ride her. I could never leave the palace or neglect my duties to the emperor. Even after the monarchy fell, it hadn't crossed my mind until now that I could take my horse anywhere. I didn't know how to embrace my liberty, although it's what I'd wanted my whole life.

I fed Raina another handful of oats, then fetched her bridle, saddle, and my riding gloves. Feliks would, no doubt, keep Anton occupied all day. If I stayed here, wondering what the Duma was discussing without me, I'd go mad.

A stitch loosened in my chest the moment Raina and I exited the palace grounds. I rode her out onto the main avenue of the city. A few peasants nodded in greeting, but the nobility weren't so friendly. When I took a side street that led to the west forest, I came across several nobles in their open carriages, converging to Countess Terezia Dyomin's mansion house.

Once they spied me, their auras lashed out with scorn. Whisperings of Sergei, Helene, and the duel at Kivratide pressed in on me like a closing box. The nobles couldn't have understood my true involvement in Helene's injury, but they knew I'd tried to stop the duel, and that Helene was shot instead of me.

At the mouth of the mansion courtyard, Countess Dyomin stood, welcoming her guests. She wore a jade-green gown that shimmered in the sunlight and perfectly offset her coiffed, raven hair. Her stiff but elegant posture spoke of pride and wealth, beauty and power. Terezia had become a widow at a young age, and before the empire fell, she was a first-class-ranking noble. Now her title meant nothing, but she kept up her charade of importance.

As I cantered by, Terezia's gaze seized mine, dagger sharp. She lifted her nose, her neck lengthening as she stood taller. "Look, friends, the summer queen of Kivratide is in our midst." A sneer curled her red-stained lips. "Isn't it astonishing how someone raised among gypsies pretends to be one of us?"

On cue, her ring of followers tittered with laughter. I glanced away, cheeks burning, and kicked Raina's flanks. We broke into a gallop toward the west forest, and I fought to shed the nobles' auras and Terezia's haughty contempt.

I rode beyond Torchev to where the terrain rose and the forest thickened. It still didn't feel far enough away. Between my run-ins with both Feliks and Terezia, memories of being excluded at the convent came flooding back. *Abomination. Unnatural.* Words my sister Auraseers had flung at me. My strange ability to sense the pain of someone's death, whether by eating meat, touching blood, or some part of the person or beast, had invoked fear and mockery from those in the empire whom I'd hoped might understand me. I felt the same now, an imposter in a city I was trying to make my home.

I ducked under tree branches and Raina leapt large roots. My muscles ached from our combined exertion. I wanted more of it, more distraction. The forest thinned, and a grassy hill came into view. I urged Raina to ride harder until we crowned the hilltop. Finally letting myself breathe deeply, I circled around to take in the view.

Far away in the valley, nestled deep in the forest, the golden domes of the palace glistened in the midday sun. The rest of the city couldn't be seen under the treetops below. The palace seemed to float on the green canopy like a castle on clouds, and the sun banded over the valley in a brilliant display of rolling light.

I could ride farther—I still had a few hours before I should turn back so that I'd arrive at the palace by nightfall—and the opposite view was equally stunning. The Riaznin countryside sprawled out before me with forestlands, pastures, and a network of hills like this one. In this direction, hundreds of miles away and out of sight, were the ridge of the Bayac Mountains, the convent, the Ilvinov Ocean, and the woods where I'd camped with the Romska. And to the east were places I'd never been: Gensi, Grishina, the Jinshan River dividing Riaznin from Shengli.

What would you do if your possibilities were limitless, Sonya?

It was something Anton would have asked me; my freedom was precious to him. But what if I had never met Anton, never become sovereign Auraseer, never involved myself in the revolution? What if nothing had ever tied me to the palace or the convent or the Romska?

I gave a little shake of my head, chiding myself. These thoughts were dangerous, irrelevant, not worth any consideration. I'd already committed to fight for Riaznin; I was just finding the best way to do that.

Riding back for Torchev, I took a route that wouldn't pass the Dyomin mansion.

❄☾⚹❄

On the palace grounds, guards with unbuttoned regimental jackets and maidservants lounged beneath a tree, tossing breadcrumbs at a chicken loose from its coop. I fought to latch on to their untroubled auras, but I couldn't shake off my tension and sense of foreboding. I'd felt it on my journey back, growing stronger the nearer I came to the dungeons' coldness.

I returned Raina to the stables and climbed the stairs to the palace porch when my ominous feeling escalated. I turned around.

A black box carriage pulled up the gravel drive. The driver sat hunched over on his bench, elbows on knees. Clearly, he'd traveled a long distance. I scanned past his weary aura and stretched my awareness to feel whoever was within the carriage. As I did, my spine ached as I fought to hold it ruler straight, my chest pulled from a lifetime of cares, my lips pursed with wariness, and a flicker of fear lit inside my belly.

"They're here," I whispered to myself, breathless with amazement. *Why have they come here?*

I rushed down the porch steps as the carriage drew to a halt. The driver stepped off the front stoop and trudged to the side door and opened it.

A gray-haired woman ducked her head under the low clearance and came outside. She had once been beautiful, though I'd never known her then, never seen her without her impressive array of deep-carved wrinkles. Despite her age, she had the fortitude of an ox. As protectress of the Auraseers in Riaznin she'd had to be strong, especially when the others like her—who had dedicated themselves to Feya and a life of stewardship—died because my actions burned down half the convent in Ormina.

"Hello, Sonya," Sestra Mirna said, her expression as warm

as cold borscht. She straightened and smoothed the folds of her dress. "I should have guessed you'd sense us approaching."

"I—" My mouth went dry. I couldn't stop staring at her. Sestra Mirna looked fiercer in my memory. I'd forgotten the soft texture of her skin beneath all those harsh, wrinkled lines. Still, I felt afraid in her presence. She surely hadn't forgiven me for all the deaths I'd caused. "In truth, I was only outside by coincidence. I should have felt you sooner. I was, um, distracted."

The sestra sighed, her breath rattling in that familiar way that said I was hopeless. "You were never one to hold your concentration for long, were you, Sonya?"

I pressed my lips together. *And you were never one to withhold your criticism.*

She turned to the open door of the carriage. "Come along, girls. Sonya isn't going to bite."

Tender affection swept through me as Dasha's golden-brown face popped out, her gray eyes large and skeptical. I gave her a wide smile. Serving as Valko's sovereign Auraseer had tested the limits of my endurance, but I'd stayed strong for the last two remaining girls at the convent. I knew if I abandoned my duty, they would be forced, in turn, to take my place. All the abuse I'd suffered had been worth it to see Dasha alive and well.

The skirt of her gray dress puffed as she hopped out of the carriage. She was seven years old with a thin nose and delicate mouth that felt proportionate to the rest of her bird-boned body. But her aura felt three times her frail size. When I'd last seen her, she and Kira had been recovering from the ague. Ironically, that illness had saved their lives because the infirmary wasn't in the half of the convent that burned in the fire.

"Why haven't you come to visit?" Dasha asked. "Sestra Mirna says you're not the sovereign Auraseer anymore because of the rebelution."

"Revolution," the sestra corrected her.

"It's true I'm not the emperor's guardian anymore," I replied, "but I've been very busy in Torchev. The day after tomorrow I'll be assisting at a trial." I felt no need to mention *whose* trial, though Sestra Mirna threw me a sharp glance. "There's still important work for Auraseers to do in Riaznin." Tugging a wrinkled pleat of my dress, I lifted my chin. I longed for the sestra to see I'd become more than the person who'd left her at the convent last winter.

Dasha looked up at me like she hadn't really listened to a word I'd said. She pulled on the tying string of her close-fitted linen cap. Some girls wore such bonnets for sleeping, but Sestra Mirna made Dasha wear one during the day to prevent her from yanking out clumps of hair—Dasha's way of dealing with the daily stress of living with other people's emotions inside of her. Most Auraseers had an equally disturbing form of emotional release.

"What do you think of Torchev?" I asked.

The pulse of Dasha's aura weakened. "It's all right here, I guess." She bit her lip and snuck a glance at Sestra Mirna, as if worried she might be reprimanded for telling the truth. "The villagers in Ormina are unhappy, too, but at least most of them like each other."

The sestra's brows drew together in a triplet-fold of wrinkles as she looked at the unkempt servants loitering about the grounds. "Yes, Torchev isn't the great city it once was."

I shifted on my feet. "Would you like to see the palace?" I asked, seeking a way to cheer up Dasha and prove to Sestra Mirna that Torchev was faring just fine. I stepped aside, as if it were possible that I alone could block such a view.

Dasha's jaw unhinged, her little mouth forming an O as she gazed upward. I'd been equally stunned when I'd first clapped eyes on the towering confection of painted tiles and gold-plated domes. "Kira, come out here and see this!" Dasha's voice bubbled with delight. "It makes the convent look like a dollhouse."

Dasha reached into the carriage and pulled out the third Auraseer left in Riaznin. Kira was ten, that awkward age when your body hasn't quite grown into your features. She had doe eyes and a full mouth with a deep crease centering her lower lip. It vanished when she smiled, which was seldom. Her eyes, nose, mouth, and ears were flushed by her constant crying—Kira's form of emotional release. Even now, a steady track of tears collected at her jawline.

"What's the matter?" I asked, inwardly chastising myself for not sensing her mood sooner. I'd been too focused on Sestra Mirna's and Dasha's dominating auras.

Kira sniffed and shyly tucked her chin-length chestnut hair behind her protruding ears. When she wouldn't speak, Dasha grabbed her arm and dragged her a few steps closer to the palace so she could see it better, but Kira stubbornly looked at the ground.

When I turned questioning eyes on Sestra Mirna, she said, "I've come to return Kira to her family."

My brows jutted upward. "I didn't know they lived in Torchev." I glanced back at Kira as she wiped her running nose. Next to her, Dasha jumped up and down off the lower porch steps, chatting merrily, though I sensed it was only a brave act for her friend. Dasha felt almost as unhappy as Kira did. "It's a shame the girls have to be separated."

The sestra's posture squared, but her aura dimmed with sadness. She took a moment to compose herself by shutting the carriage door. "Riaznin no longer lays claim on its Auraseers, and therefore neither can the sestras." She referred to the protectresses in the plural, although she was the last living one.

"What will become of the convent?" I saw it in my mind's eyes, humble and whitewashed, set against the backdrop of the forests of Ormina. A pang of longing struck inside me, even though the convent had felt like a prison next to the open road I'd traveled with the Romska. I missed the simplicity of my old life. I'd felt no fear of becoming sovereign Auraseer, I'd had no desire to lay claim to my destiny. I'd had a friend in Yuliya. That had been enough.

"The convent was once a place of worship to the goddess Feya," Sestra Mirna said, "a place of refuge for those who sought sanctuary." She drew up taller. "It will become so again.

Auraseers will continue to be born into this world, and some will still need us. Dasha does." Glancing away from me, she massaged her weathered hands. "Her family died in a village epidemic of the ague last winter."

My heart grew heavy as I watched Dasha fidget with the cap on her head. It didn't hold up her dark hair, which wisped down to the middle of her back. "So she'll remain with you— alone?"

"We aren't the only people at the convent. Thanks to Prince Anton, we have a few guards and servants."

"But Dasha will be the only Auraseer."

Sestra Mirna shrugged, as if that was irrelevant. "Yes." She wasn't gifted like us, just devoted to Feya and her charges.

A commotion rose from the great doors of the palace. I felt the pluck of Anton's aura and whirled around. I hadn't seen him since yesterday morning.

He emerged from the palace with a trail of seven attendants. They spoke over each other and ticked things off lists with quills. My former maid, Lenka, drew Anton's cape around his shoulders and smoothed his hair. Another man hurried down the porch steps and beckoned a stable hand. As everyone bustled around him, Anton focused on a document bearing a gold seal in his hands. Lenka fastened Anton's cape at his neck, and he tugged against the collar.

Everything felt too tight, not only outwardly but also within. I sensed it as my chest cramped for breath, my body itched for space, and my muscles strung with tension. Without the complete Duma in Torchev yet, Anton was doing the work of four more people, his share of the sixteen missing governors.

He glanced above his paper, meeting my gaze from where I stood below him, and his features went fluid. The corner of his lips curved. That soft, private smile just for me. Warmth rushed through my belly. I felt suddenly beautiful, despite my simple dress and far less polished appearance.

Anton motioned for his attendants to give him a moment and progressed down the stairs. But at the middle, he halted, his aura flowering with surprise when he spotted Dasha and Kira near the bottom. He had met the girls before—briefly—when he'd come to collect me from the convent. He cast me a curious look and finally noticed the woman beside me.

"Sestra Mirna," he said, descending the remaining steps. "Forgive me, I didn't expect to see you today." He might have added *or ever*. "Is everything all right at the convent?" His anxiety made my heart beat faster. With the history of attempted raids on the convent by villagers in want of its food rations, he had worthy cause to be concerned.

"We are well enough," Sestra Mirna answered plainly.

"She's come to return Kira to her family," I added.

"Oh, I see." Anton nodded in understanding at the delicate situation. He looked back at the girls, who returned his gaze with wonder. He was the brother of the fallen emperor, the person they'd been raised to believe they might serve one day.

Another carriage rolled onto the drive, this time from the stables. As Anton glanced toward it, the pulse of his aura pinched with urgency. "I apologize, but I'm needed in the city right now. I'm afraid I must go at once." He bowed a farewell to the sestra.

"What's happening?" I asked, moving in tow with him as he strode away. His attendants flocked to him again. One opened the carriage door.

"I have to settle another dispute regarding the Emancipation Act. Some of the nobles are taxing former serfs before the harvest is in, and the peasants have raided a manor house in revolt."

My breath hitched. "That's terrible." Integrating the serfs into a free economy was Anton's top priority. There were so many things he wanted to do for Riaznin, and he'd hardly had a chance to get started. "Well, I'll come with you. You need someone guarding you for threats."

"No, you need to save your strength for the trial," he said resolutely. "I'll be fine. A company of guards is already awaiting me." He took my hand, giving it an affectionate squeeze, then climbed into his carriage. Three of his attendants joined him.

"I'll see you tonight," Anton said. "We can dine together." As soon as he suggested it, he clenched a fist. "Actually, we can't. Feliks and the other governors want a report on the treasury inventory. But I'll—I'll see you soon, I promise."

My aura fell heavier, but I nodded, summoning a bright expression that would have made Pia proud. I hoped it masked my disappointment.

As the carriage whisked away, Sestra Mirna came to my

side. "The two of you seem very comfortable together. I didn't realize *how* comfortable until now." In my letters to the sestra, I'd never written about my relationship with the former prince. "Did you fall in love before or after the revolution?"

I bristled at her nosiness, as if she still had a say in my life. "What does it matter?"

"I'm just curious what triggers an interesting pattern with you. After you lived in the convent eight months, it burned. After you lived at the palace three months, the empire fell. I wonder how long this new democracy will last."

Another flare of defensiveness lit through me. She'd been here all of five minutes and was already going out of her way to make me feel like a plague to civilization. "Are you suggesting I leave Torchev?"

"I'm suggesting you take care with your involvement at Valko Ozerov's trial. From the whisperings in the city, whether the former emperor lives or dies, the outcome will cause a violent division among the people."

"And I suppose that will be my fault?" I couldn't restrain the bite in my voice.

The branching wrinkles around the sestra's mouth cut deeper as she pursed her lips. "You tend to exacerbate contention, child, though I'm not sure exactly how. So all I'm asking is that you ground yourself to your own emotions when you walk into that courtroom."

"I'm stable now, Sestra Mirna. You have nothing to fear." That's when I realized she truly was afraid. Of me. It fed the roots of her distressing aura. I was the girl she could never teach, never tame. The girl whose actions killed so many under her care. And now I didn't answer to her or the fallen empire. I had full freedom, the last thing the sestra could have wished for me.

"For your own sake, as well as Riaznin's, I pray that is true."

CHAPTER TEN

THE NEXT DAY I RAN A BRUSH THROUGH DASHA'S HAIR, MINDful to be tender with the thinner sections. We stood at the window of my old bedchamber. It provided a clear view of the gates. A carriage rolled down the drive, and my heart kicked up in a flurry, matching Dasha's cadence. She lifted on her toes and put her hand on the windowpane.

"It's not her," I said, keeping my voice steady and soothing. Dasha had awakened screaming this morning. I'd had a fitful night myself. Vicious auras seemed to slither inside the palace and slip into my awareness while my defenses were weak with fatigue. The tension in the city was worsening with Valko's impending trial. "Sestra Mirna and Kira left in a red-trimmed carriage." I worked the bristles through a tangle of Dasha's dark and wispy hair. "And Sestra Mirna will be returning alone, remember?" I added gently. I knew what it was like to lose a best friend.

Dasha fell back down to her heels and pulled her hand away from the glass. "I know." Still, she hadn't abandoned her vigil for hours. She looked at my wooden figurine of Feya on the windowsill, which she kept toting around by its head. "What did Kira ever do to deserve living in this terrible city?"

"Kira deserves to be with her family." I set the brush down. "We all do, but it isn't possible for some of us."

"*I'm* her family."

I turned Dasha by the shoulders to look at me. "You can be my family, too." I wanted what the two girls had together, that beautiful and constant sense of belonging.

"You don't live in the convent anymore. You'll be here, close to Kira. Both of you stuck in this city that will eat you!" Her agitation raked across my skin and quickened my heartbeat. She wrenched away and ran to the other side of the box bed to hide.

I let her be for a moment, unsure how to handle her. "Torchev isn't so bad, is it?" My words echoed off the oak floors and empty walls. My old bedchamber was just as barren as it had ever been, the cramped box bed its only furnishing. "We're just going through a little growing pains is all, like the leg aches you used to get at night. They hurt, but then in a few days you find you've grown taller."

A stinging sensation pricked me. Dasha made small noises of pain. I crossed the room and peered around the bed. She sat on the floor, both hands gripped in her hair as she pulled it.

I knelt down. "Dasha, you must stop that."

Her gray eyes were large and pooled with tears. "It feels better than my feelings."

My chest ached for her. I tried to think of the ultimate distraction—one that wouldn't hurt her. "If you promise to let your hair alone, I'll share something with you that only Anton and I know about."

Dasha's fingers froze. "What?"

I leaned forward, lowering my voice in a dramatic whisper. "This palace has secret rooms." Dasha blinked. "In fact, the entrance to the first room is in *this* room. Can you guess where the door is hiding?"

She released her hair and glanced about. "Behind the bed?"

"Clever girl." I smiled and gave her shoulder a little shake. "Do you think you're strong enough to help me move it?"

She nodded soberly, and I lifted her up to her feet. She was so small she only came to the height of my waist, but together we hefted back the box bed. It glided easily on its casters, but I made sure to grunt and take my time while she put all her muscle into the effort. When the bed moved away from the wall, Dasha gasped upon seeing the small red door painted with yellow daffodils.

I patted her on the back. "Go on, open it."

She did, but then her aura flooded with disappointment. "It's just another empty room."

"Oh, it's much more than that." I guided her inside. "You see this wall of mirrors? This is where princesses once practiced ballet." I set Dasha's hand on the barre of smooth wood.

Her gaze lingered on the mirror. She was a beautiful girl, and she likely hadn't seen her reflection in some time. The convent only had a handful of mirrors, but they'd been in the east wing that burned in the fire. Dasha studied her eyes, then frowned at her thin hair. "I don't know how to dance."

"I didn't either, not until I came to the palace. And then I learned how to waltz. It's easy once you find the rhythm," I said, demonstrating for her. "One-two-three, one-two-three, one-two-three."

Dasha watched, unimpressed.

An innocent and curious idea formed inside me, like a green shoot crawling out of the earth. I focused on Dasha's stubborn resistance, then felt beneath it to her sorrow and desolation. I understood her feeling of abandonment. But I was ten years older. I'd learned more. I knew joy was possible despite all the darkness in life. I let that joy fill me. I closed my eyes and heard the music from the ball at Morva's Eve. I turned in a circle, dancing with an invisible partner. My limbs moved freely, my body aligned to the lovely strains of the orchestra. I saw the light from hundreds of candles, smelled the mingling perfumes, heard the swishing of dresses, felt the auras of contented guests.

I wanted Dasha to feel what I did, the pulsing of music, the beauty of finding peace in Torchev. I imagined her at the ball with me. I hummed and swayed and opened my eyes. I glimpsed flashes of myself as I revolved before the mirror. The skirt of my dress bloomed wider. I spun faster, the music building inside me.

"Dance with me." I held out my arms to Dasha, slowing so she could join in. I pictured Sestra Mirna returning and seeing us happy together. "There isn't a wrong way to do it. You just follow the impulse and let go."

She stared at me like I'd lost my right mind, but her slipper peeked out from the hem of her dress, her toes tapping the one-two-three rhythm of the song in my mind. I took her hands. "You can feel it. I know you can."

"How are you doing that?" Her brow hitched.

"Doing what?" I twirled her around.

Her fists tightened and she pulled against my grip. "You're within me."

"Of course I am. You feel my aura."

"No, this is different." She stumbled back. "Stop. I don't want to dance. You can't make me."

My rhythm broke. I halted half-spin and paused to catch my breath. The connection between us collapsed, along with my buoyant feeling. I realized too late what had happened. Except for the brief incident in the rose garden, I hadn't used my power since the One Day War. Part of me hadn't dared. But now the instinct and method had come back so clearly. My heart pounded—I couldn't tell whether in gratification or warning.

Dasha crossed her arms, determined to cling to her bad

mood. "I want to go look out the window again."

I sighed, following her back to the bedchamber. But before we exited the ballet room, the nerves in my palm jumped with the tempo of another person's singular energy. *Anton*. My pulse raced. I'd been waiting to find a moment alone with him before the trial.

I whirled away from the red door, then rushed opposite through the lavender door to the disused nursery room, then the evergreen door to dowager empress's room of tapestries— my room—the second-to-last room in the chain that led all the way to Anton's room through the final door, painted midnight blue. I flung it open.

He turned to me, surprised, then suddenly grabbed me close and planted a fervent kiss on my lips. Heat flamed through my body, followed by a rush of blissful dizziness. I hadn't expected such a quick and intimate reaction from him.

"I've missed you," he said, attempting an affectionate whisper, then he kissed me again, longer, deeper. The trembling undercurrent in his aura told me he more than missed me; he was just as nervous as I was about tomorrow's trial—and how it would test us.

His hands traveled around my waist, and he spun me into the room of tapestries. Just as the back of my legs bumped the bed, a small sob echoed from behind me.

I pushed away from Anton and turned to see the little girl I'd left sitting on the floor of the ballet practice room. "Oh, Dasha." Her eyes were red from crying. I hurried through the adjoining nursery and rubbed her arm in comfort.

Anton followed me as far as the threshold and looked on with curiosity at the young Auraseer. The burning light of his aura refracted, bouncing in a different direction, and now radiated with sympathy. "Are you hurt?" he asked her.

Dasha tucked behind me, hiding from him.

"She's sad about losing Kira," I explained. "And she's angry with Torchev. She doesn't like it here." I worked her fingers out of her hair. "It took me some time getting used to this place, too, Dasha. Anton helped me with that."

She peeked around my torso to spy on him. "He isn't all *that* handsome."

Anton burst out laughing. "I appreciate your candidness."

Her mouth quirked upward, and she wiped her nose on her sleeve.

Anton reached into the pocket of his kaftan, procured a handkerchief, and crossed into the ballet practice room, stooping to give it to her. She studied him for a moment, then finally accepted his offering. "Sometimes the world isn't kind," he said. "I learned that at a very young age myself. Can I show you what I did about it?"

My muscles tightened as Dasha's stubbornness fought against her curiosity. At last, she blew her nose and stood, giving Anton her silent answer.

He guided her through the lavender door, the evergreen door, and the midnight blue door into his bedchamber. I followed behind, my curiosity as piqued as Dasha's.

We left Anton's room through his outer door and headed down the long corridor. He took her small hand in his. We passed the servants' stairs—the last place to exit the third floor of the palace—and the final guest room, leaving one door ahead, a great gilded door, the door to Valko's old chambers.

Panic surged through my breast once I realized our destination. I hadn't been in this room since Valko had abdicated—since he almost killed me.

Anton turned around and met my trepid gaze. "This room offers the best view of the city, but I understand if you don't want to come, Sonya. We'll only be a few minutes."

"Oh, I'm coming." I inhaled a steadying breath and schooled my features with a smile. "You can't leave me out of the fun so easily."

Two soldiers guarding the door stepped aside, allowing us to enter. The once opulent, domed-ceiling chambers spread out before us. The recessed floor in the center used to overflow with luxurious lounge pillows. Now it was empty, save for a low, round table. The great bed in the left chamber was also stripped bare to its mattress, and the golden-tiled pool in the right chamber, always filled and scented with rosemary and juniper, looked desolate without its sparkling gleam of water.

The excess grandeur that used to exist in Valko's chambers was a sad reflection of the empire's imbalance of wealth, but I still felt a little melancholy for its lost beauty.

Anton didn't say a word to Dasha about this once being the emperor's rooms, but as he ushered us inside and to the balcony door, her head turned toward Valko's golden crown with seven rubies. It was locked in a glass box on top of a pile of crates with other relics of the empire. The crown trapped my focus as well, and I shivered with a sudden chill. The humid cold of the dungeons crept into my bones, the whispered pressure of another aura far below us, like a dragon sleeping beneath the palace.

Anton opened the balcony doors. The potted plants were dying. Their leaves curled with brown edges and bent in a sad bow. I leaned against the doorframe, watching Anton and Dasha. He let go of her hand and scooped up three polished stones from one of the pots.

"When I was young, I made a rule for myself." Shaking the stones in his hands, Anton walked to the balcony's half wall. Torchev's bright domes shone in the golden sunlight. The grime of poverty lurked beneath it all, hidden behind the towering manors and charming shops lining the main avenue of the city. "Once a day, I would throw three stones, casting them as far as possible. One for my worries, one for my heartache, and one for my anger. Then I wasn't allowed to think on them any more for the rest of the day."

He opened up his hand, offering the stones to Dasha. She tentatively walked forward and reached for them.

"The trick is"—Anton retracted his hand—"you have to put all your feeling, all your energy, into each throw. Otherwise, it doesn't count and all that pain is still locked up inside you."

Dasha nodded, her gray eyes wide as she stared up at him. "I understand."

He slowly passed over the stones, as if they were great treasures. Dasha handled them with equal care. "Are you ready?" he asked.

"Yes." Her voice rang like a bell.

Lifting her up in his arms, he crossed to the right side of the balcony wall. "Over here you won't pummel the soldiers," he said. I laughed, and he tossed me a grin. "All right, now. The first stone is for your worries. You must think about everything that makes you afraid. Imagine your fears are out there"—he pointed to the distant air—"and that you will strike them down with this mighty stone. So take a deep breath, and when you're ready, throw."

I shook my head, in awe of him. "Where were you when *I* was seven years old?"

"Quiet, Sonya," Dasha said. "I'm trying to concentrate." Anton sided with her, giving me a teasing frown.

I locked my mouth shut with an invisible key.

The little girl squared her shoulders and looked back at Torchev. Her nostrils flared with a deep inhale. My spine quivered from her aura, from the fears clawing their way through her.

Her arm cocked back and she released a cry of exertion, casting the stone off the balcony. It arced through the air and fell into a leafy tree below us.

"Good," Anton complimented her. "But I bet you can throw the next stone farther."

Dasha's brows drew together as she got the stone ready. "What's this one for?"

"Your heartache."

Her chin set with determination. My eyes burned as her emotions hit the surface again. She cast the stone. It flew beyond the first one, rattling through the far end of the tree.

Anton nodded his approval. "Now the last stone, Dasha. This one is for your anger. It's the most powerful emotion, and the hardest one to release. You must use all your concentration and imagine yourself stronger than you've ever been. Show your anger it can't control you."

Dasha glanced down at the stone in her hand. She brushed her small thumb across it. Then she looked into the distance, past the target tree, past the skyline of Torchev, and deep into the horizon. Her fist curled around the stone. Our auras grafted together. My hand curled, too. I felt the innate latching, the clicking into place of our emotions. I called up my own anger, my own strength. I lent it to Dasha. I longed for her to feel empowered.

She arched her hand back, launched her arm forward, and hurtled the stone. I gasped with her, feeling the effort.

The stone flew, well beyond the tree, and landed in some unseen spot. Dasha didn't even watch it fall. Her gaze locked on the horizon, and a warm thrill of satisfaction flowed through her—it flowed through me. My chest burned with pride, as if she were my true sister.

Anton released a low whistle. "Remarkable. I've never cast a stone so far. How did that make you feel, Dasha?"

Her mouth spread in a radiant smile, and she giggled. "I think Sonya should try it."

Anton pursed his lips, looking back at me. "I don't know, Sonya might need more than three stones."

I braced a hand on my hip. "Only if I can use *you* for target practice."

Dasha leapt out of Anton's arms and ran over to a potted plant, scooping up at least fifteen stones. "You better hide!"

He chased her down and grabbed her before she could arm me. She shrieked with delight as he tossed her over his shoulder. "Let's not kill the governor of Torchev just as he takes his seat on the Duma."

She gave a playful groan. "Fine."

Anton set her down and mussed her hair. She brushed a lock out of her eye and passed me all the stones. Laughing, she tugged me to the balcony wall and pointed to the horizon that she'd fixed on. Anton picked her up again so she could see over the wall.

I threw the stones, one by one, making sure they never landed past her farthest mark. Dasha's triumph in this moment should be her own, just as her grief should be over losing Kira. I wouldn't try to will her sorrow away again.

CHAPTER ELEVEN

Sᴇꜱᴛʀᴀ Mɪʀɴᴀ ᴄᴏᴜʟᴅɴ'ᴛ ꜰɪɴᴅ Dᴀꜱʜᴀ ᴛʜᴇ ɴᴇxᴛ ᴍᴏʀɴɪɴɢ. They'd planned to leave at sunup to journey back to the convent before Valko's trial and the parade of the Duma that would precede it. The sestra didn't want Dasha subjected to all the gathered, contentious auras.

I checked both the secret chambers on the third floor, but Dasha wasn't in the ballet practice room or nursery.

"Go on and watch the parade," Sestra Mirna said to me, wearily rubbing her brow. "Dasha will turn up when she thinks we've forgotten about her. This isn't the first time she's played this little trick for attention. It happens whenever she feels life is unfair. One of these days she'll realize life is *meant* to be unfair."

"Perhaps she wants to stay here a few days longer. You should let her."

"No." She firmly shook her head. "The sooner we leave this

city, the more at ease Dasha will become. Go on." She shooed me with a wave of her hand. "Surely Governor Ozerov wishes for you to support him today. You'd best not stir up any trouble." She gave me a warning look.

I hesitated, still unsettled about Dasha, but when Sestra Mirna sat down by her knitting needles and opened a letter, going about her usual routine until the girl returned on her own, I relented begrudgingly. The sestra knew Dasha better than I did, though I wished the opposite were true.

As I turned to leave, my stomach hardened with a new pang of concern. It wasn't mine. I looked back at Sestra Mirna and glimpsed the symbol on the letter's broken seal—a peacock on a tower. "Is everything all right?"

She hurriedly folded the letter. "How many times must I tell you to leave?" she snapped, and stuffed the letter in her pocket.

My teeth set on edge. I had half a mind to make her ask me again, just out of spite, but then decided against wasting my energy. I'd need all of it for the day ahead.

⁕⁘⁙⁕

The parade stretched the length of the main avenue of the city. The Duma rode horses bedecked with flowers and silk trappings. Trumpets blared and drums beat as the governors advanced, carrying props representing the city or province they hailed from. Anton lifted a standard with the red sun of Torchev against the blue sky of the new Riaznin. The symbolic shade wove into the red and gold bunting strung along shop buildings in the city square, while rose petals carpeted the streets. Kivra-tide seemed a modest event in comparison.

Over the last couple days, three more governors had arrived in Torchev, making seven in total who would serve as judges for Valko's trial. The other thirteen would be absent. The nobles complained about the unfairness. The peasants shouted for Valko's head to be on the chopping block already. Visitors from nearby cities trickled into Torchev to witness the proceedings. The parade was meant to rally support for the Duma before-hand.

Earlier, as the Duma was preparing to enter the avenue from a back alleyway, I'd searched among them for Anton, but Feliks found me first. "I'm grateful for your forthcoming ser-vices today," he said. "Thanks to you, we'll discover the color of Valko's true intentions." His cunning aura sent a shock of cold up my spine as he stroked the blade of his Isker scythe. Parade prop or not, it felt threatening. "After all, you were at the emperor's side when he was positioned to win the One Day War *and* when he suddenly abdicated, so you've experienced Valko at his best *or* his worst."

Even now, as the parade progressed and applause rang out, unease squeezed my lungs and wrapped around my chest. Growing more nervous by the minute, I left the congested ave-nue to return to the palace by an alternate route. I should be grounding my aura before Valko's trial, not upsetting it.

I walked on, drifting farther away from the main thorough-fares of the city. The smell of refuse and waste grew pungent on the air as I neared the downstream, polluted waters of the Azanel River. Laundry hung on lines strung between the narrow alley walls and whipped on the rancid breeze. I ducked beneath them and stepped over slop buckets and broken crates.

Dread weighted my thoughts. Perhaps Feliks had discovered my role in Valko's abdication. Another slip in a public setting, and he'd surely persuade the Duma I was too dangerous to be allowed in Torchev. Riaznin would seek to contain its Auraseers once more.

A flash of darkness moved out of the corner of my eye. I jerked to look back at the way I'd come.

A hooded girl stood fifteen feet away, her body perfectly square to me and positioned in the center of the alley. She wore a black dress with a torn hemline and a cape about her shoulders. The same girl from the orchard at Kivratide.

My heart alone kicked against my ribcage. I felt no pulse from her aura.

She moved her hand to clutch the side of her hood. Her flesh was twisted with ropy scars. Swirls and strange markings dominated the remaining, uninjured skin of her forearm.

As she pulled back her hood, a tremor rocked my limbs.

I couldn't think. Couldn't speak. Couldn't even feel. Not from her.

I knew who she was, but she should be *dead*.

CHAPTER TWELVE

I BOLTED FULL SPEED BACK TO THE PALACE. BY THE TIME I arrived, dirt from the filthy streets of poorer Torchev clung to the hemline of my dress. Near the stables, the parade horses drank water from the trough. The Duma must have already returned. Citizens lined outside the palace gates. Valko's trial would begin within minutes. Fingers shaking, I rushed up to my room and changed into a clean blue dress. I wouldn't think of whom I saw in the alleyway. I had a duty to perform.

I brushed out my hair and considered leaving it down. No. I braided it again. Valko liked it loose. My reflection stared back at me from my mirror. Eyes strained. Splotches of pink on my cheeks. I exhaled, smoothing my hands across the bodice of my dress. *You can do this. Ground yourself to your emotions.*

I found my old sovereign Auraseer headdress, the last token I'd kept of my role under the empire, and cut a pearl away from one of its ropes of dangling pearls. The others slid off, pelting the ground. I had no time to clean up the mess. I left my room and slid the pearl into my dress pocket, keeping my grip on the jewel. It only gave off a faint sting—the lingering aura of its dead mother oyster—but it was something to hold onto, something to remind me of my own willpower. Something to protect me from everyone else's.

Sneaking in through a side door, I entered the great hall before the Duma or the public had the chance to come inside. I needed a few more moments alone. I breathed slowly, in through my nose, out through my mouth, and acclimated myself to the room.

The great hall had been transformed into an auditorium. Seven chairs for the Duma crowned the red-velvet dais. Valko's magnificent throne was missing, but the room still felt imperial. The painted swirls and gold leafing of the massive, domed ceiling bore all the grandeur of the former empire. Ironic that the fate of Riaznin's last emperor would be decided in the most ostentatious room of the palace.

In front of the Duma's dais was an open space, and beyond it a semicircle of chairs fanning out into the far reaches of the great hall, where there was standing room only. It was easy to determine where Valko would be situated. In the center of the open space before the dais, in a low place on the same level as the audience, was an unembellished oak chair, rather naked and desolate looking against the beautiful parquet floor. About five feet to the right sat a smaller and plainer chair, surely a chair meant for me. Not much had changed since before the

end of the monarchy. My place beside the emperor was desig-
nated, whether he was high or low in esteem.

I rubbed my thumb over the pearl's dull sting in my pocket.
I should have brought something with a more powerful bite—a
scrap of animal hide or a handkerchief dipped in blood from
the kitchens. My gaze lingered on the distance between the two
chairs. Practically nothing.

I strived to summon Anton's grim acceptance of today's necessary justice. I'd been so ready for Valko to meet his demise.
But now, after seeing him, after saving him . . .

I took my seat, posture stiff, iron ramparts around my
feelings. I couldn't confuse my emotions with anyone else's—
especially today, especially Valko's.

The great double doors opened, and the public was admitted, nobility along with the lower and middle classes. I focused
myself as their energy hit my awareness. Through the sting of
the pearl, I struggled to center myself and force their moods to
slide off me.

Not everyone sought retribution and blood. Some auras
thickened my throat with despondency or made my chest grow
hollow with despair. My gaze locked on Terezia Dyomin as she
strolled inside wearing a royal-purple gown and a scalloped-
pearl headdress. But if Terezia's mood could fabricate her attire,
the countess's opulence would vanish. She'd resemble a dreary
wilted rose. My muscles abruptly weakened as she surveyed the
dais prepared for the Duma. Her aura felt broken, as if the last
fragments of her crystalline world were shattering.

The governors entered next. I rose to my feet, but only half the public followed my example. The others remained rooted in contempt. My stomach gave a nervous lurch, sensing Anton the moment before he strode inside. He sought me out immediately, and I gave him a small smile of encouragement, which he returned.

No other governor matched his regal bearing as he followed the Duma to the dais. None other had been bred to be emperor. As Anton took his seat beside Feliks, the two men shared a diplomatic nod, but their auras bristled, shooting pins and needles across my skin. The sensation nicked deeper when Feliks met my gaze with his unsettling blue eyes.

Once all the Duma was seated, the people in the audience followed suit—or at those who had the luxury of chairs did. Some nobles grumbled at the many spots taken by the lower classes, now considered their equals. I arched my back, adjusting my position as I fought their cramping disdain and anger.

Feliks rose and smoothed the black stole of silk draped over his kaftan. Every Duma governor wore the same court robes. "Please admit the prisoner," he commanded two guards. At the rear of the dais, they reached for the ivory-handled doors.

My heart jolted. My awareness detached from Anton and tugged against my will to find Valko. Panicked, I reached too far and absorbed all the emotions in the great hall. I jerked back against my chair with a small cry of surprise. Feliks frowned and darted a glance at Anton, whose brows drew together with worry. I gave a little shake of my head, indicating there was nothing to fret about. With hot blood in my cheeks and fingers locked around the pearl, I turned my attention to the opening doors behind the Duma. Valko entered. All other auras were forgotten. My awareness riveted to him.

His hair gleamed in waves, free of the grime of the dungeons. Clean-shaven, his face appeared even thinner, and his clothes hung about his wiry body. Still, those clothes—a simple shirt and pair of trousers—were ironed and washed, and he wore them like he stood in his finest red and gold kaftan. He acted as if this were a grand reception and not a court of the Duma that replaced him.

As four guards escorted him to his humble oak chair, Valko didn't spare one glance in my direction. He sat, posture artful as he leaned against his thin armrest. His aura ebbed and flowed with a practiced pulse in my bloodstream, never quickening, never slowing. It seemed he'd labored during his time in prison to master every nuance of his emotions.

Under the steady lull of his aura, my head listed slightly. Then I caught myself and gritted my teeth. I couldn't slip up so easily.

"People of Riaznin"—Feliks clasped his hands behind his back—"you are gathered to bear witness as the Duma, your rightful governors, mete out justice upon Valko Ozerov, former monarch of the fallen empire."

Murmurs emerged from the peasants in the room, whispers of the decree they hoped for—death. Dark desire ate at the lining of my stomach. My vision grew fuzzy. I imagined the thud of the executioner's ax as it hit the chopping block. My pulse thrilled at the sound.

A flash of black rose from the dais. A stuffed portfolio. Feliks took it from Anton's lap and held it high. I snapped back to attention, shaking away the peasants' auras.

"As a nation, we accuse you, Valko Ozerov, of tyranny on no less than forty-two charges." Feliks's piercing blue eyes lowered to Valko. "Whom have you tasked for your defense?"

The tendons in Valko's neck corded as he lifted his chin. "I have no need for anyone to defend me but myself." His clear voice boomed through the domed ceiling with far more eloquence than Feliks's. I couldn't deny that I admired his level of self-assuredness and dignity. "As for my honest sentiment, that will be vouched for by my sovereign Auraseer."

My eyes widened a fraction. Valko knew, then. He knew I'd been called to act as a character witness against him. How could he not considering the distance of my chair from his?

Anton's jaw muscle tensed as he raised his voice for the first time. "Sonya Petrova is not in your service today. She is in *ours*."

No one could have missed the fierce protectiveness in his voice. Whispers of "Sonya" and "sovereign Auraseer" hissed from the people and clawed at my ears. In a sudden flood of emotion, their energy pointed at me. My breaths came short. I shrank in my chair from the pressure and turned rebuking eyes on Anton. He wasn't helping by reacting to Valko's baiting like this.

Feliks's gaze traveled between Anton, Valko, and me. If

he didn't know about my tangled relationship with the former emperor, he'd have a strong clue now.

Anton grew uncomfortable under Feliks's scrutiny. He abruptly stood and took the portfolio from Feliks's hands. "Shall we proceed with the charges?"

"Do as you will, brother," Valko answered, although Anton hadn't addressed him. "Though I must say, I'm led to wonder about the fairness of this trial when only a third of the Duma is present. I might assume you're afraid my life would be spared if I were judged by *all* the governors."

"The trial is as fair as it can be under the present circumstances," Anton replied stiffly.

"Yes, your insistence on justice, Governor Ozerov, wouldn't allow for any rule bending unless the situation were dire and you felt you could unite the people after I am dead." Valko's emotions didn't turn black or fearful when he spoke of that fate. "Let me guess, the Shenglin have invaded, and worse, they've taken our stronghold of Gensi, along with Bovallen and all the eastern border towns."

My mouth dropped. Murmurs spilled through the courtroom. The peasants' and nobles' frantic energy mounted inside me. Bovallen was the town where I'd been born, and Gensi had remained impenetrable for decades. If Shengli had truly overtaken our eastern cities, then they'd declared a full-fledged war against Riaznin. My gaze flew to Anton, waiting for him to contradict Valko, but his grip only tightened on his portfolio.

Feliks grinned like Valko's claim was humorous, but the

flat and deadly pulse of his aura proved otherwise. "What an impressive speculation, Prisoner Ozerov. What tales the dungeons' guards must be feeding you." He cast a sharp glance at Anton. "Proceed with the charges."

The courtroom quieted. The people's anticipation pulled me to the edge of my chair. Anton swallowed. Opened the portfolio. Shifted his balance on his feet. His conflicting emotions bled into me. Heightened my own. My heart pounded to the pulse of his sorrow. He loved his brother, despite their contentious history. He didn't want him dead; he wanted justice. But he couldn't have it both ways.

Anton began listing the accusations against Valko.

Withholding provisions from starving armies. Hoarding extra rations in Torchev while famine-plagued provinces went without. Outlawing literature supporting equality. Neglecting the Azanel River, though its contamination led to deaths. Not reinforcing the borderlands with Torchev's plentiful troops, resulting in a relentless cycle of razing and pillaging by the Shenglin. Worsening inequality by unjust taxation. Exempting nobility from being drafted into wars. Accepting bribes from aristocrats, rather than fair punishment, when they broke the law.

The onslaught dragged well into the late afternoon. Evidence of the crimes was presented. Documents. Letters. Testimonies. Valko's constructed confidence fell apart, blow-by-blow. By the time the prosecution was finished, his aura drooped with exhaustion and misery, but he held his shoulders straight and exact. I couldn't help pitying him. I felt his every strained muscle, the staggered beat of his heart. I sensed him more clearly than any other person in the room. The connection between our auras was real, no matter how much I wrestled against it, no matter how I hated him.

Servants brought the Duma tumblers of water. When they drank, I didn't feel the cooling quench because Valko's throat was still dry. He had yet to look at me. I fought the urge to scoot my chair closer and place my hand on his shoulder. Feliks should adjourn the court for a break. Valko needed respite. How much more could we endure?

No, not me, *him*. I was fine. I needed to be.

I gripped my pearl in my clammy hand.

Feliks did not let us pause. My skin crawled with his impatience. His focus seemed bent on declaring Valko's death sentence as soon as possible. The peasants' similar sentiment made me itch all over. I clenched my muscles. Clutched the folds of my skirt. I wouldn't scratch at myself like a madwoman. I wouldn't let anyone else's bloodlust overtake me.

"Valko Ozerov, former Emperor and Grand Duke of all Riaznin," Feliks said. "What is your defense?"

The murmuring of the assembly, which had provided a constant backdrop to the proceedings, hushed to utter silence. I watched Valko. Each person in the room watched him. My pulse thrummed as his gray eyes slid coolly over every member of the Duma, pausing when they met his brother's gaze. Anton struggled to keep eye contact.

"If you do not speak," Feliks continued, "then you have no defense, and we will move forward with the verdict."

Without so much as twitching a brow or budging in his chair, Valko replied, "I call on my sovereign Auraseer to testify."

"No." Anton stood just as soon as the words fell from Valko's lips.

"No?" Valko repeated.

"No." More murmurs erupted from the assembly. The people's conflicting energy strangled me for breath. "The Duma has summoned Sonya to assist in judging your character. She is not your spokesperson."

"What is the difference?" Valko asked. "She can declare what she feels for me *while* she testifies."

Anton's nostrils flared. His fisted knuckles went white with rage. "What she feels *from* you," he corrected, "is what we have tasked her to do—that and nothing more."

"Under our law," Feliks interjected, turning to Anton, "the accused may choose any person to testify. If he chooses Sonya Petrova, so be it." He glanced at the other Duma governors for support, and several nodded, taking sides with the more composed man of the two.

Anton's aura spiraled with amazement and heavy bitterness. He was ever a defender of the law, and now that law couldn't protect me.

Perspiration wetted my neck. I desperately tried to search out my own feelings, to separate them from the emotions of hundreds of people in the room, to filter them from Valko's. I caught Tosya's gaze. His eyes crinkled in the corners with reassurance, and he gave me a small nod that told me I could do this. I had to. The Duma needed to see my perseverance.

My legs felt fragile, brittle as I rose to my feet. I couldn't shake the feeling that this very moment was why Valko hadn't escaped his jail cell when he'd had the chance. He'd been planning to make me testify all along, even though he hadn't divined the Duma's role for me.

I rolled back my shoulders, striving to appear confident. My words scratched up my throat; I hadn't spoken in hours. "I am ready and willing."

CHAPTER THIRTEEN

ANTON'S CRESTFALLEN STARE MADE MY CHEST ACHE. *I'm helping you*, I wanted to tell him. Couldn't he see how he was losing the Duma's trust? Every time my name was mentioned, he lost his temper. Besides, the Duma needed to see my strength in any capacity.

The silent watchfulness in the great hall grew thicker. Auras ganged up on me. Scrutinizing. Vicious. Intolerant. They tried to nest within me, overtake me. I was so tired. Of pushing them away. Staying composed. Pretending I wasn't a vessel for everyone's dark emotions. I'd never been forced to remain in a place with so much combative energy this long. Each beat of my heart felt labored. I couldn't fight them anymore. I needed to use their vigor.

I opened myself up. Let a measure of the people's anger root within me. Feed my buried feelings. It hit my awareness with a jolt. A rush of unstable strength trembled into me.

I crossed the five steps to Valko and lowered my mouth to his ear. "Do not think I have any pity for you," I spat. "You're the same man who killed Pia. The same man who struck me and bruised me and held a dagger to my throat. My testimony will not help your case today." I didn't care that he was Anton's family, that he'd tried to comfort me in the dungeons after the assassin died, or that much of the nobility wanted him alive. "I will reveal you for the monster you are, and the Duma will have your head."

Feliks's authoritative voice cut in. "There will be no whispering between the witness and the accused."

I scarcely heard him. For the first time since Valko entered the courtroom, he met my gaze. Twists of blue flashed in his gray irises, and a thread of amusement spun throughout his aura. "I did not expect your pity, only your cooperation, Sonya. I thank you for it. You may rise."

Only then did I realize I was kneeling like a servant beside him. I stood abruptly, a hare dodging a trap. Anton sat on the edge of his seat, straining to hear us, his mouth contorted in a frown. "Well?" I said to Valko. "What exactly am I testifying about?"

He crossed one knee over the other, taking his time. "The Duma likes to dwell on what I did *not* do for Riaznin," he said loud enough for everyone in the room to hear. "I want you to tell them what I *did* do for the empire."

I almost snorted. "You'll have to enlighten me. I haven't an inkling of what that would be."

Valko's stare was impassive, but his aura made my blood quicken. "My abdication, Sonya," he stage-whispered, like it was some great secret. "You were there, as I recall. If I am the tyrant the Duma says I am, why did I give my government to my people?"

A sudden chill seized me. Valko must have solved how I'd owned him and manipulated him on the night he'd relinquished his throne. "They already know you abdicated."

"But do they know the peasants were losing when I called off the battle and removed my crown?"

Feliks did. He'd said as much before the parade.

"You're my most reliable witness. You were there with me in the moments leading up to my decision. You probably remember that night better than I do." The blue sparked in his eyes again. "I want you to tell them *exactly* what happened."

I stared at Valko for several seconds, my body frozen, ice cold and rigid. The blood drained from my face in a dizzying trickle. He never blinked.

"Give your testimony, Sonya Petrova," Feliks said. He was just as hungry as Valko to hear it.

I stole a glance around the room. Slid my hand inside my dress pocket. Grasped the pearl with shaking fingers. My mind raced. With all the things I shouldn't say. Things that might implicate me. But things that I *must* say to placate Valko. I slowly lifted my gaze to the Duma, heart hammering in fear. My fear, as well as everyone else's.

"Based on what I saw that night, it is my understanding

that the former emperor's guards were in a position of triumph over the peasants at the moment he chose to abdicate," I began. "Valko Ozerov believes his actions demonstrated the regard he has for his people's welfare."

Anton shut his eyes. His aura spasmed with a dread that made my shoulders bunch.

Feliks lowered himself in his chair, his attention rapt on me. This was the very topic he'd cornered me about today. "It's irrelevant what Valko *believes* he did. Tell us *your* testimony of that night. What do *you* believe happened?"

Anton sat like a spring ready to burst. His eyes pleaded with me to proceed carefully, but he didn't understand my full predicament. He was worried I would reveal what I was. *Unnatural. A manipulator. Unlike any other Auraseer.* But beyond that, I felt responsible for Valko's fate. The former emperor might be executed based on what I did or didn't say.

I flexed my free hand and glanced to Valko. While I fought my own rage and trepidation, he leaned back, expression untroubled, energy gliding on calm waves. I drew in a long breath and tried to borrow his cool collectedness.

"I found Valko standing by his balcony window after sundown when the peasants attacked the palace," I went on. I couldn't mention, of course, how he had tried to kill me. Then I'd have to explain why he'd wanted me dead. He believed I made him weak, when he wanted to be a strong ruler like his father. I didn't need the Duma musing over our complicated relationship or give them any reason to ponder why I deserved death, even if only in the former emperor's eyes. "Valko confided in me his . . . struggle over how he should handle the battle." My words fell haltingly from my lips. "He was torn that his people were so divided."

Valko tipped his head at me, as if we were sharing a fond memory. "Sonya helped me understand, in an unequivocal way, how everyone felt. I've never experienced anything as *persuasive*, anything as—"

"This is Sonya's testimony, not yours!" Anton snapped, his panic chasing through my chest.

"But I am giving my own defense." Valko brandished a hand at himself. "I can add to Sonya's testimony if it supports my case. Please tell me you *understand* your own law." He looked around the room in a mild show of embarrassment for his brother.

"He *is* within his rights," Feliks replied to Anton, and no Duma governor contradicted him. Anton roughly shifted in his chair and rubbed tense fingers over his mouth. "Though I must warn the accused that Sonya will tell us if anything he shares is false."

Valko nodded in acquiescence. "I understand her duty to both me and the Duma."

I stiffened at his unyielding effort to stake ownership of me, to reveal my role in his abdication. I couldn't understand his motive. Had he missed his chance to escape prison just to expose my hidden power to the Duma? Was Valko so bent on revenge that he wished to see me ruined rather than help himself?

"Continue, Sonya," Feliks commanded. His eyes narrowed

as they regained their intense focus on me. "What does the former emperor mean when he says you persuaded him during One Day War? Persuaded him to do *what* exactly?"

I swallowed, twisting my hands together. "It was Valko who came to the conclusion," I said, laboring to deflect my own involvement. "He decided something tremendous must be done to restore peace."

"Because I truly *felt* the people—all of them," Valko supplied. "It was almost as if, for a brief moment in time, I *became* the Auraseer."

I whirled on him, my nerve endings on fire.

Valko's collectedness didn't falter under my threatening glare. "As you speak, Sonya, I remember the night more vividly. My only wish is to make everyone understand what happened and how it changed me. I felt true compassion for my people." He turned around in his chair to address the public. "I had an overwhelming desire to help each of you on a grander scale than ever before—to such an extent that I gave up my throne after Sonya helped me *perfectly* sense your desire for independence. I don't know how she did it." He smiled, displaying a mask of humility and penitence. "That's why I want her to testify. She was there and can tell you the honest truth of my reformation. And now I will let her do so." He angled back around, returning his gaze to me.

My cheeks flamed with mortification and fury. I dropped the pearl in my pocket. I hadn't dodged a trap. I was *in* a trap, its iron jaws biting my leg.

The room quieted, which only amplified the pulse of everyone else's emotions and conflicting desires. They felt suffocatingly close, as if the people had risen from their chairs and crept up behind me. Anton's lips pressed white from his desperate need to speak and free me from saying anything more.

"I . . ." I struggled to think. What wouldn't I give right now for Anton's intelligence? Or Tosya's eloquence? What could I say to defend myself, to unravel me from this tangle?

The collective eyes of the Duma drilled into my skull. Feliks tapped a finger on his armrest. The box-faced governor from Grishina looked like she might execute me, along with Valko, if I didn't start talking.

I cleared my throat. "Valko—that is, the former emperor—gives me far too much credit for what happened that night." The heat from the afternoon sun beat against the windows. I tugged the neckline of my dress. "It's true I *did* help him feel what I was feeling."

The hook-nosed governor from Dubrov scratched his beard. I turned a fretful gaze to Anton. A crease of worry bridged his brows together. He didn't want the people to know of my enhanced ability. They would use me, fear me, maybe even lock me away. Who knew what this new Duma might do? Perhaps my unnatural gift was enough threat to merit death.

I hid my hands in the folds of my dress. "You see, I *told* the emperor what I was feeling, what the people were feeling." My voice pitched higher in my desperation to sound innocent. Heat curled at the nape of my neck and temples. I needed to concentrate, focus on something. My vision tunneled on a small slit in the velvet skirt of the dais. The servants had neglected to pull it closed.

"It is a strange thing to inherently know what makes up another person," I continued. "We call it aura, but what is that? It is more than every sensation of the body, which the mind interprets as emotion. It is more than the signature energy that radiates from the spirit. One's aura is one's essence—deeper than the body, the mind, or the spirit. And for an Auraseer, that essence is tangible. It flows like blood through our veins. It disrupts our heartbeats. We understand what it is to *be* our fellow human beings, almost as if we are inside your skin."

The leathery-faced governor from Illola shifted uncomfortably in his chair. I glanced behind me at the people. Their expressions were equally unsettled. I wanted them to understand the gift I was born with, but I was only scaring them. No one wanted to be truly understood down to their naked skeleton. They wanted boundaries, secrets. I exposed them, whether I desired to or not.

When I faced the dais once more, the slit in the velvet skirt fluttered. Small fingers opened it a fraction wider.

"Dasha," I gasped, singling out her vibrant aura.

"Pardon?" Feliks frowned. When I ran to the dais, he abruptly stood. "What is this? Do not leave your post!"

I grabbed Dasha's hands and dragged her out from beneath the platform. Her hair was a mess, all static and wispy knots. She rattled with tremors. Kneeling in front of her, I beat the dust off her dress and rubbed her shaking arms. "What are you doing here?" I asked in dismay. I hated to think she'd been suffering with what I'd been feeling all this while. "Sestra Mirna has been looking everywhere for you."

"Another Auraseer is not allowed in this courtroom!" Feliks barked, although there was no such law unless he'd just drafted it himself.

Dasha flinched, eyes wide with fright. "I didn't want to go home yet, Sonya," she hurriedly explained. "I wanted a chance to—to say good-bye." Her gaze skipped over my shoulder to Valko. She ducked her head when she caught him staring back. "He looks even younger than Prince Anton," she whispered.

I suspected the main reason Dasha had snuck in here was to glimpse the infamous emperor she might have served one day as sovereign Auraseer.

Feliks's patience met its limit. "She must leave at once! She's a distraction to the proceedings." I frowned, wondering what the governor was so keen on having me divulge when the trial was in motion again.

I glanced at Anton for help, feeling his anxious concern for Dasha, but of course he wouldn't be able to escort her away. Thankfully, Tosya stood from the audience, volunteering himself. He strode over and patted Dasha on the back. "Come along. I'll tell Sestra Mirna I caught you playing in the orchard," he said with a wink.

I tucked Dasha's hair behind her ear. "I'm sorry you have to leave Torchev so soon. I'll write you letters, I promise."

She nodded, her mouth twisting so she wouldn't cry. "Good-bye, Sonya."

I kissed her cheek, fighting back my own tears. I hated that our farewell was a public spectacle. The people's heightened curiosity made my breath hitch, my pulse trip.

As Tosya guided Dasha away, she gave a tiny wave to Anton, which he managed to return with a comforting smile.

When the doors closed, my gut folded with sorrow and dread. Dasha and Sestra Mirna would leave Torchev while I was stuck here recounting my testimony. The pressure to be truthful crashed down on my shoulders with new force. *I could run. Hide like Dasha did.*

"Your witness has been stalled long enough, Sonya." Feliks towered over me. "Finish the job."

My knees quaked. I reluctantly turned to Valko. He leaned on his armrest, stroking his chin, eyes clapped on the doors Dasha had exited. A faint sense of familiarity prickled the back of my neck. Had he met her before?

"As I was saying . . ." I cleared my throat. Valko's gaze fixated on me again. Something different sparked within him. Hope? Surprise? Resolve? My head ached. I couldn't sieve his emotions. " . . . Auraseers are *special*." No, that was the wrong word. That might give my power away. "*Talented*. Auraseers are *equally* talented."

Anton pinched the bridge of his nose. Feliks uncrossed his legs. Faces crowded the windows of the great hall. More peasants and nobles looked in from outside.

"And what did you help me feel, Sonya?" Valko's head canted, his tone patient but predatory.

"Feel?"

"When I abdicated."

Oh. My posture loosened, mind cleared. "I felt what *they* did," I said simply, though there was nothing simple about what I'd done. "I felt *all* of you that night." I looked out at the assembly. "I understood your longing to be free, to be fed, to be granted equality. Through each of your auras, Riaznin spoke her desire. And so I . . . I appealed to the emperor's compassion on your behalf."

The people's auras flooded me, as a legion of them did then, bubbling with pressure inside my chest. All my emotions from that night surfaced. All the *people's* emotions. I gasped with their pain and my sudden clarity. "You've suffered from centuries of oppression. Your sorrow is ageless. You long to be unchained." Tears sprang to my eyes. "As clearly as I could, I told the emperor what you felt." The timbre of my voice expressed their relentless heartache and yearning. "Once he understood it, he could no longer deny you. I didn't force him to do anything. Once he understood you, he let you go."

As I spoke the words, I felt the truth of them. I hadn't relayed everything—how I'd summoned the auras of the living and the dead within me, then thrust them inside Valko so he could feel everyone's anguish. The Duma didn't need to know that. But what I *had* said was honest. What I'd said of Valko was honest. I *hadn't* forced him to abdicate. I'd only forced him to feel someone beside himself—an empire's worth of someones. And once he felt them and their terrible weight, he was persuadable. He *chose* to relinquish the throne.

Sure of my stunning revelation, I spun around to face the Duma. "That is why his life should be spared. By what he did that night, *you* now have a new life, a new nation." I stood with my spine erect and spoke clearly so I could not be mistaken. "Valko Ozerov should live."

For a smattering of heartbeats, the great hall hushed in a siphon of silence. My gaze met blank stares; my words rang on deaf ears. My declaration seemed incomprehensible. But then another staggered moment passed. The people absorbed what I'd spoken. Their shock shifted to violent understanding.

Auras swarmed like bees from a burst hive. Everyone's frantic and raging energy rushed inside me. A great exhale purged from my chest. My assurance deflated.

The great hall erupted in chaos.

I stumbled back from the onslaught. I didn't know whom the people's target was—Valko, the Duma, or me.

"Order!" Feliks said. "Order!" A muted cry above the thundering voices.

A large peasant man barreled toward me. I froze. His furious aura collided with mine. I absorbed it, snarled and fisted my hands. Prepared to strike. Just as his hands reached for my neck, a young nobleman punched him in the jaw. Pain blasted through me. I gasped and ducked to the floor. Fought to escape the madness. But I couldn't shield myself from all the anger in the room. Nor could I contain it. It would break me.

More punches flew. Blood sprayed across the air and flecked the back of my hand. It amplified the onslaught inside me tenfold. Pain ruptured through my limbs. My breaths came hot, filled with greater rage. I shook harder. Cast wild eyes around. Some women joined the scuffle. Others shrieked. Continuous shouts of order rang from the Duma. I couldn't see the dais. My vision filled with circling legs. Flashing hands. People fought all around me.

I would fight *them*. Hurt them. *No.* I clutched my hair. I would make them stop.

I turned about, head dizzy, body aching. The pain wouldn't alleviate. A girl attacked me, and I shoved her away. She sprang for me again, slapped me across the face. I blinked twice, my cheek stinging with my *own* pain. Darting away, I dodged other people. Looked for an escape. Frantically groped for my pearl. Maybe it would center me. But I couldn't find the opening for my pocket.

"Sonya!"

I jerked my head up. "Anton!" I couldn't see him. I moved toward his voice, but a pair of sparring men knocked me down. "Anton!" I scrambled for my pearl once more, this time finding my pocket. Once the pearl was out, it fumbled out of my shaking hand and skittered away on the floor. I reached for it, but it was impossible to grasp beyond the trampling feet.

Someone bent to fetch it. He must have been watching to see such a tiny thing among the pandemonium. His hand closed around the pearl. Cool gray eyes. Valko.

He appeared murky through the madness surrounding me. Dangerous. Volatile. Yet I'd declared him innocent—at least innocent enough that he should live.

His aura knifed through me, cutting past the other auras raging inside. Like attracting like, his energy melded with mine. *Triumph*, his firing heartbeat told me. Triumph.

Then I realized what had happened. How I'd played right into his hand. In the dungeons with the assassin. In this very courtroom with the Duma.

I kept saving his life.

And Valko knew I would.

"Lock him away!" Feliks shouted, sounding nearer now, louder. The guards advanced.

Never tearing his gaze from mine, Valko put the pearl in his mouth. A secret between us. A place the guards wouldn't discover he was hiding a jewel. But his action felt like more than that. It felt like thievery. Ownership. Revenge. For manipulating him the night he abdicated. For choosing his brother over him.

Valko didn't swallow the pearl. His aura grafted so tightly to mine I felt the jewel's roundness lodge under my tongue. My mouth watered around its tasteless form.

"Sonya!" Anton's voice thrashed in my ear.

I couldn't sever my gaze from Valko.

A hand gripped my arm. Another hand gripped Valko's.

We were both yanked up, mirror images of each other.

"Sonya!" Anton turned my chin. My connection to Valko broke. Anton's concerned face came into focus. "Stay with me. Come back to me. You're seizing all over."

Distractedly, I glanced down at myself. My vision bounced and streaked, white stars popping in my periphery. I vaguely realized I wasn't breathing at all. Too many auras were inside me. Too much violence and anger. I couldn't hold it.

Anton said something else, but I couldn't make it out. The sounds of the room sucked away, my hearing failing. Anton's mouth moved, but his voice came slow, muffled, garbled. I wrestled to lift my gaze to his eyes, but the effort was maddeningly sluggish.

Sonya, he mouthed.

I felt empty. Of myself. My emotions. Clashing auras devoured me, burning through me until I felt like ash.

My heartbeat slowed. Anton wrapped his hand around my waist and lugged me toward the doors of the room.

The last image I saw of the great hall was its intricate parquet floor against my blue shoes. Limply and haphazardly, my numb feet dragged along its graceful seams.

Blackness flocked my vision. My knees buckled.

I gave in to the darkness.

CHAPTER FOURTEEN

THE NEXT DAY I SAT IN THE SHADE OF THE PALACE PAVILION, overlooking the garden pool, and dipped my toes in the water. The calm energy of the ornamental fish tingled my skin, but couldn't divert me from my biting fears. Riots, wars, and a girl I'd presumed dead made me flinch at the shadows.

The stretched breadth of an open, easy aura approached me. "Hello, Tosya," I said, without glancing up.

"One of these days I'm going to manage to sneak up on you."

"I doubt it. You're locked up in your room too often, courting your quill."

He chuckled and sat beside me, leaning against a beam of the pavilion. "I have to take advantage of the muse when she graces me. Her visits are few and far between. Besides, your life is far more interesting than my poetry. I heard all about the fun yesterday."

I rubbed my arm as the all the violent chaos flashed to

mind. "I'm glad you weren't there for the end."

"What, you don't think I can defend myself? I *can't*, but I'm still insulted."

Distracted, I watched the reeds below the shallow water sway and catch sparkling rays of sunlight. "How's it coming along, your new book?" I didn't want to talk about the trial. The court would reconvene for the verdict in two days, and Anton said I wasn't invited.

Tosya heaved a dramatic sigh that still managed to sound merry. "Half the time I'm sure I'm penning the language of the gods. The other half I'm no better than a braying ass. Today's a braying-ass day, so I thought I'd take a walk."

"That's often the best solution."

"And how about you?" He prodded my hip with the toe of his boot. "Why the long face? That's my look, not yours, though mine is due to this rugged bone structure." He flourished a hand from his chin to his brow. I cracked a grin at the poor joke, but didn't laugh. "Sorry." Tosya groaned at himself. "Like I said, braying-ass day."

I didn't answer Tosya's question. He knew very well why I was brooding. Despite my best efforts, I was an instigator of trouble, just like Sestra Mirna said. Anton seemed to share her opinion. After I'd recovered from my fainting spell, we'd had a heated argument about why I publicly declared Valko should live. Anton thought I'd done so because I'd lost touch with my own emotions at the trial. In spite of that, I defended my actions. For all the same reasons I stated in court, I still believed Valko should live.

Another aura scratched my awareness. I looked across the pond and found Lenka hunched over at the water's edge. She sucked in her bony cheeks, concentrating as she sifted through the tall grass. I frowned at my former maid. "What is *she* doing here?"

"Plucking a bouquet of wildflowers, it appears," Tosya replied.

My toe stirred the water in a whirlpool of resentment. "I'm amazed she appreciates any form of beauty at all. She hated Pia, you know." Nothing and no one had been more beautiful than my closest friend. "Lenka was the one who reported her missing the day she was arrested. I'll never forgive her for that." Pia was executed for treason shortly afterward.

"Well, what are you going to do about it?" Tosya's voice held a challenge.

I shrugged. "Sit here and complain to you, naturally."

His mood shifted and sent a mischievous tickle between my ribs. "I can think of more interesting ways to get even. You know, I never did see you work your mystical powers to persuade Valko to renounce his throne."

I eyed him, wondering what he was getting at. "Don't you believe I did?"

"Of course . . . I just wished I could've watched it." He played with a frayed patch on his trousers.

My brows drew slowly together. "What, you want me to meddle with Lenka *right now*? Is that what you're suggesting?"

He smiled like he was thirteen again. "Mm-hmm."

"No," I said firmly. "That's stupid." Then I grinned despite myself.

"Maybe it is. But I can't help wondering why the courtroom got so out of hand. What's the point of having the power to manipulate emotions if you're not going to use it to calm a riot?"

"I can't just snap my fingers and make everyone happy. You have no idea how hard it is to control my ability! I've scarcely used my power. Anton doesn't *want* me to use it."

"That's because he doesn't want you endangered. But maybe with a little innocent practice, you'd feel confident using it in careful and discreet amounts. You have to admit, your power would have helped yesterday."

I buried my head in my hands. "Anton would be livid if he knew we were even having this conversation."

"So we won't tell him. The truth is you have a gift that can *protect* you, Sonya, and that's all Anton wants in the end."

I considered him.

"Come on." Tosya unhitched himself from the beam and scooted closer, crisscrossing his legs. "Just do something harmless. Make Lenka jump in the pond."

"Oh, that's harmless?" I smirked, shoving his arm.

"It's no more than two feet deep. She'll get wet to her knees. It'll probably feel refreshing."

I rolled my eyes. "I can't force her to do something specific like that, Tosya. That's not how it works. I can only make her feel my *aura*. Then she'll react however she will."

He thought about that a moment. "And when Valko abdicated, you made him feel the auras of the peasants fighting in the battle?"

I nodded as a chill from the dungeons crept inside me.

"I've got it." Tosya clapped his hands. "You feel what I feel, just like you did with the peasants, then make Lenka feel *my* emotions. Unless you think you've lost your talent."

Growing tempted, I wriggled my toes through the water and peered up at Lenka. She'd gathered enough lilies in her arms to fill a large vase. I took a deep breath and pulled my feet out of the pool. "Very well," I said. The prospect of having control over something in my life was irresistible.

"Ha!" Tosya rocked back with delight. "All right, all right"—he shook out his hands—"let me get ready. I must summon the perfect emotion." His nostrils flared with concentration, and he closed his eyes.

"You look ridiculous."

"Shh, Sonya. I'm trying to focus."

"*I'm* the one who must put forth the effort here."

"Then do it already!"

I poked him in the chest. He kept his eyes shut, his brows drawn low in effort. Steeling my nerves, I turned my attention back to Lenka and folded my legs beneath me so I was kneeling. I let Tosya's emotions trickle into me.

A freeing sense of abandonment swept under my skin. I gave myself into it and my neck went limp. My eyelids fluttered in a rush of contentedness. The feeling grew stronger, surging through my chest, until it transformed into sweet bliss. I swayed, slightly drunk on the sensation. "Making my horrid old maid feel happy doesn't seem like much of a prank."

Tosya peeked his eyes open. "Send her the feeling, Sonya," he urged. "People like her don't know what to do with happiness. Trust me, this will be fun."

"You're hilarious." A peel of laughter rippled from me. "Can you follow me around all day, please? I like your company." I tossed my head back in another fit of giggles.

"Sonya, concentrate." Tosya rattled me by the shoulder. "We want to see *Lenka* lose control, not you."

I tucked my chin, striving to steady myself. "Yes, sir." I saluted him, then cocked my head at my maid. "Lenka . . . LenkaLenkaLenkaLenka."

"Is chanting part of the ritual?"

"No." I snorted. There he went again, being ridiculous. "Just trying to connect with her. *That's* necessary, I know that much." My focus trapped on Lenka's aura and it's somber pulse. "LenkaLenkaLenka."

She felt sad as she arranged the flowers in her arms with utmost care. She'd spent many long years at the palace serving Izolda, the sovereign Auraseer before me. Lenka had practically worshipped the woman. Perhaps the flowers were for Izolda's grave.

A tendril of empathy reached my heart. I understood mourning.

Lenka's hand paused as she stroked one of the flower

petals. It was hard to see her in detail from across the pond, but I swear the corners of her mouth lifted. She bowed her head, and her shoulders curled inward. For a moment, I worried some emotion had taken a wrong turn. But then she tipped her head back, basking in the sunlight, her smile growing wider. She gently swayed back and forth, embracing her flowers like they'd transformed into a dance partner. The feeling of joy built within her. She idly hummed a sprightly folk song. Her tempo picked up, and she gave a little skip and twirl.

Tosya covered his mouth, laughing so hard he couldn't breathe. His humor collided with my aura. I fell against his side and clutched my stomach. It ached from a torrent of giggles. Our silliness reached Lenka. She finally glimpsed us from the other side of the pond and didn't realize the joke was on her. As a hearty chortle racked her chest, she dropped the flowers and bent over, clasping her knees for support. That sent Tosya and me laughing harder. Tears rolled down our cheeks. We kept pointing at one another, at how idiotic we looked, then pointed at Lenka. Every moment became more absurd than the last.

"How did we not know you could do this growing up?" Tosya clapped me on the back. "Think of all the fun we missed!"

I threw my hands in the air, claiming my ignorance.

He groaned with happiness and rubbed his tears away with the palm of his hand. "I'm so glad I stopped writing today."

Lenka's hair fell out of her restrictive bun as she waved at us. She looked years younger. It felt like we three were close friends who'd once shared Romska campfires. My laughter tempered to a warm chuckle. Maybe this wasn't such a mean trick, after all.

Tosya leaned back on his elbows. "Did I tell you Motshan's caravan is in Torchev?"

I turned surprised eyes on him. "No! The Romska are here?"

"Arrived just yesterday. Smart timing, coming around the trial. They'll fatten their earnings with all the visitors in the city."

I yanked on my shoes and rose to my feet.

"Where are you going?"

"To go see them, of course."

Tosya jumped up. "Sonya, I don't think that's the best idea. The people are still agitated right now. They won't settle down until after the verdict is announced tomorrow."

"You're forgetting my power can protect me." I patted him on the chest. "Thanks for teaching me that."

He grumbled and scrubbed a hand over his face. "Anton will have my head if he knows I let you leave the palace grounds."

I crossed my arms and borrowed his line. "So we won't tell him."

CHAPTER FIFTEEN

"TRAITOR!" A PEASANT MAN WITH A PATCHED EYE KICKED DIRT in my path.

"Defender of a tyrant!" An old washwoman splashed a pail of dirty water on Raina's legs and the hem of my dress.

"I only spoke the truth," I said, my silence breaking as their anger hit my bloodstream. "I'm loyal to the democracy."

"Then why did you betray it?" A flaxen-haired peasant picked up a stone. "Leave!" He hurled it at me. I ducked just in time, but a small cluster of children followed his example. They gathered up pebbles and pelted my legs.

"Well, this is going swimmingly," Tosya muttered from his horse astride mine. He shielded his face as the pebbles flew higher.

I kicked Raina's flanks and cleared a path for us through my attackers. Our quickened pace didn't last long. We slowed near the center of the city where the streets grew congested with people at market.

Tosya scowled and brushed a clod of dirt from his vest. A peasant had missed me and nailed him. "Thanks for managing the situation back there," he said dryly.

"Oh, that was just a little adventure." I grinned, though my heart raced from our near escape. I tried not to think of my diminished esteem among the people. I'd find a way to win their favor back again. "We went looking for that kind of trouble growing up. You can't expect me to exercise my power over *everyone* who crosses me, not unless I'm truly endangered."

"Let's hope I don't lose an eye before then."

"I promise to intervene if your vanity is threatened."

We prodded our horses onward. Hostility remained, but it came from both the nobles and the peasants now, and it was no longer directed at me. "There they are!" I pointed with a smile, pushing all the aggressive auras away. The Romska were in the thick of one of their impromptu fairs.

The twins, Camlo and Durril, played their fiddle and reed pipe while Gillie and a cluster of dancers swept through the square, swaying their skirts and stomping their feet. Romska jesters and acrobats tumbled near market stalls, and tribe children wandered about, shaking tin cups for coins. Under shop awnings, Jeta and some older women sat at tables advertising miracle tinctures and card readings. And at the rear of the square, a few tribesmen, including the Romska chief, Motshan, led five stunning horses around for bartering.

"Filthy gypsies," a baron in a brocaded kaftan murmured to his companion as they strode by. "Always bringing diseases. Guard your pockets, Mikhail. They have sticky fingers."

I released an angry breath and dismounted Raina. Some prejudices never changed, even though Tosya—a Romska—had played a major role in the revolution.

All around us people sneered at the Romska's loose clothes, lower necklines, and mismatched jewelry. The colorful beads woven into their hair and sewn onto their sleeves symbolized the mystical energy the Romska worshipped rather than the seven gods—one of many reasons the people feared the tribes and found them repellent and strange. Their nomadic lifestyle was just as peculiar, but traveling was in the Romska's blood. They didn't pay taxes because they owned no land.

Thirty feet away, in the middle of the square, a little Romska girl about ten years old splashed her hands in a large fountain. She leaned forward and laughed as her dark braids dipped into the water.

I squinted my eyes and called, "Paizi, is that you?"

Her little brown face popped up, her mouth falling open with surprise. My heart lurched in recognition with hers.

I waved for her to come and say hello. She nodded and beckoned to someone behind the spouting fixture. To my surprise, Kira emerged, her sleeves wet to her elbows and a wide smile on her face.

A double wave of homesickness assaulted me, as well as concern. The pristine yellow dress Kira had worn to meet her parents in was now ragged and filthy. She walked barefoot, her feet crusted with dirt to her ankles. Her parents didn't seem to be anywhere nearby.

I tugged Raina, fighting to reach the girls faster, but the square was too crowded. Tosya took Raina's bridle. "Go on," he said. "I'll tie up the horses and meet you back here in a minute."

I gave him my thanks and pressed closer to the girls, but a woman carrying a stack of wrapped parcels collided into me. As they knocked to the ground, she cast me a reproachful glare. Once our eyes met, both our auras went black.

The woman was Countess Terezia Dyomin, her raven hair swept back with an ivory comb, her crimson dress lustrous in the afternoon sunlight. "I suppose stirring the pot at the emperor's trial wasn't enough to satisfy you," she said, looking down at me from her two-inch height difference. "Naturally, you had to race to the city the very next day to meddle in more affairs."

"What's that supposed to mean?"

"It means some of us see through to your tricks, Sovereign Auraseer."

My pulse tripped. Did she mean my power? I hadn't used it during the trial. "If you're accusing me of something, you're going to have to speak frankly, Countess." I wasn't going to let Terezia Dyomin, of all people, push me around. Practicing my power on Lenka had emboldened me.

Her gaze thinned into vicious slits. "Very well. Truth be known, we don't trust a reckless and changeable girl who defends the emperor while bedding herself with the Duma."

Anger burned through my lungs. "Is that what the nobility think of me?"

"It doesn't take genius to deduce how you moved from one royal brother's good graces to the next. The Duma may seek to strip us of our titles, but the nobility hasn't forgotten who is superior. I, for one, intend to do everything in my power to protect our way of life." My stomach hardened with her steely resolve.

"Sonya!" Kira rammed into me with a hug.

I forced a smile and rubbed the girl's back. Terezia wrinkled her nose at Kira's state of filth, and when Paizi joined us, her contempt scraped me like briars.

The Romska girl was oblivious to Terezia's irritation. She seized the moment to shake her tin cup in front of someone so markedly wealthy.

"What a disgrace." Terezia recoiled and glanced around the square to see if anyone was watching.

Camlo and Durril began another song with a frenzied tempo, growing more desperate to please the crowd. Gillie and the dancers stomped, clapped, and spun with greater energy.

Terezia composed herself, gathering her parcels back in her arms. "I'll leave you to your happy reunion with the gypsies," she said sharply. My ribs squeezed tight with her envy. It was common knowledge I'd been raised by the Romska, but I couldn't fathom why the countess would be jealous of it. "Just know their loyalty to you was bought," she added, "though I've no idea what your parents could have possibly given the nomads to persuade them to take you in."

What was she talking about? "You know nothing about my parents!" My anger flamed to fury. "They lived in Bovallen. They *died* there when they were arrested for sending me into hiding. That's the price they paid, and I won't have you mock it."

Terezia's glare hardened, but a twinge of shame bled through her aura. She shifted her stacked parcels, and I caught sight of her gold ring. It bore her family crest, a peacock on a tower—the same symbol as the seal on the letter that had upset Sestra Mirna.

I considered the countess's hatred of me in a new light. After all, I was someone who had evaded the empire's clutches until I was seventeen, then I'd survived the convent fire. "What is your connection to the convent in Ormina?" I asked, so shocked that I took no care to be delicate.

Her eye's widened. Humiliation, heartache, and fury knifed through me. All her emotions, not mine.

A loud crash sounded from across the square. Three soldiers gathered around Jeta's tables. They'd kicked one over, and the medicines and miracle tinctures tumbled and shattered. The tension in the square slammed into me as I detached from Terezia's aura.

"Your kind is not welcome in Torchev!" the largest soldier said to the women, knocking over a second table with their fortune-telling cards.

Motshan stepped forward. The Romska chief was middle-aged and intimidating in appearance with sage green eyes—a rarity among the dark-eyed Romska—heavy brows, and a scar from a stitched-together cleft lip. "My caravan comes to Torchev every summer. The emperor has never evicted us."

The soldier swiped a hand under his crooked nose and turned to stare down Motshan. "After tomorrow, the emperor's royal head will be chopped off his body." Some nobles called out disagreements, but he broadened his chest. "The Duma rules now."

My heart pounded with the growing hostility, but Motshan casually shook the ashes from his pipe. "And are *you* the Duma?"

"We're what keeps the peace in this city. What we do *is* the law."

My jaw stiffened. Violent energy gripped my aura. Twenty or more soldiers closed in from various alleyways. I ground my teeth in resistance. I wouldn't let another mob overwhelm me. Or harm the Romska.

"We will leave *if* and when the Duma decrees it." Motshan's energy flared with urgency, but he coolly strode forward. At the head soldier's feet, Jeta and the fortune-tellers scrambled to salvage what they could. The chief gave a slight nod to Camlo and Durril, and the twins set down their instruments and fisted their hands. "Until then, my people will sell our wares, trade our horses, and offer you entertainment in this city."

"You call that legitimate work?" The soldier kicked the shattered glass of a tincture vial. "Meanwhile, you poach off our lands and cut our timber. Go to some other country and take advantage of them. I hear Abdara cuts off the hands of caught thieves."

Angry shouts of agreement rose from the crowd. Equality and freedom couldn't unite the peasants and nobles, but mutual intolerance of the Romska did the trick.

Motshan advanced nearer, about fifteen feet from the head soldier. "If you cast out your guests, your guests' bad luck comes upon you." He shrugged. "Your superstition, not ours."

My breaths came quickly. I twitched as the people's fear and hatred grew more incensed. Their rage found a convenient target in the Romska. They wouldn't be arrested for harming tribesmen who weren't even considered citizens of Riaznin.

"I'll give you one final warning." The crooked-nosed soldier withdrew his saber from his scabbard. It rang out and gleamed in the sunlight. The people hushed. I froze on the balls of my feet. "Leave Torchev in peace, while you can."

Motshan's hand moved to his belted knife. "Torchev's peace has nothing to do with us," he said, stalling as long as possible while his tribe congregated. "Your quarrel is among yourselves. If you execute your emperor, you will incite a civil war. Death cannot unify a people."

"Emperor Valko *must* die, or the nobles will never yield to change!" a young peasant shouted.

Within seconds, a violent uproar broke out among the people. Their anger turned from the Romska as they yelled at their neighbors. Some shoved each other. Terezia fled to a nearby group of nobles.

Kira gazed wildly about the crowd. Thick tears poured down her face, and she rubbed the base of her throat till it was red. Paizi gaped at her, unsure how to help.

I gripped her shoulders. "Kira, look at me." I had to see to her safety, as well as Paizi's, before attempting anything else.

"I want Sestra Mirna." Kira's chin trembled.

"Sestra Mirna's gone back to the convent, remember? Where are your parents?"

"Papa's in a tavern. I don't know which one. Mama's scared of me. I tell her the baby inside her isn't well. She likes it better when I leave."

The commotion intensified. Jeta and the fortune-tellers flung the last of their wares into baskets. Six feet away, a teenaged peasant boy punched a nobleman. Kira and I jerked as his pain reverberated through us. She broke into full-blown sobs.

I drew my arm around her. "I'm going to get you out of here. Single out my aura and fix your senses upon it, all right? Force out all the other energy. Pretend you and I are behind a shield."

She released a blubbering sigh, but nodded and wiped her running nose.

"Paizi, run along to Jeta. Don't bump into anyone."

The Romska girl gave a brave grin, an adventurous spirit taking hold of her. "Bye, Sonya." Turning to Kira, she added, "Come visit my camp." She spun away, her dark braids whipping.

Kira and I fought our way forward like fish against a raging current. More fists slugged into chests, stomachs, heads, jaws. I swallowed tight moans of pain. "Don't look at them," I told her. "You'll feel them stronger if you do. Just keep clinging to me."

My awareness bounced from person to person, trying to find some safe place of landing. I avoided latching onto Kira's overwhelmed aura. I needed to protect her at all costs. That motherly instinct consumed me—and felt familiar. Terezia's emotions were this powerful when I'd brought up the convent moments ago.

A child's shriek pierced the air. My gut twisted with dread. "Paizi!" Kira cried.

I looked over my shoulder. The crooked-nosed soldier had lifted Paizi like a cat by the back of her dress.

My body flashed cold, then my nerves inflamed. "Hide," I commanded Kira, pointing to a nearby market cart. She felt the severe shift of my mood. Without a word of resistance, she did as told. Rage blazed through me as I charged toward the soldier.

Paizi wrestled helplessly as she dangled from his grasp, her eyes wild with fright. Last springtime flashed to mind. Paizi and a group of tribe children had been held hostage by the bounty hunter Bartek in exchange for me. The Romska were forced to hand me over to him, ending their many long years of protection. This moment felt like a repeat of that day, a man terrorizing an innocent child. Paizi had suffered enough abuse. I wouldn't allow anyone to harm her again.

Another man stumbled into me. I pushed him away, my gaze fixated on the head soldier. His head turned my direction. He smirked to see a slight girl coming for him.

I sensed his anger, his repulsion, his false sense of supe-riority rooted in self-doubt. I dug within his aura, beneath his physical strength, to the energy that fed his lust for control. Its adrenaline spikes radiated with fear.

I reflected his gloating smile. He hungered for power because he was afraid of the world. I would break him with it.

Paizi stopped fighting the soldier, seeing my fierce stance, my flinty gaze.

Shouts, screams, and thuds clamored around us. I pushed the air from my lungs to make room for more panic and thrust it back at the soldier. His terror rocked through me. His eyes flew wide, his brow beaded with perspiration.

I took another step forward, seizing the fear from those nearest me and channeled it into him. The soldier shuddered and dropped Paizi. She landed in a crouch, then released an amazed breath. Before the soldier could grab her again, she sprang away.

Scuffling boots charged toward us. Camlo and Durril ganged up on the soldier. Camlo pinned his arms, and Durril rammed his knuckles into his jaw.

The man grunted, and I startled with the blow he took. I was so linked to his aura that my jaw felt as if I'd also been punched.

"Stop!" My power lashed out at the twins.

They felt my intention, and Durril released the soldier at once. Camlo's arms fell to his sides. They both stared at each other like they weren't sure what had just happened. The soldier rubbed his jaw and cowered back from the twins.

I closed in on the man. "You want control of this city? Now's your chance to test your regiment's loyalty. If you play this right—without inciting more violence—you can also command genuine respect from the citizens."

The soldier withdrew his hand from the red mark on his jaw. He broadened his shoulders, his aura bloating with courage and pride, anything I fed him. He retrieved his musket, cocked the hammer, and shot upward. The people startled. A woman clapped her hands over her ears.

"Break apart this fighting or we'll be forced to arrest you— nobility or peasantry!" he shouted. "But no harm will come to you if you back down of your own accord." His regiment frowned at his sudden demand, not having indulged the full lust of their brutality. "Bring them to order, men! The market is closed for the day." The soldiers finally submitted. After some struggling from the people, they calmed the fighting and began directing everyone away. A fresh regiment poured in from a connecting street and assisted the effort.

A weightless sense of satisfaction buoyed me. I'd done what I'd failed to do during Valko's trial—quell a fight. Reluctantly, I let my connection to the soldier break. The vibrating current between our auras stilled, and my legs went weak as I came back to my own waning strength.

I fetched Kira from her hiding place, took her small hand in mine, and looked around for Tosya and our two horses. They weren't where I'd last seen them under the awning of a brightly painted shop. Worry lodged in my breast. I couldn't feel the low thrum of Raina's aura or Tosya's steady energy among the dominating, higher strains of the people.

I finally glimpsed Raina's white coat in a shady alleyway, but Tosya wasn't with the mare—Terezia Dyomin was. The countess's eyes were wide and fast upon me, her aura brimming with wonder and a pinch of terror. My stomach turned over. How closely had she been watching me all this while?

"I thought someone should watch your horse," she said, as Kira and I walked over, though her voice held no spark of generosity.

I gave a stiff nod of thanks and held my hand out to Raina. The mare ambled to me, and when I touched the side of her nose, her agitation from the skirmish accelerated my heartbeat. "There, there," I stroked her neck. "Everything's all right now."

Terezia inched closer with a surge of dark curiosity. "Does she calm under your influence?"

My hand froze on Raina. Unease pressed down on me. "I'm her master," I answered carefully. "She trusts me."

The corners of Terezia's eyes tightened. "Only a beast would."

Her words hit like acid. "And only a noblewoman would be ashamed to raise her own daughter when she had the means to keep her in hiding." I couldn't bite my tongue, even if what I'd insinuated turned out to be false.

It wasn't. Terezia blanched, took a startled step back, and then fled into the alleyway.

In the countess's wake, Tosya rushed over with his horse. "Sonya," he breathed, "there you are." A measure of relief swept through him, but didn't ease his jumpy pulse. "Raina spooked and got away from me." Wiping his sweating brow, he caught sight of Kira. "Oh, hello. You appear to be enjoying this visit to the city as much as I am." He chuckled faintheartedly, then cringed at himself. "But, of course, you must feel *more* of the strain, being an Auraseer and all. Then there's the fact this really isn't a visit since you live here." He gulped, forced himself to inhale, and turned pleading eyes on me. "Can we go now?"

As we rode off to return Kira to her family, my muscles flexed with growing apprehension. The rioting had stopped for today, but it would soon spring up again. The people's anger would reach a breaking point and they'd start killing each other, just as I'd warned the soldier.

I needed to do something to achieve lasting peace in Riaznin. And I needed to process that Terezia was the mother of an Auraseer.

CHAPTER SIXTEEN

I STRODE DOWN THE STAIRS TO THE PALACE DUNGEONS, MY gaze direct, my purpose sure. "I've come to help the prisoner prepare for his last day of trial," I told each guard who confronted me. "One of the Duma has sent me."

They gave me agreeable answers.

"Of course."

"I'll get out of your way."

I scarcely used any conscious effort to bend the guards' emotions. My intent bled out of me and into them with seamless and frightening ease. I needed to be careful with the course of my feelings. I hadn't tested the limits of my power.

The maze of the dungeons posed no difficulty. The path that led to Valko had imprinted itself on my mind. When I reached the long gallery of cells, I halted under a pool of torchlight. The last guard was a head taller than the others with three times their muscle. His thick beard covered his mouth, making his large eyes all the more prominent as they searched the gallery, ever watchful for threats.

I steadied my breathing, drew my braid in front of my shoulder, and exuded superiority. From up ahead, the guard felt the pull and turned to me. The blue of my dress took on an unearthly glow of the flickering torch fire. I plucked the invisible string between us, and the guard came.

"Sovereign Auraseer," he greeted me with reverence, ignoring there was no longer such a person or position in Riaznin.

I gave him the same story I'd relayed to the others, with one addition. "Will you do me the honor of guarding the prisoner from *that* corridor?" I pointed to a stone archway several yards away. "This conversation will be delicate, and we can't be interrupted."

My empathy ran deepest for this man who must endure Valko's presence day in and day out. He was weary, grateful for the distance I offered him. "I'll see it done," he said with a bow.

I exhaled, satisfaction spreading through me. How different it felt to be listened to, obeyed.

The gallery was now empty of guards. Up ahead, the seventh torch sconce washed a glow of amber light near Valko's cell.

I stalked forward, my shoes scuffing the straw-littered stones. My ability made me feel primal, extraordinary, absolute. With it, I could help Riaznin as I'd helped her before. Valko wasn't a danger to me. His verdict was out of my hands now. All I needed was his advice.

A soft grunting echoed within his cell. My arms burned with his exertion. I curled my hand around the first iron bar and peered inside. Valko's back gleamed in the torchlight. His body faced downward, parallel to the floor, and he lifted and lowered himself by his arms. Perspiration dripped from his hair, and my heartbeat thundered, syncing with his.

How had I ever been attracted to *this* boy? "Do you think your strength will save you from the executioner's ax?" I asked in mild curiosity.

Valko's head whipped up, his aura sharpening as he observed me. He should recognize this supremely confident Sonya and her graceful, domineering air. The last time he met her, he lost an empire.

"Good afternoon." He pushed himself upright, sitting on his knees. His chest was hard and sculpted with precision, even though he'd grown leaner in captivity. "To what do I owe this pleasure?" His old charm teased through his voice.

I let go of the bar and drifted past the next three, never withdrawing my gaze. Valko needed to know I held the power in this conversation. "You have something that is mine." How I savored the fearless ring of my voice. This Sonya didn't condescend to anyone. Her sovereignty was unbreakable.

One side of his mouth curved upward. "Is that why you came to see me—for your pearl?" He rose to his bare feet, his eyes following me as I paced predatorily. "I didn't realize a jewel from your old sovereign Auraseer headdress meant so much to you."

I flexed my hand, controlling my reaction. I'd anticipated his attempts to provoke me. "You're very presumptuous to think that's where I got the pearl."

"Didn't you? Or has my brother started giving you jewels not set in rings?" He swaggered over to me. "Rather sounds like empty promises."

Stomach tight, I gave him a caustic smile. "I came here to discuss Shengli." The pearl didn't matter. Let him keep it. "As you are well aware, the Shenglin *have* invaded and we are at war." *And nearly at war with ourselves.*

Valko nodded and strode to the wall of bars on his right in his cell. "It wasn't so hard to figure out, really. Neither is what will follow. By now, the Shenglin have surely taken our eastern borderlands and will next march on the city of Dubrov." He kicked away the straw to clear a spot. "If they take Dubrov, they'll be able to fjord the Obolv River and conquer Illola. Then there will be nothing standing between them and Torchev. Riaznin doesn't have any strongholds in the Middle Steppes." Inhaling with concentration, he lifted himself into a handstand, continuing his exercises.

I drifted closer to him. My head prickled as Valko's face reddened with collecting blood. "Are there any weaknesses we can exploit in our enemy? There must be a way Riaznin can defeat a formidable army without sacrificing hundreds of thousands of lives."

Valko adjusted his balance on his hands. "Am I still speaking with the same person who pleaded that I *not* invade Shengli?"

A vein pulsed at his temple. "Now you see what I tried to prevent by planning to attack first."

I refused to acknowledge his foresight. "Is there any strategy you didn't discuss with your council?"

Valko stepped out of his handstand and ran his fingers through his hair. He didn't grin, but his aura gave an amused twist. "Anton must be really angry with you for how magnificent you were at trial."

My defenses flared. "Pardon?"

"Is that why you're coming to me about this and not him?" He stretched his arms and shook out his muscles. "My brother still likes keeping secrets, doesn't he?"

My toes clenched inside my shoes. "Anton has *many* demanding concerns and little time to discuss every detail of his Duma meetings."

"Not even with one of his revolutionary allies? Are you being cast off already?"

My fierce hold on the bars turned my knuckles white. "I have no wish to talk about Anton."

"Clearly."

"*Shengli*, Valko. Focus."

He held up his hands, a mock surrender, and sauntered to the corner of his cell. While rummaging in the straw near his shirt and boots, he asked, "Did I ever tell you that the secret manor where I was raised is in the Eastern Steppes, just south of Bovallen?"

"No." I leaned forward.

His fist closed around whatever he was looking for. "The manor house is a day's ride from Shengli. I'm sure you know Anton lived close to Estengarde and was protected by the Esten king." He gave a dry and weary laugh. "Even while Anton and I lived in hiding, our father placed us in positions to form alliances. Maybe we were never in danger at court. We could have been separated from our family for mere strategy. I wouldn't put it past my father."

Amazed, I let go of the bars. "Are you saying you were protected by the Shenglin emperor?"

Valko ambled back to me, pocketing whatever he'd picked up. "Not the emperor. No amount of bargaining could ever persuade that man. Luckily, bribery worked on the lieutenant general of the Shenglin army. My father promised him a valuable portion of our borderlands, enough to ensure a wealthy retirement." He shrugged. "But that promise was broken when I became Riaznin's emperor and no longer needed the lieutenant's safeguarding."

Baffled by him, I brought myself center to where Valko stood. "So you went back on your father's promise, and the alliance—which wasn't even a true alliance because it never involved the Shenglin monarchy—is now gone." I shook my head with impatience. "How does that help us?"

"Jin Pao is now the Commanding General of Shengli. He's a man who can be moved upon, a man with loyalties that can be bought. And he *knows* me. It wouldn't be hard to say my father's failed bargain was a misunderstanding, an oversight that happened during my transition to becoming emperor. In the very least, I can arrange a private conversation to discuss the matter. That would be enough to position you close to him."

I stood stone still, my breath bottling in my chest. "You want me to persuade the Shenglin general to retreat?"

Valko came nearer, his body almost touching the bars. They cast striped shadows across his face. "I'm glad you're past denying you have great power."

I swallowed, only partly sorry for my slip. *Could Valko's plan really work?*

"Think of it, Sonya." His gray eyes gleamed as he smiled with fervent hope. "You persuaded *me*, a fierce defender of my nation, to remove my crown. You could work *miracles* for Riaznin."

My skin tingled. That was all I wanted.

"But even you have limitations. You can only seize control of one person at a time."

That was true. He understood my power better than I did.

"You just need access to the right person—the person with the authority to command Shengli. I've *found* you that person. Don't you see? You can end this war." His gaze championed me. "I have the utmost faith you can."

My lungs expanded to take in a deep breath. I knew all along I had the ability to inspire great change in this nation. This could be my chance. I bit my lip. "And how does this plan serve you?"

"I want what *you* do, Sonya—what's best for Riaznin."

Valko's sincerity flushed warmth through my muscles.

"But you would have to be *free* to arrange a meeting with Jin Pao."

Valko nodded. "Yes . . . I would have to be free." He studied my face, and when he spoke again, his voice came slower, more carefully. "In addition to that, the general would be more willing to speak with me if I held an esteemed position."

My lips parted in amazement. "You think I can reinstate you as emperor? You can't be serious."

Valko gripped my hand past the bars. "I should have never abdicated. You know it was a mistake to give in to the people. Has liberty brought them more peace and prosperity? From the whisperings of the guards, the citizens are in revolt with each other. They need a strong backbone—a united empire. If we don't gain control of Riaznin now, Shengli won't be our only threat. We'll be destroyed on all fronts." His eyes filled with a pain that burned through my vision. "Our culture will be lost. Our gods forgotten." My mouth ran dry with his thirst, his need. "I couldn't live with myself if that happened, not when the gods gave me a mandate—a *birthright*—to reign over this sanctified land."

"But—" Anxiety crept into me. I struggled to think past the image of a Riaznin that was no longer Riaznin but a battleground for other nations. What would happen to the convent, Dasha, Kira . . . to any new Auraseer born in this world? "How can I possibly convince the Duma to give you back your throne?"

"The Duma answers to the people, many of whom are still loyal to me."

"Then what exactly are you asking me to do?"

"If you give me a chance to live, I can rally the people."

"You want me to persuade the Duma to spare your life?"

"Yes," he replied adamantly.

I pulled my hand away. What he asked contradicted the limits of my ability—limits he'd just defined. "The Duma is seven governors—an eighth is due to arrive in Torchev by nightfall. I can't bend the will of *eight* people."

"The Duma can profess equal ruling all they want, but no one shares power. Who leads them, Sonya?"

I felt lightheaded. Valko's aura seized mine with urgency. The truth spilled out of my mouth. "Feliks Kaverin." My fingernails bit into my palms as I pictured the man's ever-watchful ice-blue eyes. He'd sought to lord over the Duma from the beginning. The council was easier to control when the governors trickled in one by one.

Valko scoffed with a wry nod. "I suspected it was Feliks. In fact, I believe Feliks was the person who hired the assassin to kill me."

"Feliks? You told Anton you thought nobles were behind the attack."

"Would my brother believe his friend was involved?"

"They're not friends."

"Listen, after you left my cell that night," Valko said,

brushing off my comment, "I discovered scars on the assassin's back from knouting."

Only an emperor could authorize knouting. It was a severe form of lashing in which barbs were used on the whip. "But he can't have been the only man you sentenced that way."

"His chest was knouted, as well."

I grimaced, thinking of the man turned over and whipped a second round when his back was already shredded and bloody.

"He was a man who bore grievances against the empire, and he'd been given food and shelter by a man named Feliks Kaverin, though I couldn't prove at the time that Feliks was also a revolutionary."

"But why would Feliks want you discreetly killed when he could have you publicly tried and executed?"

"Consider when the assassin attacked," Valko shifted closer in his fervor. "According to Anton, he and Feliks were away at an inn with the other Duma governors—a meeting *Feliks* arranged. Meanwhile, you were alone in the palace with only weary servants and drunken guards from Kivratide. What if Feliks staged the assassination to test your loyalty, to see if you'd attempt to save my life?"

My stomach quivered in unease. Feliks had also asked me to serve at Valko's trial. Another test. And another time I came to Valko's defense. He was placing me in situations that would tempt me to reveal my power. If I did, he'd find a way to use me or have me killed. The dungeons' cold stole into me, and I suppressed a shiver.

"Feliks needs to be stopped, Sonya. He claims to support liberty, but he wants to achieve it through force and make *you* his weapon. Only you can overpower him." Valko's gaze shone steady and confident. "Set me free. Then you and I can *and will* save Riaznin."

Valko's certainty was authentic, compelling. It sent a surge of energy up my spine and cut through almost all my doubts. *Almost.* "Even if I could sway Feliks in court, he couldn't sway Anton."

Valko lifted a dismissing shoulder. "Fortunately for us, the verdict doesn't have to be unanimous."

My head ached as I fought to think through Valko's plan rationally. "I never said I would do any of this. I *can't*, in fact. The Duma has dismissed me from further service." *Or at least Anton has.* "I'm not allowed to attend the rest of your trial."

"That's no matter," he said calmly. "With your power, gaining access to the courtroom shouldn't pose a problem."

"Still, I . . ." I rubbed my throbbing temples, trying work through my dilemma on my own. If I followed through with Valko's plan, I'd be going directly against Anton. I'd risk our relationship and break his faith in me.

"Give me your hand, Sonya."

My muscles stiffened. I buried my fingers in the folds of my dress. "Why?"

Valko smiled like he had when he sat in the corner of Raina's stall, while I groomed her mane and he spoke freely—when he trusted me and I'd trusted him. He smiled without ownership, without the weight of an obsessive lover, or the sneer of power-hungry tyrant. He smiled like a true friend, in the way that confused me most. "I believe you wanted this back," he said, reaching into his pocket and retrieving my pearl.

My heart drummed in warning. Taking the pearl back felt like I was agreeing to something, but I couldn't piece together what that was.

The small jewel caught the flickering amber light of the torches. I itched to hold it again. I raised my hand from the folds of my dress and cupped it before Valko.

He set the pearl in my palm. It still held the heat of his body. His hand lingered, sliding under mine, closing my fingers over the pearl.

"I believe in you, Sonya. You're a girl who can do impossible things. No one like you has walked this world. I regret not realizing that sooner."

My limbs eased from the terrible tension that had strung them taut for days. Valko understood the extent of my power—and he wasn't afraid.

He placed his other hand atop our joined ones. His gray eyes burned pure and without cunning. I couldn't unravel myself from the vines of his aura. Pressure built inside me, pulsing with sincerity, powerful conviction, and remorse—the sentiments I most identified with.

"If you help me live," he said, "I will make everything right again. I will have *you* at my side. Together, we're undefeatable."

His cocooning hands closed tighter. My skin prickled with a separate energy my foggy mind couldn't interpret. Valko's aura was too tangled in mine. Even the shouts and arguing drifting about my ears felt far away, like they echoed from a distant chamber in the palace. Valko's head bent nearer, more intimate. "We—"

"Sonya!" a guttural voice rang out, filled with anger and betrayal.

My awareness widened. Ripped apart from Valko. I flinched out of his grasp.

The pearl fell to the dungeons' floor, bounced down the gallery, and rolled into a crack beside a pair of polished boots I recognized immediately.

With a sharp intake of breath, I glanced up at Anton.

His highborn features twisted into an expression of raw pain. I'd never seen him so livid. "Why in all the gods' names are you here?" he asked. "I've been searching everywhere for you."

Panicked, I didn't know how to justify myself. The truth was my best defense. "Another brawl broke out in the city, and I'm worried about Shengli."

"So you turned to *him*?" Anton pointed at his brother, shirtless and smug as he watched us quarrel.

"Would *you* have discussed it with me?" I asked. Anton's rage ignited my own frustrations.

His energy shattered with hurt, but he swiftly pulled

himself back together. "How did you get past the guards?" He braced his hands on his hips. "I've told them not to let you down here."

What? I gave him an incredulous stare. When I didn't answer, too furious he didn't trust me, he nodded with a bitter laugh. He knew I'd used my power.

Valko smirked, leaning his weight on one leg. "If you must know why Sonya came to me, it's because she regrets siding with the weaker brother."

Anton's eyes smoldered and slowly turned on him. He stormed past me, reached into the cell, and grabbed Valko by the nape of his neck. With one clean movement, he smashed his head into the bars.

"Anton!" I cried, shocked by his violence. Valko's pain ricocheted through me.

Anton gave him another hard shake. I winced with dizziness. Valko's eyes glistened with moisture, but he didn't struggle or back down from his brother's stare. His smile was venomous, triumphant, nothing like the boy in the corner of Raina's stall. I ached for both brothers, for the peace they could never share.

"Well done, Anton," Valko said, voice ragged. "Father would be so proud to see you now. You share his ruthless blood, after all. Mother wouldn't even recognize you."

The wedge between them drove deeper, cutting like shards of glass into my bones. Stifling a cry, I fell to my knees. Neither brother saw me. They couldn't even truly see each other. But

I saw them—felt them—acutely. Beneath their anger, Anton's remorse and Valko's insecurities wrapped around my nerves, beat through my heart, and clawed inside my lungs, choking my breath.

Anton let Valko go, shoving back from him, and dragged his hands through his hair.

Valko gripped the cell bars to prevent himself from collapsing. "You say you want justice and a fair trial." His lip curled with contempt. "But the truth is you're too soft to kill me yourself."

Anton's jaw muscle bulged at Valko's goading. His aura burned hot. I grabbed his trouser leg; I couldn't bear it if he struck Valko again. The guilt would only haunt Anton later and hurt me. "Stop this!" I croaked, scarcely able to speak. My aura was so entangled with both of theirs, I felt myself splintering, ripping apart—every organ, every cell—as their fragile and buried bond of brotherhood severed. "Please."

"Sonya." Anton's eyes widened to find me fallen in pain. He pulled me up, supporting me, and swiftly led us out of the gallery.

"Aren't you forgetting something?" Valko called, his voice echoing around us.

Anton's brow hardened as we looked back. Valko's head jutted out from the bars, the torchlight sputtering in his eyes. He nodded to the ground outside his cell where my pearl lay in the cracked stones.

I gave a tight swallow. I couldn't deny how much I craved the sting of the pearl. But I wouldn't turn back for it, not with Anton watching, not with Valko so sure he held me in the palm of his hand.

I wouldn't come for the pearl again.

CHAPTER SEVENTEEN

ANTON LED ME BY THE HAND, HIS GRIP FIRM, HIS EXPRESSION closed, fixed. His energy pulsed with determination and urgency. Neither of us spoke a word as we passed the curious guards and left the dank corridors of the dungeons. On the main floor of the palace, he pulled me onward, guiding me toward the kitchens. I couldn't ascertain his mood. It wasn't exactly anger—it was an emotion stronger than that. It trembled through me with adrenaline. It rattled inside my eardrums like the roaring of blood.

My stomach cramped with guilt. "Let me go, Anton. I'm fine. Nothing dangerous happened with Valko. We were only discussing the politics of Shengli."

His brows creased together. "It doesn't matter anymore." His voice was low, as if speaking to himself more than me.

"Where are we going? What is this about?"

"I need to show you something."

I relented without a struggle. I'd braced myself for a heated argument with Anton, not this ominous mood. I had no idea how to react.

We entered the kitchens where we came upon the staff plucking chickens. A feather swirled up and brushed my arm. I jerked away. It burned like a hot iron with the bird's deathly aura. Anton seemed to understand and took more care leading me through the room.

We left through the outer door, and his gaze darted around to make sure no one was watching. He hurried us through the side gate. We exited the palace grounds onto the courier's lane with arching cherry trees.

"How much farther?" My legs shook from my need to eat, as well as Anton's trepidation.

"We're almost there," he said flatly.

Up ahead, a parked wagon came into view, harnessed to two draft horses, facing away from the palace.

My heartbeat sped faster, matching Anton's. "Is this what you wanted to show me?" I asked when we were within ten feet of the wagon.

A man stepped down from the driver's bench and gave a nod to Anton. It was more than a gesture of greeting; it held the solemn promise of a pact. The man's stubbed nose and intelligent brown eyes looked familiar. Finally, I recognized him. He was the curator Anton had hired. "Are you smuggling out relics of the empire?" I asked Anton. I had no qualms either way, but I didn't understand why he was so alarmed about it.

"Yes." He glanced about in all directions, ensuring we were still alone. His emotions overflowed with conflicting sorrow and resolve. He took both of my hands and gazed back at my eyes. "Sonya, please listen. There is no time to argue."

My nerves tingled with dread.

"I need you to leave with this man. I trust him. He'll take you somewhere safe outside the city."

"What? No." I shook my head, pulling back, but Anton held my hands fast. "What are you talking about?"

"Your life is in danger. You have to leave Torchev."

"*Everyone* is in danger here," I protested. My body felt numb except for my throbbing hands in his grip. "I'm not leaving."

"Feliks confronted me while you were out today, Sonya."

"About what?"

With great effort, Anton restrained his voice to a whisper so the curator wouldn't hear us. "Feliks knows what you are capable of!"

My skin flashed with ice. "How?"

Anton released me and turned away, the last of his composure coming undone. "He's puzzled together clues from several moments—the misfire in the rose garden, the dead assassin who tried to kill Valko, my brother's abdication." Rubbing a hand over his face, he added, "What you and Valko said in court finally confirmed your true involvement—in everything."

My stomach rolled. "And you didn't refute it?"

"Of course I did!" Anton whirled on me. "But Feliks doesn't believe anything I say. He knows I'd do anything to protect you."

I forced myself to breathe deeply and gather my senses. "Everything will be all right. I can protect myself. I know how to control my power now. There's no need for me to leave."

"You can *alter people's emotions*, Sonya," Anton said, voice hushed, tone severe. "Your gift hinders a person's free will. You're a threat to the democracy." I flinched, struck by his harsh words. "That's surely how Feliks sees it," he amended. "He's a man who will stop at nothing to achieve what he wants. And he doesn't trust where your loyalties lie."

"I'm not loyal to Valko." My hands bunched into tight fists.

"You have to go, Sonya." Anton's brows lifted with pleading, with pained acceptance. "You can't guard yourself from everyone. The people are calling you a traitor. They'll come after you and take justice into their own hands."

"Would *you* leave if your life was also threatened?"

"I'm a Duma governor," he replied, as if that position welded him here, for better or for worse.

"Well, I don't need a title to be as committed to Riaznin as you are," I bit out, my stubbornness blazing. "I'm not going to run. I've spent my whole life hiding. Torchev is where I belong."

"Sonya—"

I spun away and strode back toward the palace. A few seconds later, a horse and rider galloped down the lane, coming my direction. I halted, my awareness casting wide for his aura. A cool and strong energy coursed into me, its current direct and unbendable.

I sucked in a steeling breath. "Feliks is here," I called back to Anton. "Tell your curator to leave before he's caught."

Anton quickly motioned to the man, and I heard the crack of a whip. The wagon rushed away without me. Hurrying to my side, Anton pressed his arm against mine and formed a line of defense. But as Feliks galloped nearer, I saw no soldiers accompanying him. Still, I shifted to the balls of my feet, searching for a way to overpower his will, if necessary.

Feliks closed the distance between us, then drew his horse to a halt. Anger knotted my muscles when I saw the mare he was riding was Danica—one of the three white horses that pulled the troika last winter. Feliks felt entitled to just about anything that was once the empire's.

"Good afternoon." he said, his voice ringing with a pleasant tone, as if he'd just stumbled upon us on this picturesque lane rather than hunted me down. His ravenous energy shot pins and needles up my arms. He felt he'd triumphed over me at last. "May I speak with you alone?"

"No," Anton replied, the word thrown dagger-sharp.

I cast Anton a look that said I could take care of myself. "Whatever you have to say to me can be said in Anton's presence, too," I told Feliks. "Though I'm in no mood for a lengthy conversation," I added, still bristling from Anton's attempt to remove me from Torchev. "Let's be direct and transparent. You know I have the power to manipulate another person's emotions. You've set me up in more ways than one to discover it. So before you threaten those I love to make me stay in line"—I shifted closer to Anton—"let me help you consider my talents in a different light. I can *help* the Duma."

Anton's aura split with alarm. "Sonya—"

I locked my focus on Feliks. "Your march on the palace didn't win the revolution; Valko's abdication did. And you know what part I played in that."

Feliks studied me a moment, then dismounted his horse. He walked closer, his face coming out of the leafy shadows. When the sun hit his eyes, it didn't warm the ice-blue shards in his irises. "I'm listening," he said.

I inhaled, drawing my shoulders back. "With my power, I stopped a riot today in the city square. The Romska came and—"

"You quelled the soldiers?" Feliks's gaze intensified.

"Yes." I lifted my chin. "So you see, I could be of great use to you."

Grudging admiration coursed through him, but he arched a skeptical brow. "I came here thinking I'd have to persuade you, but now I see you are ready and willing."

Anton stiffened beside me. "Is that what you've been plotting all this while—to use Sonya as your weapon?" He loomed over his old revolutionary ally, giving him a dark and challenging stare.

Feliks wasn't intimidated. "Didn't you once do the same?"

"I've realized since then Sonya pays a great cost for using her power."

"Yet she hasn't stopped using it, has she?"

Anton drew in a pained breath, then turned imploring eyes

on me. "Sonya, you cannot force Riaznin to be at peace. No one person can achieve that." His voice quieted to a soft, rumbling plea. "If you try, it will break you."

I angled away from him, my knees locking in determination. He had no idea what I was capable of. "If you let me continue to live in the palace," I said to Feliks, "and if you allow me join your meetings, I'll do as the Duma commands."

He raised a warning hand. "You are not in a position to bargain. Your power is impressive, but you have yet to gain my trust. Here is how we will take you up on your offer—"

Anton briefly closed his eyes. "Please tell me the other governors don't know about this." His anxiety frayed my nerve-endings. Even Danica felt it and stomped her hoof.

"We'll keep this arrangement between the three of us, so long as Sonya conforms."

"Conforms to what?" I said, annoyance growing.

"Whatever I ask of you." The governor looked down his nose at me. "Let's start with you ceasing the soldier brutality, just like you did today. The soldiers are overstepping their roles as law enforcers."

"My power can't control the masses like that. I have to work on key people." Valko was one step ahead of Feliks, having already figured that out. "And I can't promise no one will get hurt."

"If the violence continues, the people will turn on the government. Once the riots stop and peace is restored, we can convince our citizens to stand behind us as we face the greater threat of Shengli." Feliks's gaze bored into me. "No one is to die in this city, do you understand?"

I crossed my arms. "This coming from the man who felt the lives of the peasants were dispensable as he marched on the palace."

He leaned closer. His voice lost its steadiness and turned as cold as his eyes. The freeze scraped up my spine. "I've proved what sacrifices I'm willing to make to stand behind this democracy. You will do the same. If the soldiers so much as bruise another person, it wouldn't be the first time a wildfire seized the west forest where the gypsies camp every summer."

Anton's mouth slackened. "That's indisputable tyranny! It goes against everything we fought for in the revolution."

"It's leverage," Feliks replied evenly.

My throat closed tight. "The Romska have nothing to do with this. Leave them alone. They're neutral in Riaznin's politics."

Feliks shrugged. "Perhaps it's time they took a side . . . as you should."

I gasped in disbelief. "So Torchev citizens can't be hurt, but the Romska are expendable?"

"That depends on you, Sonya. Do as I say—demonstrate your allegiance—and no one you care about will be endangered."

My eyes glistened with fury.

"Come along, Anton," Feliks beckoned his fellow governor. "We have one last mess to clean up. That nobleman, Sergei

Ivanov, and the peasant boy who started all that commotion at Kivratide have finally finished their duel. They're both dead. I've just received word. Their bodies were found in an abandoned mill off the Azanel River."

I remembered Rurik's shock and remorse when he'd fired upon Helene instead of Sergei, the pang in Sergei's aura as he'd tended to his injured fiancée. *Both boys dead?* My heaviness felt so familiar. I hadn't done enough, sensed enough. I could have turned the boys' anger to compassion at Kivratide. I could have prevented more deaths.

"We'll leave you to your new employment, Sonya." Feliks tipped his head in farewell. A subtle but menacing grin crossed his face. "Thank you for being so obliging."

CHAPTER EIGHTEEN

I RODE RAINA AT A BREAKNECK PACE ON THE ROAD TO THE Dyomin estate. I needed to find Kira. Her parents were former serfs and now tenant farmers on Terezia's land. Kira was in as much danger as the Romska. Feliks knew I also cared about her, which meant he would soon threaten her, too. I couldn't wait to find out when that would happen. She and the Romska needed to leave Torchev tonight.

I found her playing in a ditch a half-mile away from her cottage, the same place she'd insisted I drop her off earlier today. "Haven't you gone home yet?" I asked.

She smiled bravely, but her eyes clouded with tears. "I usually wait until nightfall after Papa's home and asleep. Mama's mood improves then."

I studied her hollowed cheeks and thinning frame. Kira was looking nearly as bird-boned as Dasha. "Don't your parents feed you?"

She lifted a shoulder. "They're not eating much either, so there's little to spare."

My chest tightened with anger. Kira's parents were as poor as any peasants in Torchev, but they might at least *try* to do something for their daughter. But it didn't matter anymore. I wouldn't give them a second chance. Not with Feliks's threats hanging over an innocent girl's life.

I held out my hand. "You're coming with me."

✳❀✺❀✳

Brightly painted wagons flashed through the greenery of larches, spruce, and pines. The Romska's encampment was in the west forest just beyond the Dyomin estate. The nomad's growing energy buzzed along my veins. I picked up speed, but not so much as to jostle Kira from the saddle. We made a loud and dusty entrance into a sunny meadow in the forest. Caravan wagons and tents in all varieties and colors took up residence.

I spotted Paizi first. She darted around small campfires, bubbling pots, and under wash lines to reach us. "You came, Kira!" she said, cheeks bright. "Come see the rabbit I caught. I'm hiding him in a trunk so Camlo doesn't skin him for dinner. Let's give him a name."

I helped Kira dismount, and she cast a tentative glance at the encampment. "It's all right," I assured her. "The tribes raised me and you can sense for yourself that they're a kind and safe people."

She breathed deeply, looked around her again, then nodded,

her aura calming. Paizi took her hand, and the two girls dashed off together.

Wasting no time, I led Raina to the round pen, gated her inside, then hurried to the center of the encampment, my aim the caravan wagon painted with the brightest colors. It belonged to Motshan.

✤❂✤

The Romska chief's pipe hung from his mouth, caught in the chink of his scarred cleft lip. He lifted his chin with a shrug at my declaration that he and his people must leave. "Trouble cannot catch a traveler," he replied. "It merely nips at our heels. The Romska have spent centuries avoiding trouble. We do not need your warnings. I'm well aware of the danger in Torchev."

"Go to Isker or Orelchelm," I pleaded. "You'll turn a better profit there. Any place has to be friendlier than here."

"We've been to Isker and Orelchelm." Motshan pulled his pipe away. "We've even been as far as Illola in the past weeks. Every city is the same—raids, looting, soldiers and peasants and nobles all fighting for power, mayors and town officials unable to control the madness. The Romska must make a living. Torchev is as good and as terrible as any other place."

Beside me, Tosya rubbed his brow, as frustrated with Motshan's stubbornness as I was. He'd been in the middle of visiting with the chief when I'd barged in.

"It's not widely known in Torchev," I said, "but Shengli has invaded Riaznin. They've taken Gensi, Bovallen, and the entire eastern border. It's only a matter of time before they march on the capital."

Motshan's sage-green eyes narrowed as he absorbed this information. "We could be safer in Torchev," he replied, still refuting me. "At least the capital is fortified."

"No place that is fortified will take you in here! You *must* leave. It isn't just the threat of the people and the Shenglin. You're being targeted—even now. Governor Kaverin leads the Duma." I quieted my voice so the other Romska wouldn't here me. "He's threatened to burn down your encampment if I don't . . ." I released a heavy exhale. I didn't want Motshan to fear me by learning of my power or tell him his tribe was endangered once more because of me. "Just know that what the governor has asked me to do is impossible. Please leave before you're hurt."

Tosya's scrutiny pierced through me. He'd surely guessed that Feliks had discovered my deeper ability.

Motshan fell silent, his aura chilling mine. For the first time since the bounty hunter had taken Romska children hostage, I sensed terror stir within the chief. I hoped he was finally considering my warning.

"Can you take Kira with you?" I asked. Maybe if I spoke as though Motshan had already decided to leave, he *would* leave.

"No." The smoldering leaf from Motshan's pipe burned through my nostrils. "The Romska are done protecting Auraseers."

My eyes rounded on him. "But Kira's life is threatened, too."

"I cannot risk my people again, not for one of the Gadje."
Gadje. Non-Romska. The tribes had a deep-rooted distrust of
outsiders, fueled by centuries of persecution.

"Is that why you won't help her, because she doesn't have
Romska blood?" I scoffed, anger blazing through my limbs.
"You're just as discriminating as the people who refuse to trade
with you."

"We have no right to take a child from her parents, whether
they're neglectful or not."

"You took *me* from my parents."

"Your parents *gave* you to us. The Romska are not thieves,
no matter what the people say. We follow a strict moral law, and
we have no intention to kidnap a child."

"She will die if you abandon her here!" When Motshan's
aura didn't bend, my willpower grew stronger, so fierce it
vibrated along my bones and made them quiver with energy.
"I'll do what I have to if you don't—"

"Sonya—" Tosya warned.

Motshan watched me carefully and drew a long inhale on
his pipe. He blew a ring of smoke above my head. My eyes
watered, but I clenched my jaw and didn't flinch. "You must
have been hard pressed for your power to unleash inside you,"
he said.

He knew? I glanced at Tosya, but he shook his head. My
anger faded, my pulse quickening with yearning. I'd harbored

questions all my life, questions about who I really was and why I had gifts no one else did. "When I had to defend my life, my, um"—I cleared my throat—"my power manifested." My cheeks burned. I felt vulnerable, unsure how Motshan would think of me now for having this strange ability. "But I've used it to save other people, too."

Motshan's aura drooped with a solemn and defeated energy that made my shoulders curl. The tribes must not have wished for my stronger gift to develop over the years. My power was too dangerous. *I* was too dangerous.

"Is that why the Romska agreed to raise me?" I asked, remembering Terezia's scornful words. Apparently the tribes weren't easily swayed to take in just anyone. "How did you know I had this ability as a child?"

Motshan puffed on his pipe again. The smoke swirled away on the breeze. "Do you remember a wild stallion named Yashma?" I nodded. Yashma sired many Romska horses. "When he was younger, Yashma was wild and wouldn't tame for the very best of our horsemen. But he calmed in your presence . . . he even let you touch him. The elders and I knew then and there what you were." Motshan's reverence raised the hairs on my arm. "The Romska worship energy. Auraseers can sense it, but legends tell of rare Auraseers who can also *shift* energy. It is a terrible and wonderful gift. We felt it our sacred duty to protect you."

"Did my parents know?" I asked, my voice quieting with emotion. "Did they even love me?"

Tosya squeezed my shoulder. "All parents love their children, Sonya."

"It's different for Auraseers," I replied with bitter sadness, thinking of Kira's family, how they feared her, and Terezia, who had the wealth to hide and harbor her daughter, but still gave her away. All this time I thought my own parents risked their lives so my life could be free. But what if they never held such ideals of liberty and only wanted to protect themselves?

I blinked back tears. I wouldn't cry. Not for the childhood I'd always wanted, the parents I'd wished for every time the Romska passed me to different caravans with the changing seasons. I'd known no stability, no true home. What I knew of my own heritage was largely a product of my own imagination, what I wanted to be true.

"I have to go," I announced, stuffing back my emotions. None of this mattered. I was what I was, an Auraseer, a girl with great power—power that endangered those I loved. "Please heed my warning and leave before nightfall. You aren't safe here."

I turned and walked briskly away, keeping my head down and my jaw strung tight. I had to prepare myself for what was to come tomorrow—Valko's verdict and the resulting riots that would surely overrun the city. Controlling the soldiers, containing the madness, that was my responsibility now.

Tosya followed as I strode to the round pen to fetch Raina. "Sonya, talk to me. What is Feliks trying to force you to do?"

I fisted my hands. "It doesn't matter. Please make sure the Romska leave tonight."

"I will. I'm going with them."

I halted, whirling around so quickly Tosya almost barged into me. "What?" My heart gave a hard thump.

His cheeks flushed at my stunned reaction. I was too startled to sift through his aura to discover the reason. He swept back his hair and said a little sheepishly, "I'm running for Duma governor." When my eyes grew even wider, he added, "Of the Romska—representing them, that is."

My mouth struggled to form words. "Whaa—how?"

"Well, I *am* educated." He shifted on his feet. "And I'm the Voice of the Revolution, so clearly I'm loyal to the democracy."

"But did the Duma agree to admit a Romska governor?" I couldn't imagine Feliks warming to the idea. He didn't even see the nomads as citizens.

"Anton says he'll present a strong case for the tribes being treated equally like any group of people in a city or province—people who are granted representatives on the Duma. The Romska simply aren't tied to one place, but we've lived in Riaznin for centuries."

My expression of surprise softened, tempered by my awe of Anton and Tosya. The two friends proved to be what they'd always been—idealists. Now they had a new crusade: bringing equality to the nomadic tribes.

"So you're on your way to have this approved by the Greater

Council?" I asked. The Romska elders met early in the fall when all the tribes convened for a few weeks.

Tosya nodded, kicking at a loose stone in the grass. "Should be a fun challenge"—he held up his finger—"though I refuse to believe an impossible one." He gave me another grin, and then shrugged. "Anton will also have his work cut out for him if he hopes to persuade the Duma to let me join them."

"Anton must really believe in you." I found myself rubbing the healing wound on my arm. The scab had almost fallen away. I was sure now there was no lynx-shaped scar beneath. "Of course he does . . . I just wish he'd place his faith so implicitly in me."

Tosya tilted his head, prodding for more, but I didn't mention how Anton had tried to make me leave the city today.

Several yards away, Paizi hopped out of a caravan wagon, a fluffy bundle with two long ears tucked in her arms. Kira emerged after her, her mouth and fingers stained with berry juice, her smile unbridled. "Hurry," Paizi said to her, "We have to free Fonso before Camlo discovers him. He loves rabbit stew!"

The girls ran off into the forest together, the late afternoon sun gilding the tall grass and wildflowers with gold. My chest panged at the thought of Kira forced to return to her family again. "Can she play here a while longer?" I asked Tosya.

He nodded, shoving his hands in his pockets. "I'll take her home before the caravan leaves Torchev." His eyes filled with sympathy. "I'm sorry about Motshan. If it were up to me, I'd bring Kira along with us."

I looked up at my oldest friend, all legs and arms and the biggest heart. "You'll make a fine governor, Tosya." Wrapping my arms around his torso, I gave him a long hug. "Take care of yourself."

I prayed Riaznin would hold together long enough to let Tosya fight for his people.

CHAPTER NINETEEN

I SAT ON A GRANITE BENCH BENEATH A CHESTNUT TREE AND watched the continual influx of guests arriving for Valko's verdict.

Little drips of collected rain spilled from the leaves and splashed my unbound hair. I shivered. The air was warm, but the dungeons' coolness penetrated my bones.

When the guards declined to admit anyone else, the remaining public flocked to the windows and garden doors of the great hall to listen from outside. The threat of another riot hadn't scared them off; their curiosity outweighed their fear.

A peasant man with a swollen eye approached me with three of his friends. I tasted their bitter wrath on the back of my tongue. "Once this trial is over, we'll have no more imperialism tainting this city, including you, Sovereign Auraseer." The man's lips pulled back over his teeth as he said my old title. "You are not welcome in Torchev, and we will see you removed from it." He spit at my feet and walked away.

I pinched my eyes closed and released a slow exhale. In my mind's eye, I saw the pearl on the cracked dungeons' floor. I felt Valko take my hand and tell me to do the impossible. I sensed the dark thrill of him encouraging me to use my full power, to be who I was born to be.

A bell tolled. My stomach turned over, empty and nauseated. Fifteen minutes until the proceeding would begin.

My legs grew restless. I longed to be in the courtroom. I was tired of being shut out.

Valko's spidery aura wasn't cold now. It skittered tepidly across my shoulders. The guards had brought him out of the dungeons.

I took a steeling breath. I struggled to weaken my awareness of Valko by latching onto the auras of the guests, but all I felt was his pulsing confidence lifting my chin.

I waited for his arrival in the courtroom. When the bell tolled ten times and the proceeding began, I waited longer. Valko would sense the perfect timing. He would let me know.

Peasants and nobles stood at attention in divided groups outside the wing of the domed hall. Soldiers holding muskets stationed themselves between the people.

My heart pounded, sending a rush of panic through my veins. I tried to shake my trepidation. Valko didn't have to manipulate me into doing what needed to be done. I would draw from my own strength. Everything I'd ever been accused of, I'd embrace it.

I belonged to no one—not my parents, not the Romska, not the convent, not the empire. I alone decided the limits of my power. I would exceed them. If any one person could save Riaznin, I could. All I needed was for Valko to pave my way.

A rift in my energy made my back straighten.

Valko's aura plucked mine, dark and hungry.

I touched two fingers to my forehead, then my heart, making the sign of the goddess, Feya. Then I stood, smoothed the folds of my violet dress, and struck a direct path for the great hall.

Bystanders surrounded the courtroom's garden doors. I pushed through them. A booming voice—Valko's voice—echoed from within. He was beginning his last defense.

Six guards blocked the entrance. Six might dam back any more of the public from entering, but they were a tiny force next to me.

"You know who I am," I said. "It is my turn to give the last word at this trial."

I was a storm of defiance, a channeler of emotion and dark energy. I would use it like the weapon it was.

"Stand aside," I commanded. "The Duma is waiting for me."

The guards didn't question my claim or even exchange puzzled glances. They felt what I felt, wanted what I wanted. They parted in perfect formation. I entered the great hall like a monarch, a goddess, a proud Auraseer.

I walked up the aisle between the cramped rows of chairs. Valko stood ahead in the cleared space before the Duma, his back turned to me. As the murmurs of the people built in my wake, Valko's words died on his breath. He slowly turned and met my fiery stare. A slip of a grin crossed his mouth. Did he think his fate was guaranteed? How amusing.

I brushed past where he stood, relishing in his confusion when I didn't deign to acknowledge his presence. I strode to the foot of the dais, to the barrier between me and the eight governors. It was just a step, a lifted platform a few inches off the ground. The barrier was nothing. I ascended it and came face-to-face with Feliks. He stood, not to be towered over.

"Sonya." Anton rose in anxiety, in warning.

Don't look at him. I can't look at him.

He wouldn't understand what I was about to do. I hoped he would someday.

"Do you wish to say something, Auraseer Petrova?" Feliks asked, his voice as brisk as his piercing blue stare.

"Yes, as a matter of fact, I do. And you will listen, Governor Kaverin."

A spasm chased through Feliks's right eyelid. My gaze narrowed, trapping him in his fear. *You should be afraid.*

His chest caved a fraction, but he folded his arms in defiance. "Go on," he challenged.

Feliks knew what I was, what I'd done on the night Valko abdicated. He knew I'd persuaded a tyrant to bow down to my words.

"Do you think you're also beyond empathy?" I asked. "I can prove how much I understand you."

He arched a brow and hardened his aura like a boulder.

"I know why you broke the pact of the revolution." My voice was a hiss so no one but himself could hear me. The courtroom fell in utter silence, straining to try. "You spurred the peasants' anger and marched on the palace in hopes to seize the government yourself. But you didn't anticipate the peasants would almost lose the battle and Valko would relinquish his crown when his soldiers were winning. You never got your moment of glory, and now you're trying to win it back by ruling Riaznin under the guise of a democracy."

Feliks didn't call the guards to bind me in chains. He offered a lazy shrug, though the ice was splintering at his feet.

"The most terrible truth about you is that you're responsible for the deaths of thousands of people." I cocked my head like a vulture. "If you hadn't caused the peasants to march, they would still be alive."

His pale eyes darkened, though he kept his emotions imprisoned behind the rock of his aura. "Death is a certainty in any war," he said. "You cannot find understanding for what I do not regret."

I slid closer, near the flexed tendons of his neck, and brought my mouth to his ear. "You forget, Governor Kaverin, that my delay on that night also allowed those deaths to happen. You and I are stained with the same blood, and beneath it the same black shame. I understand it exquisitely." *And you will, too.*

I felt to the depths of him, to the darkest feelings buried

beneath his pride. A spark of remorse was there. I fueled it into a blaze of harrowing guilt. When I pulled back from him, his eyes shone, obscuring my own vision with tears. "I am sorry you have to carry this burden," I said, letting him feel the full weight of it. "We never knew how heavy it would be, did we?"

His lips trembled. He gave an infinitesimal shake of his head.

I placed a reassuring hand on his arm. "Sit down." Now that our auras were fully connected, I felt Feliks's aching joints in my legs, his knotted back against my spine. "You are weary, Governor Kaverin, and you've done enough. I will see this trial through for you." Feliks collapsed in his chair, grateful.

"Sonya, what are you doing?" Anton's voice. Panicked. Distraught.

I can't look at him.

Squaring my jaw, I turned my power on the other Duma governors. They perched on the edge of their seats, confusion in their eyes, warning bells in their auras. Unlike Feliks, they didn't understand what I had done. They only saw me as an Auraseer who had somehow gained the confidence of their dominant leader.

"The prisoner has summoned me to give his last defense," I said. Without looking behind me, I pointed to Valko. I knew right where to direct my hand; I felt the energy flow between us. My claim was a lie, but Valko wouldn't refute me.

I studied each man and woman in the Duma. Finding empathy for them didn't pose a challenge. I identified with their cowering before Feliks. Hadn't I done the same for too long?

No governor raised his or her voice in resistance to my words.

None but Anton.

"Sonya, you've already given your witness of what happened during the One Day War. We heard you, and we've taken into account your testimony. There is nothing more you can say to add to Valko's defense. We are all but done here."

I didn't look at him, but I heard Anton's desperation leak past his grumbling command.

I dug within myself for strength, strength I'd formed without parents or a fixed home, the strength of an ability I'd learned to wield without the convent's help or any teacher. "This trial is *not* done," I replied defiantly. "You *will* hear me."

I am someone important, too.

My chest constricted with Anton's hurt. My stomach hardened with his fear. I stood tall and ground my teeth against his feelings. Riaznin was divided. The people needed to see a strong hand of power, hear one assuring voice to bring them unity. I revolved to face the public assembly and angled back my shoulders.

"After my last defense, I will propose a verdict," I announced, my tone clear, my words clipped with polished enunciation as they rang into the dome of the great hall. "Then we shall see if the Duma agrees," I added, complying with the law, at least for appearance's sake.

I felt Anton's aura yank mine, and I twitched, half-turning

to him. I resisted the final rotation and held my bearings on the lip of the dais. Out of the corner of my eye, Anton's shoulders tensed with anger and franticness. I inhaled a sharp breath and stepped down to the parquet floor to take my place at Valko's side.

"Well done," he murmured.

"I'm not finished yet."

His mouth quirked. "I eagerly await the grand finale."

A dark fire stoked in my belly. I'd had enough of Valko's arrogance. "Do you really want what I can offer you?" My whisper raked on hot breath. "Do you understand the consequence?"

He nodded, desire smoldering in his gray eyes. "We would be a match to be reckoned with. No one would stand in our way. We can stop Shengli and bring peace to Riaznin. We can begin a new dynasty of power."

"And you truly want to touch that power?" My brows lifted with challenge. "The last time you did, you cowered before me."

"Sonya," Anton called again. I ignored him.

"What have you decided?" I whispered to Valko. "And please note, for the future, I'm not forcing your choice."

Murmurs of confusion sprang up among the people. They itched for the trial to continue. Their curiosity piqued, then grew irksome because they had no idea what was happening.

"Do you feel everyone?" I asked Valko. "*I* do. Half of them want your blood. And if you survive, they'll seek to kill you themselves. If you want a pleasing outcome—a verdict in your favor and a clean exit from this courtroom—then you must agree to what I propose here today without a struggle."

Valko studied me, cool gray eyes, his desire for me more rampant than ever. He recognized my move for power, my chance to demonstrate who held whom by the collar. He wanted me most when I was furthest from reach. "Do what you must, Sonya. I trust your allegiance."

I smiled like a predator, in the way that taunted him most. I would show him I held supremacy over my own life. I wasn't loyal to him. He was just a means to bring me to the Shenglin general. "Very well."

As I turned to the dais to begin my defense, I made one small but terrible mistake.

My eyes captured Anton's.

CHAPTER TWENTY

"SONYA." ANTON TOOK A SLOW STEP FORWARD. I WINCED from the pain of his aura. "You're not responsible for everyone's fates. You can't hold that burden."

"Yes, I can. I have to."

I crawled inside his aura to the root of all his feelings and found his trembling faith in me. I gave it a firm, unshakeable foundation. In the end, he and I wanted the same thing for Riaznin—peace. "You must let me give Valko's defense, Anton."

He didn't have a choice. All the fight in him drained away. His noble bearing wilted, and he glanced from me to his brother. "Be just with him," he said, in his final struggle to speak. He lowered his head for a moment and took a shuddering breath. When he looked up again, his eyes filled with courage and perfect hope in me. How I wished he'd found that conviction on his own.

He swept fallen hair from his eyes and returned to his

chair, sitting tall, attentive, submissive. His gaze upon me didn't waver.

My lip quivered. I wanted to be someone Anton could take pride in, someone who worked as his equal partner, not someone who stole his true character. But I couldn't retreat from my purpose now. The fate of the nation depended on me.

I gathered the full muscle of my ability. I couldn't risk the hundreds of peasants and nobles turning on each other like they did last time.

Breathing deeply, I cast down all defenses around my aura. I welcomed everyone's feelings inside me and found empathy for them. The Duma in their daunting undertaking to bring order to Riaznin. The nobility in all they'd lost and their unsure place in the world. The peasants in the restitution they desired for being abused so long.

My heart thumped stronger, faster. Blood surged through my head. Energy rippled along my nerves. My lungs expanded in my culminating effort to breathe. The pressure of all the forging connections built inside me. All my muscles seized up. My body shivered to make room for their radiance. Thrilling pain shot through my limbs. In a wide burst of energy, I captured everyone's auras.

I gasped, my eyes round with shock and coursing pride. I'd done it. As if I were a tree, hundreds of auras branched out from me and drew life from my roots.

My shoulders slowly relaxed. I willed my body absorb the pain of so much vitality inside me. I didn't fight the auras as

Valko had during the One Day War. I let their pulses ease through me and acclimate to our union. I breathed sympathetic feelings into them. Harmony. Contentedness. I twisted their anxious concern into calm confidence, so calm it was almost paralyzing.

My pain lifted. My body stopped shaking. My heartbeat steadied. I stood tall and triumphant like a queen.

The only person whose emotions I didn't tamper with was Valko. I couldn't suffer myself to join with his aura, though I would if necessary. If he were wise, he wouldn't resist me.

The varnished parquet floor gleamed beneath my feet. I moved across it to the center of the cleared space and addressed both the people and the Duma.

"You have heard the lengthy crimes of Valko Ozerov, Former Emperor and Grand Duke of all Riaznin. Some people say those who died because of him cry out for his blood. That is the only payment they will accept, the only course for revenge."

As I spoke, Valko remained standing, his posture elegant, his hands clasped behind his back. He didn't want to leave the stage.

"But what will Valko Ozerov's death bring us?" I asked. "Will it resurrect our dead, or will it only make him a martyr of the empire?" I paused, inviting everyone to understand me, bending their lust for vengeance into waves of compassion. "Do we wish the rebirth of our nation to be forged in blood and hatred? We are hypocrites if we spill blood for the blood he's spilled."

Peasants and nobles nodded in agreement. The Duma leaned forward, captivated by my words.

"Now, you might ask, if we spare his life, will he escape *all* punishment? Does the law mean nothing?"

From across the clearing, Valko turned questioning eyes on me. I returned his gaze with a subtle but vengeful smile.

The energy inside me rushed through every space of my body. My vision throbbed, flashing white with its pulsing. I felt holy, unstoppable, vindicated past all my plaguing uncertainties.

"I submit that the prisoner be banished from Torchev, beyond any sphere of influence, outdistancing anyone he has hurt." In the far northeast of Riaznin was a cold and barren wasteland where the Romska had stopped traveling to because its villagers were so focused on survival that they wouldn't pay for entertainment. "I submit that Valko Ozerov be banished to Sanbriel."

Valko's eyes flew wide.

Neither the people nor the Duma broke into murmurs of debate. Their silence descended eerily. Their stares reflected their steady thoughts, their placid emotions. I fed them tranquil feelings. Kept their auras anchored to my own. Our hearts thrummed together. Our lungs filled and purged with shared breath. They felt contented with my words.

"Banishment, Sonya?" Valko's voice stained with light humor but dark betrayal. "You truly believe I deserve that?"

I glanced unwittingly to Anton. Without his pensive and

intelligent gaze, he looked nothing like himself. I gave a hard swallow, but didn't loosen the chains of my power. "You deserve nothing less," I answered Valko flatly.

He considered me a moment, then his gray eyes sparked with cunning. He lifted his chin with a pride that had to be false, despite its sure and acrid taste in my mouth. Valko thought he knew my game, but he didn't.

I approached the dais of the Duma. "Is this your verdict, banishment and not death? All in favor raise your voice."

One by one, the governors' answers rang out, pattering down from the dome ceiling. The word they spoke was the same: "Banishment."

Two men hadn't uttered so much as a whisper. Feliks and Anton. They were already outnumbered, but their votes would be the most respected by the people.

"Governor Kaverin." I turned to Feliks, channeling the overflowing strength inside me and directing it at him. "What do you say?"

He shrank under my stare. Moisture collected above his lip. Remorse for the deaths in the revolution still racked him. "B-banishment."

I looked four chairs to his right. "Governor Ozerov." *Anton.*

His face appeared satisfied with the ruling, except for his strained eyes. He balled his trembling hands and struggled against my power.

My love for him made my heart fissure. *Let me finish this,* I tried to tell him, as if my emotions and the hundreds of auras inside me could shape words in his mind. *Agree with the verdict. You never wanted your brother dead.*

Anton's lips parted. He made a small, conflicted noise.

I moved closer. Touched his knee. His gaze painstakingly rose to mine, his pupils dilating. Guilt flooded me. My throat grew thick to see Anton so frail of mind. But I had to follow through for our shared dream of a free and united Riaznin. I willed him to feel my conviction. My plan would work.

My voice fell soft so only Anton would hear. "If Valko is banished, it will set a course of action for me to bring peace to Riaznin." Leaning closer, I said the one thing that could ultimately persuade him. "Once peace is restored, I will be safe. That's what you want, isn't it?"

Sweat glistened at his temples. He gave a shaky exhale and unballed his hands. "Banishment," he said, loud enough so the court would hear him. "Banishment," he echoed to himself, a quiet and lost refrain.

The fissure in my heart split to a chasm, pain ripping from all sides. The hundreds of auras sang inside me from my conquest, feeding me with the resolve to continue. I held them fast, but my own aura withered. I felt terribly and utterly alone.

The room was so hushed I heard the swish of my dress as I turned to face the assembly. "It is done. Valko Ozerov is banished."

No cries of victory. No riotous mobs. Just the pulse of the collective, repressed energy.

"Guards"—my voice was a raw carcass of emotion—"escort

the prisoner away. He leaves for Sanbriel now."

I hated that I found sympathy in Valko's eyes. I needed him to be spiteful so I wouldn't feel a sliver of remorse. He deserved this fate. I wouldn't admit, after all I'd done, that I deserved the same. We were nothing alike. Mirror reflections were deceiving—at first glance, similar, but in truth, reversed. I wasn't the tyrant.

I wasn't.

CHAPTER TWENTY-ONE

FOUR GUARDS STOOD BY AS VALKO AND I APPROACHED HIS carriage. He paused to run his fingers along the brass latch. "I've heard tales of the great aurora that can be seen from Sanbriel," he said. "I've always longed to see how the gods play with color and fire in the sky. That marvelous sight will be their gift to me—a sign they're pleased their ordained ruler is free."

"You are not free. I never promised you that. I never promised you anything." Heat writhed through my body. I felt like I was burning alive, though the flames scorched with something darker than pain. I pressed my lips together, striving to keep hold of all the auras. I couldn't release them until Valko was gone.

His brows lifted with amusement. "Call what you've done for me what you like, Sonya. I will call it freedom if I'm no longer in the dungeons." He glanced at the guards and lowered his voice. "Shall I arrange for General Jin Pao to meet us in

Sanbriel?" His gaze swept over my face, his energy flowering with desire to obtain power again and the person who'd opened that gate for him. He touched a lock of my hair.

"Don't." I flinched back from him.

His constructed calm flashed to anger in an instant. He jerked me to him and crashed his mouth down on mine. I squirmed, but his grip was unyielding. His other hand snaked around my waist and chained our bodies together.

Just as the guards were coming to my assistance, Valko broke away from me, the skin around his mouth raw and red.

"You demon!" I spat, wiping my lips on my sleeve.

His gray eyes glinted with malevolence. This was the same man who'd killed Pia without second thought, the man who wasn't bothered when I left a dead man in his cell. "Demon?" he echoed, canting his head with musing. "Who are you to judge me for using force when I want something? That was a clever stunt you pulled off in the courtroom, though not as impressive as when you shoved all of Torchev's emotions inside me." His voice cut with bitterness. "I'll never forget that feeling—sensing my people's needs so clearly. It's convinced me I need to take more ruthless action. So I can thank you for that." He gave me a pleasant grin, but his jaw muscle rippled with tension. "Though it was rather a rape of an abdication, wasn't it?"

My eyes burned. "You're vile, you know that?"

His brow arched, and he gave a mock bow of submission. "Just trying to match you, measure for measure. I've always told you we're perfect for each other."

My skin tightened, crawling with disgust and rage. At Valko. At myself for believing we could have ever worked together to bring peace to Riaznin. "Leave. Now. I never want to see you again. Our partnership is over, do you understand? I hope you rot in Sanbriel." I'd find access to General Jin Pao without him.

I expected Valko to blanch, to beg me to reconsider. His plan depended on me. But he only flared his nostrils with hatred, his aura black and vindictive. "Bravo, Sonya." He smirked. "You're just as merciless as I am."

My stomach twisted, but I gave a steady exhale. "At least you'll live. That's more than half the nation thinks you deserve."

I motioned for the four guards to surround him. Valko managed a little saunter in his step as they pulled him into the carriage. As it rolled away, I exhaled, shaking from expending my last ounce of strength. I fought to strip my aura from every taste of him, every remembrance of his touch, every dark game he'd played with my mind.

I stumbled into the stables, feeling anything but glorious for my actions today. I didn't care that Valko was gone. I cared that I'd betrayed Anton in order to save his brother, a vindictive boy who wasn't worth my trouble in the end.

I penned myself inside Raina's stall without pausing to greet her or stroke her white mane. I hid in the dark corner and kicked aside the small stool that Valko had once frequented. Drawing my knees to my chest, I buried my head in the folds of my violet gown. I wanted to drown myself in the smell of sweet hay and wash away the foulness of who I was.

Valko was right. I *was* just like him.

I invaded people, stole their liberty, silenced their voices, warped their defining emotions.

I hadn't done justice today. I hadn't brought peace. My power hadn't given me supreme independence. I'd released a villain from death. I was a bringer of doom. A tyrant, equal to Valko. And I'd lost everything. The trust of the boy I loved. Any chance of respect from the Duma governors. Any lasting esteem from the people. Feliks wouldn't try to use me for my power now. I'd proved myself disloyal to the democracy. He'd have me hunted and killed. I doubted I ever had any real chance of preventing a war.

The glow of the auras within me diminished to the sickening pulse of revulsion. My gut roiled, sweat dripped down the back of my neck, my body flashed ice cold then flaming hot. The people's energy felt diseased with corruption—brought on by me.

I couldn't compel a nation to be peaceful when I couldn't even stand these auras inside me for an hour. Everything I had done today had been a terrible, miserable mistake.

I let the auras go, shaking from the wrenching separation, and I wept.

CHAPTER TWENTY-TWO

ABOVE THE SMELL OF HAY, THE SHARP SCENT OF CLOVES AND poison-sweet blossoms laced the air. A dark figure passed in front of Raina's stall. My head jerked up, strands of my hair caught between my clenched fingers. The public assembly had already left the palace. Had Feliks sent his soldiers to find me?

I crept around Raina and reached out with my awareness. My muscles tensed as I prepared to defend myself. I felt so weak.

Footsteps. The soft crunch of straw on the ground. The skittering of a mouse.

I felt no auras. None that were human. But that figure that passed—? That smell . . .

Had someone else come for me?

I braced my shaking hands against the stall gate and peered slowly around the corner.

She stood ten feet away in the shadow of a stone column,

her black hood drawn up. My heart kicked. Breath seized. *Nadia.* One of my peers from the convent. One who should be dead.

Her expression was as haughty and unmoving as ever. She'd hated me, my wildness, my unnatural gifts. I'd hated her back. Her scalding superiority. Her viciousness.

I stared at her, still disbelieving. My body was ice. I couldn't make my legs move. Somehow she'd survived the convent fire. Feya forgive me, that didn't bring me peace.

I desperately grasped for Nadia's aura. Nothing. Not even a flickering pulse.

She stepped into a beam of mote-filled sunlight and pulled back her hood. Her raven hair skimmed her shoulders. I gasped. Struggled harder to breathe. Tried not to avert my gaze from her face.

From her left eye to her jaw, tattoos swirled across her skin. The etchings weren't new—marking her skin had always been Nadia's emotional release—but the terrible burn scars wrapping across one side of her face, down her throat, and under the neckline of her dress were. Proof of the suffering I'd caused when the convent burned.

I didn't need to sense her aura to understand what she wanted now. Revenge.

Nadia had come here to kill me.

She walked toward my stall. Slowly. Unnervingly patient. I whimpered. Fumbled with the latch. It was stuck. I shook the gate. She came nearer. Five feet away. I frantically tried to climb the gate. Slipped back down. Hissed when a splinter of wood scratched my arm.

Nadia was at the gate. I scrambled backward. Bumped into Raina. Nadia blocked my exit. "Please, please!" I held up my hands. "I'm *sorry*. For everything. I beg you to believe that I am. Please leave me in peace!"

"Peace?" she echoed wryly. She sounded vicious, ripped apart, like the word she spoke sifted through broken glass. "What peace do you deserve?"

"I know what I deserve. You don't have to taunt me with it."

"You know only a *fragment* of the damage you've done. Your selfish carelessness has ruined far more than yourself."

"I know my sister Auraseers died because of me." *I know I can never atone for it.*

She leaned against the gate, penning me in with my feelings—for I felt none from her. That blindness rocked me with terror. My integral sense was cut off. "You don't know what it's like to be trapped in a room full of girls while they burn by fire," she said. "I felt every pair of lungs fill with smoke. Every frantic prayer go unanswered. I writhed while everyone's skin blistered and charred. Meanwhile, you slept in the snow. And when you awoke, you left for Torchev to live out *my* destiny."

My shoulders crumpled inward over my chest. I closed my eyes and released a tight breath of pain. *Make her stop talking. I can't hear this.* But my power couldn't help me now. Nadia had no aura to hold on to, no emotions I could sense to bend. I couldn't escape.

"How—?" My throat closed, paper dry. "Why didn't Sestra Mirna tell me you were alive?" I cast about me for a weapon—a pitchfork, a whip, even a horseshoe. Nothing.

Nadia shrugged, but her jade green eyes narrowed—in malice or pride, I couldn't tell. "Sestra Mirna doesn't know. For two days, I lay nearly dead in the rubble of the east wing. While the sestra and the youngest Auraseers were away at market, a villager found me and took me to his cottage. For months, he and his wife nursed me back to health. I made them promise not to tell the sestra about me."

"Why?" I choked out a whisper, my body quaking. Why would Nadia keep her existence secret from the sestra when revealing it would help Nadia win back her rightful role as sovereign Auraseer? Sestra Mirna adhered to the letter of the law. She would have made me trade places with Nadia, who was the eldest. Everything would have turned out so differently. The revolution would have failed. No Duma would exist. Valko would still be emperor.

Would that have been better?

"Why?" Nadia repeated, leering at me. "Why should I tell *you* anything?" Her ragged voice shredded thinner to a spine-chilling whisper. "Why should a murderer be sovereign Auraseer?"

"Stop!" I cried. Her accusation echoed through me. *Murderer. Murderer. Murderer.* "Don't say that. I didn't mean to hurt—" *Didn't mean to kill.* I shook my head. My eyes burned with tears. "I'm not sovereign Auraseer, not anymore."

"No, you are *nothing*. And you're no longer necessary."

I flinched with another whimper. But it was true. It stung so deeply. There was no hope I could ever mean anything to anyone now. Not the Duma, not Anton, not Riaznin.

Nadia glanced over me with scorn. "I wonder what the emperor ever saw in you before you showed him your power."

"How do you—?" Perspiration flushed my body. Somehow Nadia knew everything about me, including my stronger ability. How closely had she been spying on me these past weeks? "What's done is done," I said, fighting to ground my emotions. "Why are you here?" I demanded.

"Why are *you* here?" Nadia pressed me. One corner of her scarred mouth lifted in a cruel smile. "I can't imagine anyone welcomes you in Torchev anymore, not even your beloved prince."

My chest panged. I stumbled backward another step. Her words clashed against my ears. I pictured Anton's strained eyes when he'd struggled against my power in the courtroom. He wouldn't want me back now, not after my betrayal.

Nadia reached for the latch and swung the gate open.

I startled. "Stay back!" I launched myself farther away. Raina snorted in agitation and cocked her rear hoof.

Nadia coolly walked forward and stroked Raina's nose with familiarity. The mare relaxed, even nickered.

I tripped back another step, my nerves strung taut. I strived to anticipate Nadia's next move, waited for her emotions to shift, to warn me when she'd attack. But she was empty. Of feeling, intention, energy. I was defenseless. "Why have you been following me?" I lashed out at her. *Why hadn't she tried to kill me in the orchard at Kivratide?* "Were you hoping the democracy would fail and you'd have your chance to serve the empire, after all?"

"Is that so far-fetched?" She ran a fingernail up to the auburn star on Raina's brow. "A people's government is absurd, and it's failing right before our eyes."

My stomach sank. Another truth. This dream of liberty *was* failing. People were revolting. I'd persuaded Valko to abdicate, but Riaznin wasn't ready for equality. "Even if it does fail," I said, clinging to my stubbornness, "the people won't unite under Valko. Give up your futile dream, Nadia." My voice rang out harsher than I'd intended, but I needed her to go. Horribly scarred or not, Nadia was still the same vicious girl who took pleasure in tormenting me. She was poisoning my mind, cornering me with my worst fears. I couldn't run away from my black thoughts in her presence. I had no one's emotions to latch onto but my own.

Nadia seethed, circling Raina as she advanced on me. I backtracked, my breaths coming in tight, fitful bursts. My legs bumped into a low stool. I snatched it up and held it like a battering ram.

"Isn't this your dream, too?" Nadia inched nearer, not intimidated. "You may have not always wanted to be sovereign

Auraseer, but you can't pretend you don't want that power back."

"Being sovereign Auraseer wasn't power." I retreated two more steps. "It was slavery."

"Then why do you keep saving our emperor from death?" Nadia forced me backward until I hit the partitioning stone wall.

"I'm loyal to the democracy," I said on a thin breath. "I'm fighting for freedom and equal rights."

She scoffed, expression savage. "You're fighting to save your own skin! This government will not protect you or any other Auraseer." She grabbed the stool, yanked it out of my grasp, and flung it out of reach.

My eyes rounded, my empty hands trembled. This is when she would kill me. I scanned her cape for the bulk of a hiding dagger or pistol.

Nadia crowded closer. Our skirts brushed. "How long can your prince defend Dasha's home at the convent when he wields only a fraction of the Duma's power?" I shifted sideways, but only wedged myself into a corner. "How long can Kira stay alive in Torchev when the new laws cause more strife among the peasants? At least Auraseers were esteemed when the emperor depended on our talents to safeguard him. Now we have *no* respect. If the people continue to self-govern, their fear of us will become our ruin. So don't criticize me for wanting my rightful role back when you're fighting for the same."

"I've banished Valko!" My throat scraped with my shouting. My own feelings clawed into me. Anger, fear, and terrible regret. "I do not want him back!"

Nadia's cracked lips pulled into a tight sneer. "When this nation lies in ashes and all those you love are dead, you will regret those words!"

Her hand moved toward her cape. My heart jumped. I shoved her backward to the ground. She landed hard, reflexively jerking to one side. If I hurt her wounded body, I was glad of it.

I fled across the stall to Raina and yanked myself up on her back. My heels jabbed her flanks. She reared up on hind legs. Nadia thrust herself out of the way so she wouldn't be trampled—and just in time. Raina's front legs crashed down, and we tore out of the stables. Dust and straw gusted up behind us.

I couldn't stay here any longer. Any attempts I'd made to fix this nation had failed. I only made everything worse.

I had to leave Torchev forever.

CHAPTER TWENTY-THREE

MY HEART POUNDED AS RAINA AND I RUSHED THROUGH THE
palace gates. My dress fluttered against my horse, a streak of
violet against white. Nadia's words bounced through my skull,
twisted, crowing, blending with my thoughts. *You're no longer
necessary.*

I gritted my teeth and crouched low, pushing Raina harder
and faster down the avenue. The streets were thick with depart-
ing crowds from the palace. But I couldn't bear to face anyone,
so I swerved left, taking the road to the Dyomin estate, and
beyond it, to where the Romska caravans had camped in the
west forest. I longed to be with people who were separate from
all the chaos I'd caused. I prayed they hadn't gone yet.

A gilded box carriage came into view farther down the road.
As I galloped past it, Terezia Dyomin looked out the window.
My aura seized with her hatred, deep and new and terrible. I let
it sweep into me and latched onto its strength. I steered Raina

closer to her horses. They gave a frenzied neigh and drove her carriage off the road. It stalled as the wheels caught in the choking underbrush.

I set my jaw and rode onward. I didn't care if Terezia hated me for banishing Valko. I was done with others treating me with contempt. I'd tried my best to help this city, and the people had given me nothing in return.

Raina and I fled past the Dyomin estate and around the bend. Soon the cobblestone road turned to a dirt path. I followed it into the forest.

Branches clawed me as we ripped through the trees. Raina's energy still burned with vigor, but my fatigue of the day overwhelmed me. I hung onto her back by sheer grit. Gasping for breath, I trained my bleary gaze ahead, searching for the bright Romska wagons.

We rode into the meadow where their encampment had been. Now there was nothing, only patches of beaten grass. I circled the perimeter in vain. Tears scalded down my cheeks. The Romska were gone, Tosya was gone. I wanted to be journeying with them, lost in never-ending travels. I wanted to be far away from Torchev, from myself, from the monster I was becoming.

My energy gave out. Raina's hoof caught in an empty fire pit. I couldn't hold her mane any longer. I lurched sideways, skidding off her, and crashed onto the ground. Raina darted away, her nerves frayed. I rose to my bruised knees and called her name, but it was useless. She rode on and on until the forest swallowed her from view and I couldn't sense a whisper of her aura.

I crumpled forward on my hands and knees. My anger turned inward. I ripped out clumps of grass in frustration. I was better than this. I had to pull myself together. I wouldn't let Nadia or my own self-loathing drive me out of this city. I'd fought long and hard for my place in Torchev. I wouldn't give it up. I couldn't. Kira was still here. Even if the Duma rejected me and Anton could never forgive me, a little girl still needed my protection.

I dragged myself to my feet and wiped my black hands on my dress. I wasn't a child. I wouldn't run away. I wouldn't submit before anyone.

Nadia was wrong. I had glorious power. And I didn't need to stand behind Valko or the Duma or anyone else to use it.

I took a step toward the palace, and my knees almost buckled beneath me. I groaned with irritation at my weakness. I needed strength—or something to draw strength from.

I closed my eyes, feeling for any life in the forest. I sensed the scurrying of small beasts, the flutterings of birds. Then the high-humming energy of a person crept up on me. I latched onto the aura and felt my vitality surging back.

A throaty voice pierced my eardrums. "What have you done, girl?"

Slowly, I opened my eyes.

My head throbbed, rocking my vision. I hazily made out a woman draped in a petal-pink gown. Terezia Dyomin. She must have followed me after I'd run her carriage off the road.

She clutched her emerald necklace and had the audacity to come nearer. "What venom did you speak at the trial?"

"I spared the life of your beloved emperor," I replied, curious at the violent pulse of her aura.

Terezia took a step nearer. "You do more than read emotions; you meddle with them. I saw you do it in the city square *and* in the courtroom. You're not a normal Auraseer."

I stood taller. "You don't have the right to judge me. You have no idea what *is* or *isn't* abnormal for my kind. You didn't keep your daughter long enough to find out."

"You demon!" Her arm tensed, as if she might slap me. If she tried, I would beat her to it. Terezia was just like Kira's mother, my mother, any Auraseer's mother—people who deserted their daughters because they weren't brave enough to raise them. "You cared more for yourself than for your only child."

"You're wrong. I loved her." Her stark honesty made my breath hitch. "My husband refused to let me keep her once he knew what she was. I tried to save her from the convent, but when I offered her to the gypsies, they said they only welcomed Romska-born into the tribes. Why they took *you*"—Terezia's gaze wandered over my fair hair—"has mystified me, but I realize now that the Romska must have learned of your power. It's the only explanation."

"You could have stood up to your husband and kept your daughter," I said stubbornly. "Where was your strength when you needed it?"

"You have no idea how vicious my husband was. The late Emperor Izia had him in his pocket. The count's good standing was more important than his own flesh and blood. I may have lost my family, but I won't lose my people and what we're entitled to. If the Duma won't defend the nobility, we'll protect ourselves."

I frowned at her. "And how does a countess manage that?"

Terezia lifted her chin. "I carry a dagger with me at all times." She withdrew the weapon from a pocket in her skirt. "Life in Torchev has grown too dangerous to be unarmed."

I'd never seen another dagger like the one in her hand. The blade was cut from quartz crystal, and smaller crystals jutted out like claws at the top of the hilt, surrounding a glittering silver-gray gemstone. The dagger looked ancient. It must have been a priceless family heirloom. I suspected half the reason Terezia kept it on her was to ensure nobody stole it.

She adjusted her grip on its black hilt. "If I must choose between two evils, the democracy or a reestablished empire, I choose the empire."

I felt the flint-like shift in her aura, the sudden scathing edge. "Are you here to confront me about my supposed inconstancy?" I asked with a derisive laugh. "Go back to your petty, crumbling life. Maybe you'll come across a miserable creature named Nadia who shares your vain dream of a reborn empire."

"I have my own supporters. Scores of them. They're not about to stand by while you undermine everything we've worked for. The Duma is naive if they think they can use an uncontrollable girl for their gain. You're a danger to everyone. They should get rid of you themselves."

My eyes dropped to the dagger in Terezia's hand. It trembled in her grip. My heart tripped faster. My skin flashed fever-hot with her dark and desperate energy.

"I haven't come here to harm you," the countess said, a sheen of sweat on her brow. "But you should know my followers are ruthless. You need to leave Torchev before someone you care about gets hurt."

Who I cared about in this city totaled two people—Anton and Kira. At the thought of either one of them being harmed, my voice dropped to a severe tone. "Do you know how tired I am of being threatened?" I stalked toward Terezia, closing the five paces between us.

Her lips went chalk-pale. She stumbled and lifted her dagger in defense. "Stay back! Don't come near me."

"You came here seeking *me*, invading *my* privacy." My temper escalated. "Don't tell me to back away."

"Stop, I'm warning you! Leave me alone." Every line of her body tensed to fight.

My muscles momentarily seized with hers, but then I broke past the hold.

"Come a step nearer," she said, "and I'll be forced to hurt you."

I gave a feral smile. "If I wanted to harm you, I wouldn't have to touch you; I could control your aura from across this meadow. You saw what I did in the courtroom. And if you dare threaten those I care about one more time, I will see you and the nobility utterly ruined, do you understand?" I moved in closer. Fire rushed through my veins, my heart, every limb, joint, and space of my body.

"Stop!" Terezia pleaded again. She swiped her dagger at the air between us, a pathetic attempt to intimidate me.

"No," I commanded. "You stop!"

The dagger froze in her grasp. Her hand halted. She went silent. Her eyes narrowed on the stilled crystal blade, then me.

"Stop being such a weakling," I went on. Her hatred became my hatred. Her frenzied emotions rattled mine. I turned all her feelings against her. "Don't come here with threats you aren't prepared to draw blood for yourself. Don't complain about the democracy when you won't give it a chance. And don't pretend you cared about a daughter you feared and didn't fight hard enough to keep. Stop all of this—stop it all!"

Terezia's hatred peaked. She gave a cry of rage. In one quick motion, she arced the dagger to her own throat and cut a clean line across its base.

Deep pain burst through me. I stared at the slit on the countess's neck. I still couldn't comprehend. For a fraction of a second, it looked like nothing more than a graze. Then blood cascaded from the wound, coursing across the gash in abundance. Terezia's body went limp and collapsed to the ground.

I gasped in horror. Fell to my knees. "Terezia?" I held her throat. Tried to stop the blood. It poured through my fingers, a warm flood of crimson.

Her body convulsed. Her eyes bulged as she stared at me. I willed her blood to clot, her skin to heal. But I didn't have that power.

Terezia's mouth moved to speak. She gurgled on a strangled breath of air.

"Shhh, shhh." I held her throat tighter. My hands shook, soaked in red. The blood pulsed out in waves, running down the countess's neck and staining the grass beneath her body.

She mouthed a word I couldn't make out. But Terezia looked so insistent that I let up the pressure on her throat. "Inessa," she rasped. Her sorrow compressed my heart, so much stronger than her dwindling pain.

Her body shuddered with another horrible tremor. One last wash of blood gushed from the slit in her neck. Then Terezia froze, lips parted, staring past me to the open sky.

Quaking with shock, I faced the truth of what I'd done, the truth that was smeared all over my hands.

CHAPTER TWENTY-FOUR

HOURS PASSED. THE SUN CROWNED IN THE SKY, THEN FELL into the depths of the murky forest. Soon full darkness would be upon me. Gray clouds converged, blotting out the stars and the moonlight. I didn't have a candle, a lantern—anything to kindle a warm glow to guide me homeward.

I wiped another rush of tears onto my sleeve. The cloth was rumpled and damp from my ceaseless flow of misery. My backside ached from sitting on the root-ridden earth. I dug my palms into my eyes and rocked back and forth, my knees bent tight to my chest.

"I'm sorry," I whispered to Terezia for the thousandth time. I pulled my hands away to look at her, hoping against hope I'd somehow find her alive again. But her voice was just as silent as her aura. "I'm sorry," I said again, stretching out my pale fingers to reach her hand.

My own hands were clean of her blood now. I'd washed

them in the stream, along with every last lingering trace of her aura. But when I'd returned to Terezia's stiff body, my guilt compelled me to feel, once more, her hands, her blood, what I'd done. The whites of Terezia's eyes gradually faded to black as the sky met the darkness I knew was coming.

The leaves in trees above me took shape, backlit by a haze of amber. I blinked, more tears streaking down my face, my muddled senses so inwardly focused that I didn't recognize the light for what it was, nor interpret the thrum of energy surrounding it.

The light built, the leaves' delicate edges growing sharper, crisper, the shadows swinging and bouncing across branches and other clusters of trees. Finally, the light grew so brilliant that it pooled over my face. I could see nothing beyond its bright golden glow.

"Sonya?" A rumbling baritone voice struck a chord of longing within me.

I squinted, lifting a shaking hand to shield the light. The pool of gold shifted so I could see past it.

A face peered down at me, a young man sitting in the saddle of a white horse. His thin upper lip looked full from my upward vantage. His brows were drawn tight with worry. A lantern suspended from his outstretched hand.

Anton.

I imagined how I must appear to him. My hair in tangles, flecked with dirt and brambles. Ash from the Romska's fire pit smeared across my face. Eyes red from crying. The worst guilt etched onto my countenance. I couldn't bear to look at him, but I couldn't look away. He was here, despite everything I'd done at Valko's trial.

This moment was a bizarre repetition of how Anton and I had first met. When he'd guided the troika up the snowy lane of the convent, he'd found me in a similar condition, marked with the filth of death, my crimes fresh.

The hard glint in Anton's eyes shifted, absorbing his panic as he glanced between me and my victim. A riot of feelings swept his aura. I raked through them, desperate to know what he must think of me. Percussive fear. Vice-gripping protectiveness. Bleating confusion. The knife-twist of his complicated love for me, even now. How he sustained his affection was astonishing. I felt the difficulty inside him, the white-hot anger underlying his emotions, adding an anvil of weight to my shame. "Sonya, what happened?"

I opened my mouth. Couldn't think to explain. "You found me," I said instead, my voice bruised from hours of weeping, my head prickling with fog. Nothing felt real. I couldn't wrap my brain around all that I had done and seen in one day . . . the trial, Valko gone, Nadia alive, Terezia dead.

"You were spotted leaving the palace grounds with Raina." Anton dismounted Oriel, the third white horse that pulled the troika last winter. I recognized the stallion's copper socks. A second horse was tied to Anton's and stood in the darker recesses of the lantern's light. *Raina.* Somehow, he'd recovered her.

Anton's gaze flitted over our surroundings, then drifted

toward Terezia, stopping short of her empty eyes.

I shivered, the summer air incapable of reaching my bones. "I—I didn't know what to do with her body," I said, my least disturbing confession of the day.

He set down the lantern and crouched before me. "Are you hurt?" He scrutinized the bodice of my dress, as if I might be concealing a stab wound. When he found none, he angled me around to gently probe at my back. I briefly closed my eyes against the warmth of his touch, the way it heightened his aura inside me. I didn't deserve his tenderness.

"I'm fine." My throat closed. Clenching my hands around a fistful of my skirt, I forced my breath to carry my voice. "I killed her."

Anton went perfectly still. The fringe of his hair swept his hardened jawline. The wind whistled around us, rustling leaves in the treetops. It sounded like rushing water. His pulse slowed to a deliberate, painful throbbing in my body. "Sonya, you're ash-pale and trembling from head to toe. You're not in your right mind."

"I killed her," I repeated, summoning steel in my gaze. "I'm forged for destruction. I can't escape what I do to people."

Anton's arm rested across his bent knee. His fingers rubbed together, as if sifting through my words for the lie he desperately needed to hear: I was innocent of this crime. Against his will, his eyes slid to the lifeless form beside us. This time his gaze lingered. In the grass, between my body and Terezia's, lay her dagger where she'd dropped it. Anton carefully picked it up and turned it over. The crystals of the hilt sparkled, reflecting the firelight of his lantern. Only a thin streak of dried blood dulled the translucent gleam of the blade.

"It's really not so hard to believe, is it," I asked, "knowing I'm capable of this? I don't have a spotless history. This is what I am, it's what I do."

"You're not telling me everything. Terezia must have threatened you."

"I told her to stop speaking, stop threatening those I cared about." My cry found no reverberation in the dark forest. "I wanted her to stop so violently that my command caused her to slit her own throat. I killed her just by thinking it."

He wouldn't relent. "It was self-defense, same as with the assassin."

"I'm not sure it was." I wiped my sleeve under my nose. My sobs came faster. "I don't think she meant to kill me."

"She had a dagger."

"She'd carried one for days. It's no excuse!"

"No, you didn't mean to do this."

"I *did* mean to scare her, to make her leave me alone. I just didn't think she would—" I glanced at Terezia's bloody neck. Bile rose up my throat, and I began rocking again.

"Stop, Sonya." Anton gripped my shoulders. "Stop. You're in a state of shock. You need to calm yourself. We can work through this."

"I don't see how."

"I have a plan. Please follow it this time." He swallowed, his aura gathering courage. "Here." He removed a small purse of coins from his belt and slid it into my dress pocket. "Take the Krichev Road to Isker. It's faster and less traveled. It's the route Motshan always told my mother to take."

"What are you—? Motshan knew the empress?"

"They sometimes traveled together when she went to visit me and Valko. He knew how to keep her protected while also being discreet."

My mouth slackened. I could hardly imagine the two of them in the same room, much less the same caravan.

"If you ride hard, you should be able to meet up with the Romska in two days. Tosya said the caravan is headed that way." Anton removed his cloak and flung it around my shoulders. "This will keep you warm at night. Tuck your braid beneath the collar during the day. Then you won't be spotted so easily."

I stared dumbly at him, at his razor-edged calm, so at odds with the wild panic coursing through me. "You can't make—" Lightheadedness assaulted me. "No. I'm not leaving."

"Sonya, breathe. Breathe and listen to me." He crouched low so our eyes were level. "The Duma is having you hunted. Feliks told the governors about your power. They came back to their own minds after you left the palace, and they realized you'd outsmarted them."

"Good," I said, my trusted stubbornness rousing my logic. "Then they know they can't control me."

"They'll find a way to. You showed Feliks you can indeed overpower a large group of people. He wants your help more than ever, despite your intervention at the trial."

At his mention of the trial, his aura darkened and he lowered his gaze. If our circumstances were different—if I hadn't killed a woman and the Duma wasn't after me—we would surely be having a raging fight right now. Instead, I sensed Anton's conflicting feelings of urgency, tenderness, and fear. "Feliks says he'll provide for Kira's family if you cooperate."

I arched a weary brow. "Is that how Feliks is phrasing his threat now? I preferred his plainness. His threat is the same as before—he'll harm Kira if I don't become his weapon." *He'll harm you.*

Anton nodded, studying the tremble in my shoulders, the ashy filth on my face. "Sonya, you must leave Torchev. This situation has become far too dangerous for you. If Feliks can't control you, he'll seek to have you killed."

"I dare him to try." I attempted a sardonic laugh, but it caught in my throat and sounded like a dry sob. How terribly false it felt to pretend I was expertly skilled when my power brought such devastation. "I will be useful to Riaznin on my own terms. I don't need the Duma to spell out my tasks or try to wield my power through me. I can master it, I promise you. This was a mistake." I gestured to Terezia with a steady arm, but my fingers quivered.

Anton's grip on my shoulders didn't soften. "What if the next mistake involves your life?" He took a long breath and encased his heartache in iron will. So many times he'd tried to persuade me to leave Torchev. But now his aura was inflexibly sure.

"You're giving up." My voice broke, and Anton's pain tore through my own misery. "You're giving up after everything I've done to fight for us."

"I've fought, too. Please believe that." His hand lifted to touch my cheek. "Sonya." My name fell sacred from his breath. "I love you. I always will."

"No. Don't."

He smiled sadly and lifted his other hand to brush my cheekbone. "Stay with the Romska. I'll find a way to be with you as often as I can."

I gazed back and forth between his eyes, my panic heightening. "I scarcely see you as it is." Anton would never abandon his duty. He hadn't missed a single Duma meeting or left one early, even when they ran half the night. "You'll never leave your seat at the capital. Shengli will attack Torchev, and you'll be killed when I could have stayed and saved you."

"You are not responsible for my life."

"You cannot say that when you shoulder responsibility for mine."

He frowned, but I knew that frown, the frustrated tug of his lips, the aching desire beneath it to protect me at all costs and the stubborn refusal to believe he needed me to do the same for him. "I'm not the one who is truly in danger, Anton. You are." I pulled his hands away from my face, but held them tight. "I can protect you. I can protect *all* of Riaznin."

My conviction ran so deep that Anton's tense hands went soft and malleable in my grip. "Our nation is about to crumble." I scooted nearer to him, keeping his focus trapped, masking the tremor in my voice. I had to be strong. I had to make him see reason. "But there is hope. *You* could lead the people. Remember how you did that at Kivratide? You wore that wreath crown that made you feel ridiculous, but you looked so grand. Did you see the way the people's eyes followed you everywhere? You reigned with kindness but sure vision."

I didn't mention the brewing contempt at Kivratide or the incident in the rose garden; those were small considerations compared to how mad things had since become.

"You held Riaznin together before the Duma ever came into power. And I supported you. When you were too stern, I made you laugh. I helped you understand the people's perspective, their feelings. They related to you more with me at your side. I made you more approachable."

I ran a finger over Anton's brow, smoothing his last crease of worry away, along with my lingering guilt. What I was doing was necessary, the only way to save us—to save everyone. "I can help you rise to power. The people have no faith in the Duma, but they *would* unite behind you. I can compel the governors to withdraw from their positions. You wouldn't have to contend with Feliks any longer, and he wouldn't be around to threaten me."

I leaned close and pressed soft lips against his mouth. "Think of it. We could rule together and protect our nation.

Riaznin would be *strong* again. Doesn't that sound wonderful?" I brushed a lock of hair off his face. "I wouldn't have to leave, and everyone would be safe. You could be *emperor*," I whispered. "You could be the person you were raised to be. You've never really given up on that dream, have you?" I brought the buried longing for power within him to the surface.

Anton's gaze darkened, nostrils flared. "No, I haven't," he agreed. Our pulses thrummed in synchronicity, as if we shared one heart. My hope blazed brighter. All I needed was for his submission to be long-term. I couldn't hold him forever under my power. His belief in this saving plan for us had to root so deeply that his outlook permanently changed.

"Kiss me, Anton," I said, stroking his ear. "Everything will be all right." My arms wound around his neck. My mouth hovered above his. Our lips grazed when I spoke again, so quietly my words were more vibration than sound. "Kiss me."

His eyes closed. He gave a shuddering breath. His aura burned with more than heated desire. It trembled with the yearning of a dream denied years ago. But now that dream was within reach—a peaceful Riaznin united under Anton's imperial rule.

The placid tempo of his aura snapped. He grabbed the front panels of my cloak and roughly pulled me against him, my face to his face, my mouth to his mouth. He kissed me—dark and hungry and wild. It was the surrender I'd always wanted from him, the part of himself he kept guarded, tamed.

I kissed him back with fiercer need. We belonged together.

We were meant to rule side by side.

His hands yanked through my hair. Mine dug across his back. We gasped for breath, drawing our lips apart in quick bursts, only long enough to frantically inhale and exhale. Our bodies pressed tighter. We still weren't close enough. As we jostled nearer, we bumped the lantern beside Anton. It wobbled, but didn't tip over. My eyes flashed open and caught the amber firelight bouncing over Terezia's dead face a few feet away. I closed my eyes and kissed Anton harder.

He lowered me down to the grass and spread my cloak open like a blanket beneath us. His mouth trailed down my throat to the wide neckline of my dress. I arched my back as a shower of prickling warmth washed over me.

My gaze opened to take in the starless night. Leaves rustled at the edge of the meadow, capturing a faint glow from the lantern. Tree branches creaked in the breeze. If I kept my head turned from Terezia's lifeless body, all my surroundings felt darkly magical and perfect.

Anton's hands slipped behind my back to the laces of my dress. He wrestled impatiently to loosen them, and I feverishly unbuttoned his kaftan. He wore an undershirt beneath it, and I untucked it from his trousers and ran my hands over his bare torso. His head collapsed against my collarbone as he took a heavy breath, then he pushed himself back up, his chin sliding against me, his mouth returning to my mouth.

His teeth cut my lips as his kiss explored deeper. I'd never felt so free with him. He was nothing like the shy boy who asked me to leave his room while he was dressing, the boy who blushed when he saw me in my nightgown, the boy who gave Sestra Mirna a solemn promise that his intentions toward me were honorable. That was a boy whose kisses came slowly so I could feel his tender affection, a boy who wanted a life with me but who also respected my freedom to choose it, a boy who labored for my safety above any other consideration.

In fact, the boy I was kissing didn't feel like Anton at all.

He finished untying my laces and slid my dress off one shoulder. As his hands moved to clasp the other side of my neckline, my fingers went still on his stomach. "Anton . . . stop. We can't. Not like this." Not when his will wasn't freely his own.

As soon as I said *stop*, Anton froze, his mouth on my jawline. He didn't go rigid like Terezia had when I'd halted her dagger. Anton froze of his own volition. His consideration for me and my change in consent—a deep respect so aligned with his true character—broke the spell of my power over him.

The muscles of his stomach hardened under my touch. He hastily moved off of me and sat back, his aura pulsing with confusion and disconcertedness. His eyes went golden in the lantern's light. He looked like himself again. "Sonya . . ." He gave a little shake of his head, staring down at me. "This isn't how I wanted us to—"

"It's all right." I pulled up into a sitting position. My loose dress hung on me by the grace of one shoulder. I clutched it there. "You've done nothing wrong." I touched his knee with my free hand, trying to calm him. "Let's go back to the palace."

He nodded slowly, but then his frown deepened. His gaze turned to Terezia's body and the two white horses that had wandered a few feet away. When he looked at me again, his eyes carefully narrowed as he studied every inch of my face.

The pulse of his aura went flat with disillusionment.

My heart hammered in my chest. Panic gripped me. I was losing him. "Anton, listen to me. I know what you must be thinking, but—"

"*No.*"

The livid energy behind his word struck me as if I'd been slapped.

He jerked to his feet. "Don't say anything," he said savagely, pointing a warning finger at me. "I know exactly what it was you were trying to do. You don't honor who I am if you believe I'll bring this nation under imperial rule again."

I stood, holding my dress against my chest. "I'm fighting for the same thing you are—" The night breeze shivered against my back where it was bare from my neck to my waist. "—to save Riaznin."

"By *compulsion*, Sonya!" Anton paced away from me and dug his fingers through his mussed hair. His unbuttoned kaftan flapped in the wind.

I walked three steps toward him, then halted when he motioned for me to stay back. Anxiety raced through me. I struggled to find some means to reclaim his trust. "Our nation is facing its worst crisis. Riaznin needs more than a democracy now. I was just trying to help." I reached for his arm, but he pulled away. "Anton, forgive me. I only wanted you to understand my reasoning."

His expression was diamond hard, almost hateful. "You wanted to force it."

My chest ached with his deep hurt and sense of betrayal. "Please . . . I'm sorry."

"Leave," he said flatly, defiantly. Then his brows hitched, his nostrils flared with pained emotion, and he gave a weak shrug. "You—you're breaking me. I can't do this anymore."

My heart rose up my throat. "Anton . . ." My voice was a shocked whisper. All my weakness from the day returned and compounded tenfold. My muscles went limp. Tears tracked down my face. His eyes glistened when he saw them, but he set his chin and looked away.

I reached for him again, but then my nerve endings pricked with alarm—with separate feelings. Auras of other people. They crept into my awareness.

I flinched. Jerked my gaze in a circle. Struggled to see past the lantern's glow to the dim night beyond. I made a move for the beckoning dagger in the grass, but then clenched my hand in resistance.

The Duma's hunting party had arrived.

Anton understood, though not so much as a rustle had sounded in the quiet forest. His pulse quickened, falling into syncopation with mine. "How many?" he asked.

I strained to sense the intruders' variations. Each aura

exuded a different pulse of energy. Some reverberated faster. Others buzzed low like the roar of a distant waterfall. They choked my breathing. "At least three." I glanced at the dagger again. The auras had one thing in common—deadly intent. "Feliks lied to you. These soldiers mean to kill."

Anton's body corded with tension. "How far away are they?"

I shook my head. Tremors overtook me. I had to go. Now. I couldn't use my power again, not after what I'd just done to Anton. "H-half a mile." I wrestled to gauge the strength of their auras. "Maybe . . . maybe less."

Anton's energy spiked, but his features went cool, sharp, unyielding. Single-mindedness pumped through him. He grabbed Terezia's crystal dagger, ran to the horses, and sliced the rope tying them together. He quickly led Raina to me. "Turn around," he commanded.

When I stared dumbly at him, he dropped the dagger, grabbed my shoulders, and spun my back to him. He cinched the laces of my dress. His hands were rough. His conflicted feelings rushed through me every time his fingers swept across my skin or his knuckles caught the ridge of my spine.

My throat tightened with longing, already missing the tenderness with which he used to touch me. I would never feel it again.

Once Anton knotted the laces, he let go of me, almost pushing me away. His steely gaze turned to Terezia's body. He strode to her and stooped to examine her dress. "Where does she keep her sheath?" he asked, voice clipped.

I studied the taut lines of Anton's body silhouetted against the light of the lantern. "She pulled the dagger from her pocket."

He found it and withdrew an engraved silver sheath. At any other time I would have paused to admire its beauty, but now I just felt grateful the sheath would encase the dagger and shield me from Terezia's blood.

Anton unfastened his belt, looped the sheath onto it, and passed it to me. "Put this on. Quickly. I won't send you away unarmed."

My power was far more deadly than this weapon, but refusing the dagger seemed a futile argument at this point.

He grabbed his cloak from the ground and hurriedly shook off the debris of moss and broken twigs. He flung the cloak around my shoulders, and his scent of musk and pine settled around me, buried in the cloth. I looked up to Anton's eyes, pleading for him to return my gaze, my love, my last apology.

I knew I had to go, but when he brought Raina beside me, I faltered at the thought of leaving him forever. The next thing I knew, Anton's arms were around me. He scooped me up with surprising strength and hoisted me onto the mare's back.

"The Romska are journeying by way of Ormina to reach the caravans at the seashore. The tribes are safer in greater numbers. Together, they'll travel to where the Romska Greater Council is held in the autumn. I told you how to find them. Take the—"

"Krichev Road to Isker," I finished, my voice hollow.

At last, his gaze lifted to me.

Defiance froze my heels at Raina's flanks. In the far reaches of the forest, the trees quivered as faint torchlight bobbed through the leaves. I latched onto Anton's beautiful face, his fathomless brown eyes, the fierceness with which he still sought to protect me, even after all my betrayals. "I can't . . ." My voice was a whisper-worn croak. "Anton, I can't . . ." *I can't leave you.*

Behind the rigid contours of his body, the torchlight grew in illumination. The trees in the distance became more distinct against the brightness. The auras of those in the hunting party met mine with greater strength. They were fast approaching. My fists tightened with their urgency. My stomach gave a ravenous lurch. The hunters must know there were people out here.

We were out of time.

Anton placed his hand on my thigh. His anxiety flooded into me, tripling my own. "Go, Sonya!" he whispered.

His touch bled warmth through my dress to my skin to the core of my aura. I committed every fluctuation of sensation to memory, every spark of energy that made him *him*. My eyes burned hot. Water blurred my vision. "I can't," I said again.

I felt the slight tremble in Anton's fingertips, the warring inside him. Then he blinked hard and reclaimed his resolve.

He stepped back, letting go of my leg. I shuddered as a chill swept over my skin in the space where his hand had been. I understood his silent answer: *You can. You must.*

Releasing a shaky breath of determination, I grabbed clumps of Raina's mane and locked my thighs around her girth.

"You can't be found alone here," I said to Anton. I wouldn't have him swallow the repercussions of my crime. Even now, Terezia's dead eyes fixed uncannily in my direction, and my gut roiled with a resurgence of dread.

"I'll be fine," he replied stiffly. "I know what must be done."

"Please watch over Kira." I hated the thought of abandoning her.

"Of course."

My heart drummed with the skidding pulse of the hunting party, with the stinging loss of Anton's affection, with the dream of Riaznin we'd once shared and worked so hard for together. My mouth couldn't shape the word, *Good-bye*. "Don't forget me."

"Sonya . . ." Anton's grief burned in his eyes. He glanced behind him at the threatening advance of torchlight, then back at me. Rage, hurt, and sorrow pierced through him at our separation, at my terrible breach of his trust.

I clung to every breath of his aura, every memory of my life with him, every imagining of the future we could have had. "I love you." Tears rolled down my face. "I'm so sorry."

"Go!" His voice was hoarse, bitter, aching.

I kicked Raina hard in the flanks.

We galloped away into the night. I felt Oriel's energy receding as Anton rode him in an opposite direction of the hunting party.

As soon as we had vacated the meadow, the blazing light of torch fire bled across the deserted Romska camping grounds. A few seconds later, the shrill whinny of a horse split the air, like the animal had been drawn to a sharp halt. Two other horses and riders thundered to the middle of the clearing. Raina and I tore faster into the dark forest.

The bark of a man's rough voice called out to his companions, "I need assistance at once! I've found Countess Dyomin!"

My breath hitched, my shoulders racked inward.

I wouldn't use my power ever again.

CHAPTER TWENTY-FIVE

I STRUGGLED TO SHAKE OFF THE HORROR OF MY REMORSE. I forced my feelings into a locked box in my mind. Cleaving to the stalwart and tenacious energy of the forest, I became what I needed to be in order to survive, in order to outdistance my heartache and guilt.

The hours passed into days. I found the Krichev Road and approached a small river town. I purchased a saddle and trappings, a pair of ankle-high boots, and thick wool socks so I wouldn't feel the brush of the leather and the death of the beast. I drew on a new pair of gloves to protect my hands from the reins of Raina's bridle, and then continued onward.

Numb inside, I allowed only the mare's aura to penetrate my awareness. I closed my ears to the circulating rumors and discord among the peasants. News had reached them of the emperor's banishment. Many didn't trust the Duma for making such a soft decision in court. Outside the town, I passed a country estate. The windows were broken and doors left ajar. Crumbled, smoking beams of a recent fire marred a wing of the main floor.

I told myself it wasn't my problem. None of the tensions in Riaznin were anymore. I couldn't help now. I'd tried to, and I'd failed.

Travelers passed me. I tucked my fair braid inside the collar of the cloak and kept my head ducked. Journeying alone wasn't safe. I'd heard horrific stories about what happened to Romska girls who wandered too far from their caravans.

When a regiment of soldiers appeared on the road between Torchev and Isker, I jerked Raina aside into the cover of trees. The men traveled on without spotting or apprehending me. I breathed only a short-lived sigh of relief. Feliks was surely having me hunted. He wasn't the kind of man to lose graciously.

Another evening fell. I ate a little food from my pack. I should have reached the Romska by now. I needed to pick up my pace tomorrow. I curled up against the cradling roots of a giant oak and turned the crystal dagger over in my hand. It may have belonged to Terezia, but it seemed designed for me. I sheathed the dagger and tried not to touch it again.

⁂

I awoke in the middle of the night to a tickle on my brow. I swiped at it and felt the vibration of fluttering wings. A moth flew off my face. I adjusted Anton's cloak around me, trying to get comfortable again. As my eyes were closing, I spied a shadowy figure a few feet away. My muscles locked in fright.

I forced a shallow breath. This was just my wild imagination.

A breeze swept through the forest, kicking up dried mulch. The shadowy shape changed. A large wing unfurled on its right side. I blinked. It wasn't a wing; it was a billowing cape.

I'd been found.

I whipped out my dagger. Sprang to my feet. Charged the figure with a cry of fear and fury. It was Feliks. He'd come for me.

The figure jolted in surprise. Dodged left to miss my strike.

My foot caught on protruding root. I fell to the ground. Lost grip of the dagger. It tumbled three feet away, landing in a dim patch of moonlight.

My attacker ran for it.

"No!" I scrambled on hands and knees to beat him there.

As he darted ahead of me, I grabbed his leg. He went sprawling and landed face-first beside the dagger. I lunged for it. Grabbed the hilt. The blade flashed as I drew it up and rolled to my side, ready to stab. My attacker seized my forearm. He was a hooded blur of black before me in the darkness. All I saw were the whites of his eyes.

We wrestled for control of my weapon. Raina stomped and whinnied in fright. I bent up my legs, squirming in the tight space between us, and kicked my attacker hard in the stomach. He gave a low grunt and flew backward. I heard his head thunk the hard ground.

I spun up to my feet. Hurtled for him. Lifted my dagger. Skidded down to my knees to deliver a killing blow to his chest.

My attacker's arms rose to protect himself. "Sonya, stop!" her ragged, winded voice cried out. *Her.* A girl's voice.

My dagger froze in the air. I panted. Sought to orient my senses. All of this had happened when I'd just awoken. My mind was still muddled. Now I realized I couldn't feel my attacker's aura. Not even a flicker of energy.

I yanked off her hood and sat back so I didn't block the glimmer of moonlight. Her features came out of shadow. Tattooed skin. Ropy burn scars. Jade eyes.

My heart thundered. I gazed at her in disbelief. *Nadia.* Not Feliks. Not the Duma's hunters.

I didn't lower my dagger.

"You followed me from Torchev?" My voice rang hoarse and out of breath.

Her brows screwed up in panic. She shifted to sit up.

"Don't move!" I brought the dagger closer.

The scars on her neck stretched as she swallowed.

"You better explain why you're here," I said. Fear strung my nerves tight. For all I knew, Nadia wanted me dead, too.

"I'm journeying back to the convent," she replied weakly.

"And so you're following me?" I exclaimed. "I'm not traveling there." *Sestra Mirna would never have me back.*

"But you're en route to meet the Romska at the seashore past Ormina," Nadia said in a rush, eyes wide, mouth trembling. "The same road leads to the convent."

Dark understanding descended upon me, pounding blood through my head. My hand cramped around the dagger hilt.

"How do you know I'm planning to meet the Romska?" I loomed nearer, my voice lowering to a deadly octave.

Nadia went pale, mist gray in the moonlight. She shook all over. "I know you didn't mean to do it."

I jerked the dagger to the base of her neck, the same place where Terezia had slitted hers. The moonlight glinted off the crystal blade. "Do *what*?" Had Nadia come here to kill me because she'd seen me kill?

Tears pooled in her eyes. She bit her lip—in nervousness, deliberation? "Burn the convent," she whispered. Her words crackled up the scarred lining of her throat.

A startled breath purged out of me. I pulled the blade away. Pushed back so I sat two feet from her. Stared in amazement. I still didn't drop the dagger. I didn't know what to do anymore. It was more shocking to hear Nadia declare the convent fire was an accident than to accept the truth she'd survived it.

She sat up slowly. The tendons in her neck drew taut. She looked ready to spring at any moment if I made another move. "I followed Prince Anton when he went searching for you," she said. "I found you both in the west forest." She paused, lifting her brows a little. Was she embarrassed? Without being able to sense her aura, I didn't know if it was an act. I'd never seen Nadia flustered before. "I kept my distance when I heard you and the prince, well . . ." She waved her hand, making a vague gesture.

Heat flushed my cheeks, and I shifted uncomfortably. "So you didn't see"—I cleared my throat—"anything?" I found myself scowling at her, but I would stomach the fact that Nadia had eavesdropped on such a private moment if it meant she didn't see Terezia dead in the grass.

She looked affronted, as if even her spying had moral boundaries. "Of course not. I was crouched behind the trees surrounding the meadow. I saw nothing, only heard your voices. I came upon you when you were"—she waved her hand again— "and then readying to leave."

Jaw clenched, I examined the sincere and solemn expression on her face for any signs of falseness. My palm ached from gripping the dagger hilt too hard. My awareness strained to sense Nadia's emotions once more and revealed nothing. "So you found out where I was traveling and left Torchev to follow me—after you were so insistent I leave you to your rightful place there?"

The moonlight only revealed the unscarred portion of her face. The trees shaded the rest of her. She looked like the old Nadia I knew—beautiful—except her features weren't sharp with malice like usual. "We both know neither one of us belongs in the palace anymore," she said.

I eyed the artful sag of her shoulders, the picture of defeat. "So why torment me if you were planning to leave all this while?"

"I wasn't," she answered evenly. "I wanted to punish you. I wanted what I could never have back. It was foolish."

My eyes narrowed. It wasn't like Nadia to speak so self-deprecatingly. Then again, until now she hadn't come to terms with losing what she'd labored so hard for. I thought of Dasha throwing stones off the balcony and Kira running through the meadow with Paizi. My chest tightened, knowing I'd likely never see them again.

I finally comprehended why Nadia had followed me. Besides herself, I was one of three Auraseers left in Riaznin— and the only one near her age. Despite all the enmity between us, I was the closest person Nadia knew who might be able to understand her, whether her aura was blocked to me or not.

"Why can't I sense you?" I asked, the biting edge of my voice gone.

She lowered her eyes briefly, then sat up straighter, clasping her hands in her lap. Her visible eye glittered in the moonlight. "You're not the only Auraseer with an unusual gift of power, Sonya. Mine manifested during the convent fire when I felt our sisters suffering and dying all around me."

I tugged at the laces of my cloak, my stomach tightening in guilt.

Nadia's expression remained serene as she watched me fidget. She held her swanlike neck with exact posture. "As a measure of defense," she continued, "I fought to blind my awareness to the other Auraseers' auras. I didn't realize until we met again in the orchard at Kivratide that I'd caused the opposite to happen—permanently, it seems."

My brow wrinkled. "You can't reverse it or lower that . . . shield?" I couldn't think of a better term.

Nadia blinked slowly and shook her head. "So, you see,

while I'm able to sense you, you'll never be able to sense me." Her chin lifted the slightest degree, and the hint of a smile curled the corner of her mouth. I knew that look of arrogance. She was the old Nadia for a moment then, always seeking to be superior. I settled into a more comfortable position. Although her confession was disturbing, at least her pride was something I could rely upon.

"So now you wish to live the rest of your life at the convent?" The place where Nadia had studied so diligently, where she'd hated the holding chamber of our existence as much as I did.

"Sestra Mirna has records of my parents and the place where I was born. I need to return to the convent so I can find my family."

I suppressed a scoff. Of course, only when Nadia's dream of being sovereign Auraseer was obsolete did she seek out her father and mother.

My palms ached with dread and my stomach went rock hard. What if Terezia Dyomin had been Nadia's mother?

Had I killed Nadia's last living parent?

The breeze ruffled her shoulder-length hair. She tucked it behind one ear as she studied me intently. "What is it?"

I held my breath, heart pounding, and studied her features. I searched for any similarities she had with the countess. Terezia and Nadia both had the same raven hair, but that shade was common enough in Riaznin—and in the convent. They had different surnames—Dyomin and Firsova, but it wasn't exceptional for a girl's name to be changed at her family's request. There was just as good a chance that Nadia *was* Terezia's daughter than she wasn't—and no way to tell except by asking Sestra Mirna.

"Nothing," I replied, though Nadia could surely sense my pressing guilt. When she continued to scrutinize me, I stood and shook the debris off my cloak and sheathed my dagger. Her expression eased, seeing my weapon put away.

"How much food did you pack for the journey?" I asked, working to keep my voice light.

"None," she admitted. "I was too rushed to turn back and steal a horse from the palace stables. Any more delay would have lost me precious time catching up to you." When I frowned and scanned around us, she said, "The mare is tied to a tree a quarter-mile away." It took me a moment to sense the low thrum of energy from another horse besides my own. "I knew she'd awaken you if I brought her too close," she added, as if her tactics for stalking me were the most natural thing in the world.

I exhaled, deciding not to argue about Nadia's thieving. It was the least of my concerns now. "Good." I swept back a strand of loose hair. "Then we won't have to share my horse."

She went still. "Pardon?"

I brushed the dirt off my sleeves. "I'd rather we journey together than have you creep up on me in the night. Either way, I can't seem to get rid of you. We'll leave at first light, agreed?"

Nadia gave me a wary look, like I was the one to be distrusted in this new arrangement. Strangely, her inability to emit an aura was the one aspect of traveling with her that brought me peace. I wouldn't be able to harm Nadia if I slipped up with my power again.

I held out my hand and helped her to her feet. We came face-to-face. Her jade eyes held the challenge of my offer. "We are agreed."

CHAPTER TWENTY-SIX

AFTER THREE HOURS ON THE ROAD THE NEXT DAY, MY STOM-
ach was as empty as my knapsack. Nadia and I detoured to a
nearby town for provisions. It would set us back a good two
hours from reaching the Romska this evening, if I'd guessed
their distance correctly. I hoped Motshan would allow Nadia to
accompany the caravan as far as the convent. If he didn't, she'd
likely trail behind them anyway.

I kept glancing over my shoulder to make sure she was still
there and hadn't leapt off her horse to attack me while I wasn't
watching. Neither one of us was in the mood for conversation,
though Nadia's mood was just a blind guess on my part. Her
aura was as eerily silent as ever.

The mare she had stolen was Danica, one of the three
troika horses. Between thoughts of the troika and Anton's cloak
around me, I felt the echoes of his touch, heard his low voice
say we were over, saw the last broken look he gave me. My

betrayal sank deep inside to my tangled web of regrets. I could never go back, never change what I had done. All that was left was for me to strive to become a good person, a difficult task when Nadia proved to be as frustrating and entitled as ever.

"But this will cost half my remaining rubles," I said, looking in dismay at the new clothes she had gathered in a tailor's shop. "We've already bought you new boots."

"I need a new dress and cloak, Sonya." She plucked her tattered skirt with a sulking frown. "This belonged to the villager's wife who took care of me. The woman was twice my size. I look ridiculous!"

"We'll be with the Romska by nightfall," I replied. "They'll share clothes with you." Nadia wrinkled up her nose like that might bring her disease. "Plus, if the caravan keeps a steady pace, you'll arrive at the convent within a week. Sestra Mirna will provide you necessities."

"Perhaps you've forgotten"—Nadia sneered—"but the east wing with all the bedrooms and wardrobes burned. Any new clothes the convent has received since then will be in Dasha's or Kira's or Sestra Mirna's sizes."

I threw up my hands. "Fine. Buy your stupid wardrobe."

She selected a smart, indigo blue dress, not as simple as a peasant's sarafan or as gaudy as a dining gown, and an ankle-length, hooded cloak that was a drab shade of brownish-green—a practical choice, I realized. Such a color blended well with leaves, shrubs, and bark. Nadia was prepared to hide away again if she needed to. I just couldn't determine why, and her absent aura didn't offer any clues.

Before we'd entered the town, we left our horses in the forest off the road. A matching pair of such fine pedigree would attract unwanted attention. As it was, Nadia and I had to duck into shadows or behind carts whenever soldiers marched by. We kept an ear to the gossip in the market as we purchased hard biscuits and apples for me, cheese and salted pork for her. I caught whisperings of the missing former sovereign Auraseer who had left Torchev the same day the emperor was banished.

Musket fire shot out more than once. The scuffles happened out of sight, but the victims were near enough that I jerked each time with their radiating pain. Thankfully, their wounds weren't fatal. When the third crack of gunfire blasted, I gasped, doubling over. But Nadia looked untroubled by any discomfort. She arched a brow and said, "Are you still so fragile, dear Sonya? You never tolerated the market well, did you?"

"This is nothing like the market outside Ormina," I snapped, although the sestras' failed methods to acclimate me to crowds weren't much less unpleasant.

Nadia shrugged and ate a piece of her dried pork, chewing slowly, as if she were instead savoring a roasted leg of duck. "This is delicious. You should try some." She extended her hand, then quickly retracted it. "Oh, wait, I forgot, you can't eat meat. It disturbs your delicate senses. Such a shame." She brushed past me, licking her lips.

My muscles burned with acid anger. It wasn't fair how she could trigger my emotions without emitting any aura. I bit off a chunk of my bland biscuit and scowled at the back of her head. I may have entertained a brief fantasy of strangling her.

"We need to find a tack shop," Nadia called over her shoulder, her fingers trailing over a display of fox furs she knew I couldn't touch. "Danica must have a new bit for her bridle. She's been chewing the one in her mouth."

"That's because she's distressed. She doesn't like the way you ride her. You need to give the reins more slack and be more sensitive to what she's trying to communicate to you."

Nadia smirked, eyes narrowed. "You see, this is the difference between you and me. Not much has changed since we studied at the convent. I model discipline while you cave to any emotions you feel, whether or not they belong to you." She lifted her chin and gave me a haughty stare. "Danica needs a new bit."

I flexed my hands and steadied my breathing. I wouldn't prove Nadia right so easily. "We've stayed in this town long enough. We're lucky we haven't been discovered."

"It'll be quick."

I exhaled the simmering rage inside me. *One week, Sonya. Then she'll be gone.* "Fine," I said.

But it wasn't quick. Nadia wasn't satisfied with the offerings in the marketplace, so we took to the backstreets to find the shop a peddler recommended. Here, the discontent in the town cut at my skin with a sharp edge of danger.

A window shattered above us in a narrow alley. Two peasants leaped down with handful of jewels. A large soldier with a prominent jaw emerged into the alley after them, saber drawn.

A jolt of fear lit through me. If he saw us—

"Here!" Nadia yanked me through a cracked-open door and shut it with a quiet click. She dragged me to the corner of a dim and cramped lobby, then shoved me behind a ragged chaise lounge and crouched beside me. This place must be a brothel with its thick perfume, tinkling laughter, rousing desire, and sickening dread. The lobby was deserted, but I sensed the auras of eager guests and weary residents upstairs.

Seconds later, the soldier's pounding boots grew louder, and a harsh clang rang out. He must have kicked over a pail in his pursuit of the thieves. At last, his boots picked up speed, running off until they faded into the distance.

Lightheadedness seized me. I'd been holding my breath. With an exhale, I turned to scrutinize Nadia. I couldn't understand why she'd gone from threatening me in Torchev to protecting me once we were outside the capital. What if her motive for traveling with me was darker than the excuse of safety?

She stood, smoothing the skirt of her new dress. "Why didn't you work your special sorcery back there?" She waggled her fingers, as if conjuring a spell. "You could have made that soldier fall in love with me rather than test my stamina . . . though, I suppose, both are related." She preened her hair.

I rolled my eyes and pulled myself to my feet. I hated that Nadia knew about my enhanced ability. "I don't do that anymore—use my power." I couldn't hold her gaze, so I angled away and fidgeted with the frayed neckline of my violet gown. I'd been wearing the same clothes since Valko's verdict. I should have bought something new like Nadia. I'd probably have to wear one of Gillie's old dresses once we reached the Romska, and she was all curves while I was bones.

When I looked at Nadia again, she was giving me an unnerving stare. I wished to the gods I could sense the emotion beneath it. "What?" I asked.

"Just wondering what caused you to become so tight-laced since you meddled with the emperor's trial."

Memories blazed to mind. The savage kiss Valko had given me. How he'd compared my role in his abdication to rape. The cascading blood from Terezia's slit throat. Anton's eyes when he'd discovered my betrayal. "I've decided my power should only be used during rare times of desperate need," I answered, though I doubted I'd justify anything in that category anymore.

Nadia pursed her lips, turning up her nose at me. "Well, I'm so glad we didn't die by a saber just now. I'm not sure what else would have convinced you our situation was desperate." She skirted around the chaise lounge and nodded to my knapsack. "Enjoy your apples. You've probably bruised them all."

She didn't deign to speak to me while we waited in the brothel to make sure we were truly clear of the soldier, nor did she utter a word as we slunk out of town in the most direct route possible, foregoing a new bit for Danica. I treasured the silence while it lasted. Soon enough, Nadia would find something else to belittle me about.

We rode our horses westward. The forests gave way to

rolling plains. I prayed we wouldn't run into any more soldiers. There were fewer and fewer places to hide along the road. We stopped only once to stretch our legs, let our horses drink from a pond, and eat more provisions. We didn't ration our helpings. We'd meet up with the Romska tonight and feast around their campfires. I ate another apple, giving Raina and Danica the last few, and then Nadia and I set off again.

The travelers on the road dwindled as the afternoon pressed toward evening. Despite the lowering sun, the day grew hotter, the air thicker with humidity. We removed our cloaks and tied them in rolls behind our saddles. I rubbed sweat off the back of my neck, and kept my gaze trained ahead, my senses alert, searching for any signs of the Romska. My skin tingled, ready for any prick of recognition, any pulse of familiarity.

We rounded a bend. Up ahead, a small hill crouched between towering pines. At the crest of the hilltop, a deep patch of shade beckoned me, promising shelter from the heat.

I prodded Raina to ride faster, outpacing Nadia and Danica as I came nearer to the hill. In the depths of the shade, the lanky figure of a man swam into vision. He strolled along with his back to me and his hands in his pockets.

I gasped and pulled Raina to a halt. Then I leapt to the ground and ran full speed, barreling into my friend's surprised arms. I'd mistaken his easing aura for my own desire for respite.

I laughed, though I felt like weeping. "Tosya."

"Sonya?" he asked in shock. He drew away, his brown eyes narrowing as they swept over Anton's cloak, the palace horse I'd just dismounted, and what must be an expression of staggering relief upon my face. "Why are you here?" My chest constricted with his worry and confusion.

Nadia rode up on Danica, stopping six feet away. Earlier, when we'd watered our horses, she'd taken the opportunity to scrub her hair. Now it fell in gleaming waves and looked far more elegant than its previously stringy incarnation. She sat tall with flawless posture and stared down at Tosya like a battle-ready queen. Even her scars looked stunning, shimmering pearlescent in the fading sunlight. She was nothing like the girl who'd been so infuriating today.

Tosya's brows lifted ever so slightly as he gazed back at her. A current of warmth traveled from my neck to my ears, flushed with his piqued interest. I scratched my dirty hair, smoothed a rumpled fold of my dress, and looked longingly at Nadia's indigo gown.

I cleared my throat—twice—to reclaim Tosya's attention. "Tosya, this is Nadia, an Auraseer from the convent in Ormina." His brows jutted up another notch, and his gaze focused on Nadia's scars. "Nadia, this is Tosya, my oldest friend and the poet who penned *Lament of the Gods*." When Nadia's eyes didn't widen in recognition of the work, I added, "The poem that drove the revolution."

Her eyes rounded to my satisfaction, and I suppressed a smirk. I'd just introduced the most politically opposed pair I could have dreamed of throwing together.

Nadia glanced at my smug expression, and a cunning look

of challenge swept across her face. She dismounted her horse with the grace of a ballerina, glided up to Tosya, and dipped into a plié of a curtsy. The ragged edge to her damaged voice softened to a delicate purr. "I'm honored to make your acquaintance, Tosya."

CHAPTER TWENTY-SEVEN

"WHAT DO YOU MEAN WE CAN'T TRAVEL WITH YOU?" I openly stared at Motshan. He may as well have just slammed a door in my face. *Where can I go if the Romska won't take me in?*

Tosya, Nadia, and I were seated across the chief around a private campfire near his wagon at the center of the camp. Night had fallen in the time it took to walk the two miles' distance to catch up to the caravan. Tosya said he'd lagged behind for quiet contemplation, "as poets do," he'd added with a wink. He was probably just saying that to impress Nadia. I suspected the real reason was he felt like an outcast among his own people. The Romska disapproved of the education he'd received among the Gadje, and Motshan hated Tosya's hopeful plan to represent the tribes in the Duma. I felt the chief's aversion grow at every reference Tosya had made to it tonight.

Nadia set down her spoon in her bowl of mushroom dumplings, Jeta's signature dish. "Is this about me?" she asked

Motshan, batting her eyes like a court lady. Tosya had warned Nadia that the Romska distrusted strangers. "I'm only traveling as far as the convent."

I frowned slightly at the other Auraseer. Tosya sat between us on a log, and Nadia made sure to position herself so he was seated next to the unscarred half of her body. The campfire's glow haloed her lovely profile, and she kept sending Tosya furtive smiles—especially when I was looking—that made his pulse quicken. I shifted protectively toward my friend. Tosya fell for anybody.

Motshan sucked in a long draft from his pipe. "My decision is about Sonya," he replied to Nadia, though from the way my stomach knotted with his suspicion, I doubted the Romska chief would have let her journey with the caravan, with or without me. "My scouts have warned me that the bounty hunter, Bartek, is searching for you." Motshan's sage-green eyes slid to me.

My ribs wrenched tight. Bartek was a monster. He'd caught and tortured Pia just to bait her lover. Bartek was the same man who'd held innocent tribe children hostage, forcing the Romska to give me up to the empire last spring. No wonder Motshan was refusing to protect me. He didn't want to endanger his people again.

Nadia picked up her spoon and blew steam off a dainty bite. "A bounty hunter won't pose a threat, not if Sonya's with the caravan," she said casually.

I shot Nadia a warning glance.

"What?" she said innocently, looking between all of us. "I'm sure they know about your special power, Sonya."

My gaze was sharp enough to fling knives. I turned to Motshan and swallowed. The last thing I needed was for him to think I went around telling everyone I could manipulate aura.

He crossed his arms, the embroidered sleeves of his jacket folding over each other. "When you touch dark energy, you tamper with the natural balance of the world," he said.

"I won't anymore, I promise. I'm done playing with power." Tosya wrinkled his brows at me. I still hadn't told him what had happened with Anton and Terezia, only that Feliks wanted to use me as a weapon, so I had to stay on the run. "If I live a peaceful life with the Romska, I won't even be tempted to use it. All we have to do is deal with the problem of Bartek. He's a man driven by money. Maybe we can pay him off with something valuable."

A log snapped in the fire, and embers swirled before Motshan's eyes. "The Romska tried bribing him before. Bartek wasn't swayed by anything, even our finest horses. His ambitions go beyond money; he also wants power. He desires respect and consistent employment from the ruling government in the nation." Motshan took another puff on his pipe, and his aura chilled me with foreboding. "My scouts say the *Duma* hired Bartek to hunt you."

My scalp prickled with unease. I doubted it was the Duma. Anton wouldn't have allowed it. *Feliks* had hired Bartek. I just didn't know whether the governor wanted me captured or killed.

Motshan hunched over, elbows on knees, and scratched his stitched cleft lip. "I'm sorry, Sonya. Even though you're one of us, the Romska can no longer be your guardians."

My brows drew together. "One of you?" As much as the Romska had shown me kindness, I'd always felt separate from them. They were tribal to the core, bound together by blood.

Motshan stood, crossed over to me, and clamped a warm hand on my shoulder. "Why do you think we really took you in as a child?"

I thought of Terezia's daughter, rejected by the nomads. "Because you knew I had power, and you wanted to make sure I didn't abuse it."

Motshan nodded, his eyes losing their harsh glint. Deep affection permeated his aura . . . deep affection for *me*. "The elders also took you in because we believe only Romska-born hold such power. Our legends speak of rare Auraseers with your abilities. Your gift is a sign that somewhere in your lineage you share our blood."

I gazed at him without blinking. Warmth slowly spread through my body. My throat grew thick with emotion. "I'm *Romska*?"

He nodded, the lines around his eyes crinkling, though he didn't smile. This was a farewell, not a homecoming. But somehow that didn't matter.

The warmth inside me built into strong and sustaining heat. Long-wrought tension eased from my muscles. I was no longer concerned if my parents knew about my power, whether it made them afraid, or if their love for me outweighed their fear. My bond to the Romska made up for all that. As much as Auraseers were my people, the Romska were, too. I belonged with them.

Motshan gave my shoulder a pat, and the pipe-smoke scent of his clothes wafted down on me with memories of journeying alongside his caravan wagon, his tobacco smell mingling with damp earth, pine needles, and the morning mist. "I'm sorry we can't risk protecting you again, Sonya. You may spend the night here"—his gaze lifted to include Nadia—"then you'll both need to be on your way in the morning."

Tosya sat up straighter. "I'm going with them," he announced in determination. "Two girls shouldn't travel alone," he added, broadening his chest.

I arched a brow. If we ran into trouble, *I'd* likely be the one defending *him*.

Nadia cast him a challenging smile that made my eye twitch. "Perhaps you can show me how to wield a dagger, Tosya. Unless a poet doesn't have any experience with a blade."

Tosya gave Nadia what he probably thought was a ruggedly brave stare. To me, he looked like he'd just sat on a thorn. "I do know a few helpful techniques," he replied, his voice suddenly deep and raspy.

I wanted to throttle them both.

"It's decided, then," Tosya told Motshan. "Sonya and I will see Nadia safely to the convent. Then I'll help Sonya get settled"—

he waved a vague hand through the air, and I imagined a dark cave I'd live in for the rest of my life—"and meet back up with the caravan in time to join the Greater Council in the autumn."

"Very well." Motshan scowled at Tosya like he hoped he'd stay away and stop badgering him with talk of democracy, governors, and Duma representation. "You may take Hanzi." Hanzi was a sandy Esten trotter that Motshan had won in a bad barter. The stallion was as sluggish and stubborn as a mule. He was also the ugliest horse in the herd.

"Wonderful!" Tosya beamed. He never was a horseman.

"Within a day, you'll reach more forestland," Motshan continued. "Once you do, travel off the road and stay hidden in the trees. Journey at night and sleep during the day. Bartek was the empire's greatest bounty hunter, and now he'll want to prove himself to the Duma." Motshan looked at me. "Do you understand who you're up against, Sonya?"

Taking a deep breath, I curled my fingers into the log I sat on. "Yes. And I know he won't stop looking for me." I bit my lip and glanced at Tosya. "You shouldn't come."

His false bravery whittled away, but in its place came something I cherished more, his loyalty. With it, Tosya gave me a brotherly smile and covered my hand with his own. *"The mighty isn't one, but many,"* he said, quoting words he'd penned, the very mantra of the revolution. With a smirk, he added, "At least the mighty is two."

"Three," Nadia clarified with a light smile, brushing her knee against his.

"Yes, three." Tosya laughed. "The mighty is three."

I studied them, my gut forming a knot of despair. If Bartek ambushed us, we wouldn't stand a chance.

"The mighty is three," I echoed.

CHAPTER TWENTY-EIGHT

As Motshan promised, by the end of the next day, Tosya, Nadia, and I reached forestland. We traveled off the road and continued journeying through the first night. Picking our way through the trees, we took care to be quiet. Our slowed pace meant it would take us even longer to reach the convent, but we hoped the delay would bring us greater safety.

For the first two days, Nadia teased Tosya, throwing him light remarks that disputed his views on democracy and bantered off his flirtatious quips. But by the third day, Nadia quieted when Tosya started talking about his new book of poetry, listening rather than dominating their conversations. She stared at him softly when she didn't think I was looking. Her laughter lost its artful lilt when he said something funny, which was most of the time. Instead, she snickered, giggled, and, once, even belly laughed. She stopped traveling on the left side of him and let him see the scarred and tattooed half of her face.

I watched the two of them, so comfortable together, and a brush of loneliness flitted across my empty hands. Tosya deserved better than the cruelest girl at the convent, but he seemed just as rapt with Nadia as she was with him.

"Sonya tells me you'd like to find the whereabouts of your family," I heard him say to Nadia one afternoon when I'd just awakened from sleeping. I rolled over on my bed of dried pine needles and saw him lying on his side next to her. She lay sprawled out on her back, and he was propped up on one elbow. He twirled a long blade of grass between his fingers.

Nadia's smile fell at Tosya's remark, and she looked away from him. The sun pillared down through the canopy above us and made her jade eyes turn hemlock green. "Yes," she said. "Sestra Mirna keeps a locked chest of records in the library. Fortunately, that room didn't burn with the other half of the convent."

Tosya shifted a little closer to her. His aura made my body tingle and my mouth go dry with breathlessness. "Once you find your family, I hope you'll write to me and tell me where I can look for you."

Nadia turned to him, blinking slowly, her lips lifting in a subtle curve. "I'd like that."

He traced one of the tattooed swirls on the edge of her forehead where it melded into her most prominent scar. She released a shiver, her chest rising and falling. Tosya's head bent down and she arched up, leaning closer to his lips.

I sprang. "Anyone hungry?" Tosya and Nadia jerked apart.

"I saw some blackberries down by the stream. Come on, Tosya. You can help me pick them." I hauled him up by his arm and marshaled him away.

"Oh . . . all right." He craned his head back at Nadia. "We can finish what we were, uh, talking about later."

My grip on him tightened. "Maybe we'll find blueberries, too."

❦

The afternoon clouds converged and bruised the sunlight, bringing a summer sprinkling of rain that bred a torrent by evening. We decided against riding through the night and tucked under an overhanging boulder to keep dry. Tosya started a campfire, insisting no one would be able to see our firelight past the tempest. Nadia fell asleep with Tosya's cloak wrapped over her own. At least they hadn't kissed.

I frowned at her closed eyes, her beautifully thick and dark lashes. Was Nadia really sleeping? Maybe I could crack into her aura while her defenses were down. I fought to feel something from her, but there was nothing, only the bewildered pulse of Tosya sitting beside me. "Why don't you like her?" he asked.

I wrinkled my nose. "Why do *you*? She's fiercely loyal to the empire."

"She was raised to be," he said with a shrug. "She never learned any other ideology. People's opinions can change. I think Nadia's are beginning to."

I absently poked a stick in the campfire's ashes. "She used to torment me, you know."

"She could say the same thing about you. Half her body bears scars to prove it."

"Are you really siding with her?"

"Why does there have to be sides? Why are you so threatened?"

I jabbed my stick into a coal, trying to bust it apart.

"Sonya?" Tosya touched my arm. His concern bled into me and opened my mouth.

"You're the last friend I have, and she's taking you away!" I dropped the stick and slumped against the rock wall.

The sky rumbled and unleashed another onslaught of rain. It splattered on the stony ground and hissed, bouncing into the campfire.

Tosya leaned back next to me. "Are you ready to tell me what happened with Anton?"

I looked down at my hands and rubbed at the dirt caked beneath my fingernails. The past few days, Tosya hadn't pressed me about my other reasons for leaving Torchev. Still, he knew I wouldn't have left just because of Feliks's threats.

"I can't be the person I was," I replied. "That Sonya does more than overpower emperors. She . . . I—I conquered wills. I stole people's freedom." I angled away, my vision burning and blurring.

In a hushed voice, I confessed what had happened at Valko's trial and later with Terezia and Anton. Tosya listened quietly. Although he felt distraught, his emotions weren't colored by horrified surprise. Perhaps he'd expected the worst to surface in me someday. "I can't ever return to Torchev." I swallowed hard and faced Tosya again.

His brown eyes pulled heavy at the corners. "Anton asked you to leave?"

"He *demanded* I leave."

Tosya nodded, giving a lengthy sigh. He drew his knees to his chest and watched the rain pour. His aura spun deep in thought, prickling warmth around my head. When he spoke at last, his words came slowly, carefully, like he hoped he wouldn't offend me with his honesty. "Maybe you should try a little harder to understand Anton's reasoning."

"I'm an *Auraseer.*"

"That doesn't necessarily mean you've mastered empathy," he replied. "You *know* Anton's history—one way or another, he's lost all of his family. Maybe in all your months with him, you were too wrapped up in your own mourning to distinguish it from his."

I fidgeted and tugged my cloak tighter around me.

"Anton's deepest desire has always been to have a sustainable relationship in his life," Tosya continued. "And then *you* came along and managed to achieve something no other person could, not even me. You gained Anton's full trust. When you broke it, Sonya, what choice did you give him but to fall back on his instinct for survival? Of course he asked you to leave."

My hand inched to the spot on my arm where Valko had cut me on the One Day War. The wound had healed completely. All that remained was a vague, pink patch of skin that meant nothing. I would never bear a mark to match Anton's, never be the girl the fortune-teller spoke of, never have a relationship with him stronger than the family he could never depend on.

"Anton didn't trust me, not fully." I lifted my chin a little. "He *feared* what I was. He didn't want the people to know what I could do to them—or what I had *done* for them. He didn't want me to be *me*." My shoulders wilted. How could I pretend Anton's offenses were anywhere near my betrayals? "I don't blame him. In the end, I treated Anton no better than Valko did."

As soon as the former emperor sprang to mind, I rubbed my brow, trying to divert my thoughts from him. I didn't need to see myself mirrored in Valko. He wouldn't hold any more power over my life. He was gone, banished, en route to Sanbriel—far beyond my reach.

"Anyway, none of this matters," I said. "I'll never see Anton again. I'll never win back his trust." I kept my gaze trapped on the searing flames of the campfire and hoped they'd burn the threatening tears from my eyes.

"I don't know." Tosya gave a light shrug. "Anton gave up his dream of ruling the empire to plot a revolution with a lowly poet. He just might surprise you."

I couldn't help a small smile. Tosya was such an optimist. I gave his knee a little shove. "You know I love you, right?"

He drew his lanky arm around me, and I leaned my head against the side of his chest. "I love you, too, Sonya."

The rain fell in rippling sheets for another minute or two,

and then it let up to a steady patter. I turned my cheek closer to Tosya and started to drift off to sleep.

As my lashes batted closed, my gaze cut to where Nadia lay resting on the ground. Her jade eyes were open, sharpened, alert. Riveted on me.

CHAPTER TWENTY-NINE

THE STORM BLEW OVER BEFORE DAWN. THE SUN ROSE SO HOT in the sky that I wished the rain back again. While we waited to travel until night, Tosya, Nadia, and I decided to wash our damp and dirty clothes. We rode our horses deep into the forest, following a trickling stream in hopes it would lead us to a larger body of water. When the trees grew low and thick, we dismounted and let the horses walk beside us. Tosya's and Nadia's hands slipped into one another's grasp.

I almost didn't mind.

The stream led to a river. The river spread into a moss-green pool. Surrounding it were lush, leafy trees and a waterfall that cascaded in levels down a boulder-ridden hill. A young doe sipped from the pool's edge, but leapt away when our party emerged onto the shore.

Tosya discovered there was an upper pool at the top of the hill, so Nadia and I separated from him. That way, we could wash our clothes and he could wash his and no one would be alarmed—or inadvertently aroused—by too much bare skin in the process.

Nadia stripped down first, not ashamed in the least of her body. She stretched and combed her fingers through her hair, closing her eyes as she stood and basked in the sunlight. I frowned, wondering if she was trying to flaunt her perfect shape or make me feel guilty for the terrible scars that twisted from her neck to her thigh, running down her left side. For the thousandth time, I questioned what she felt behind the impenetrable wall surrounding her aura.

She swung around to look at me, her raven hair fluttering in the breeze. "Let's go for a swim while our clothes soak," she suggested without smiling.

I bit my lip, my insides squirming with unease. Without Tosya around, Nadia's countenance looked more threatening. I didn't wish to feel more vulnerable by getting naked. But she'd never let me hear the end of it if I shied away now. "All right."

She dipped her foot in the water, watching me while I removed my belt with the crystal dagger, took off my boots, and reached for the laces of my violet dress. A lump formed in my throat. This was the first time I'd untied those laces since Anton had cinched them together for me. My dress fell to my ankles with a dull whoosh, and I wrapped my arms around my stomach. I was sure I looked sickly thin after only nibbling on nuts, berries, and hard bread for days. My toes curled over each other, my ears burning hot.

"Oh, Sonya, relax." Nadia smirked. "We bathed in front of one another all the time at the convent." She sauntered over and picked up my dress. "I'll start this soaking. You jump in first."

I didn't jump. I waded in, shivering and glancing over my shoulder at her. I wouldn't sense it if Nadia decided to creep up on me and dunk my head under the water.

We swam for over an hour. Nadia proved as graceful a swimmer as she was on dry ground. At first, I clung to the edges of the pool, glowering at her. But then I adjusted to the frigid temperature of the water, and my mood improved. I paddled out into the deep middle and flapped my arms and legs to stay afloat in one spot.

Nadia snickered. "You look like a dog treading water!" She splashed me, and I had a sudden urge to dunk *her* head. "Try broader, stronger strokes, like this." She demonstrated. "Don't fight against the water; make friends with it."

I gritted my teeth, but did as she suggested. After a couple of minutes, I got the trick of it.

"That's better." She flicked another light splash at me.

Despite my stubborn instinct to dislike her, I grinned and splashed back.

Next thing I knew, we were in a full-blown water fight. Me. Nadia. Laughing. Screeching.

Maybe Riaznin really was coming to an end.

We swam a few more minutes, then scrubbed our dresses against the rocks before hanging them over a branch to dry.

Nadia and I wrapped ourselves in our cloaks and sat on the pebbled shore. She positioned herself behind me and combed out the knots in my hair with her hands. She had a soothing touch. I didn't expect that.

I looked down at my fingertips. They were still wrinkled from the water. "Yuliya told me Sestra Mirna used to be a midwife. Is that true?" For once, I felt comfortable enough with Nadia to bring up questions that had been pressing on my mind.

Her hands kept weaving through my hair. "Yes. Villagers from Ormina used to come to the convent to deliver their babies."

"Were *you* born there?" I asked as casually as possible, knowing Terezia's daughter wasn't. The countess had tried to save her child from living with the sestras.

"Only peasantry resorted to using convent midwives. The one thing I know about my parents is that they were nobility."

My chest fell. So much for ruling out Terezia as Nadia's mother.

"Dasha was born at the convent, though," she added. "I was twelve at the time. Sestra Mirna locked up the infirmary wing. She'd never done that before. It made me wonder if Dasha's mother was a noble, unlike the others."

"Was the woman that ashamed?" I scoffed. Typical aristocrat.

"Maybe." Nadia's fingernails scratched against my back as she worked through a stubborn tangle. "I *do* know Dasha was the only Auraseer born at the convent. Her mother must have realized her daughter would be gifted. Sestra Mirna says that can happen."

"What can?"

"A mother sometimes develops temporary abilities with an Auraseer in her womb."

I lifted my brows, then fiddled with the overlapping folds of my cloak. "How would that feel, do you think, that mother-daughter connection?" My heart pounded inside my chest. I hoped that was a natural enough segue into what I really wanted to ask.

"I don't know." She sectioned my hair and started braiding. "Resonant, I guess. Like your auras reflect one another."

"I sense that with almost everyone, even people I don't like."

"Meaning the emperor?" Nadia's voice darkened a smidgen.

"Yes," I conceded with a sideways tilt of my head. "*And* Feliks Kaverin *and* the palace cook *and* Terezia Dyomin . . ." A bead of water rolled down my brow from my still-wet hair. "Have you ever met the countess?" My heart kicked harder. "Not formally, I mean, but did you ever see her when you were lurking about Torchev?" Maybe Nadia *had* felt a deep resonance with her, and Terezia was indeed her mother—a mother I'd killed. "She's a very intelligent and proud woman. Her aura has a particularly strong energy."

"*Had*, Sonya." Nadia's voice went flat. "Her aura *had* strong energy." She gave my braid a little yank of playfulness—or maybe frustration. "I think I know what you're trying to get at, and I wish to the gods you'd learn to speak directly."

My hands curled in my lap. "I don't know what you're talk-ing about."

She sighed, finished plaiting my hair, and dropped my braid against my back. "I overheard your conversation with Tosya last night."

I stiffened. "You did?" I knew she did.

"You saw me awake, so we don't need to pretend."

My toes dug into the pebbles. "What exactly did you hear?"

"A whole lot of drivel about Prince Anton and his broken heart . . . and, of course, your confession to killing Terezia Dyo-min."

My lungs compressed, unable to draw air. I spun around, studying every inch of Nadia's face for what she might be feel-ing—shock, rage, hatred, fear, deep and endless pain? But the unscarred half of her face was only smooth and placid. Her fea-tures didn't betray any powerful emotions, just slightly rounded eyes at my reaction. "It's all right, Sonya. I understand you didn't do it on purpose."

Growing dizzy, I finally forced a breath. Oxygen flooded my brain in a rush of pins and needles. "Did you lie to me?" My body shook with anger, terror. "You were there when it hap-pened, weren't you?" I sought to claw through the void of energy surrounding Nadia. I needed access to my power.

Her wet hair hung in inky waves where it grazed her shoul-ders. She raised a single eyebrow and stared unflinchingly at me. Was she mocking, defiant, astounded? "I *wasn't* there when it happened," she replied. "I saw nothing. But if I had, would you blame me for lying? Last time we discussed the night you left Torchev, you had a blade at my throat."

I tensed, waiting for her to do something drastic. Attack me. Run for my dagger. For the first time since we'd journeyed together, I didn't have it on me. It was in its sheath on my belt at the water's edge, twenty feet away, beside my boots and knapsack. "Why did you dare to travel with me if you knew what I did?"

"*I didn't know*, Sonya. But there *are* other reasons I could have chosen not to trust you with my life." I averted my gaze from her scars. "I did, in the end, for the same reason you let me accompany you. You knew your power wouldn't work on me."

She stood in one swift motion. My heart slammed with fear. I scrambled to my feet and jerked a step toward my dagger. Nadia frowned. "What's overcome you? Your aura is as frantic as a fly caught in a web." Placing a hand on her hip, she added, "You confessed your sins to Tosya last night, then slept soundly in his arms."

I shifted on my feet. "I've known Tosya most of my life."

"And you know what he's *feeling*," she added. I flexed my balled hands and nodded. Her eyes narrowed—whether in scorn or contemplation, I couldn't tell. "It really drives you mad, doesn't it, not being able to sense me?"

"Wouldn't it drive *you* mad?"

Her brows came together with a slight pinch. "Perhaps." She whirled away and strolled down the shore nearer the water.

My calves tightened, ready to spring, but Nadia stopped ten feet short of my dagger. She lowered herself to the ground and laid out on her side, her head pillowed against her unscarred arm. "I'm going to rest until our dresses dry," she announced with her back to me.

I picked at the end of my wet braid and watched her for a long minute. She didn't move. She couldn't be asleep yet, but her hip rose and fell with her slowing intakes of breath.

I crept down the shore and walked around her body so I was between her and my dagger. I sat beside her, adjusted my cloak, and then lay on my stomach, my cheek against my folded arms. I struggled to relax and steady my heartbeat.

I supposed if Nadia wanted to hurt me, she could have done it weeks ago in Torchev. I just prayed that if Terezia *were* Nadia's mother, Nadia would never find out.

"Sonya?" she asked quietly, without opening her eyes.

"Yes?"

"I'm sorry . . . for how I treated you at the convent."

I blinked, caught off guard. My stomach tightened with buried pain.

"I wanted to be the best in all things." Her eyelids cracked, but she kept her gaze lowered. "The most skilled. The healthiest. The strongest. If I was the best, I could outlive the other Auraseers and one day leave. I could live in a place where I could finally *breathe*, where I wouldn't have to fight for perfection because I would have already achieved the highest ranking." She brushed her thumb across a shiny pebble. The breeze fluttered through her hair. It was beginning to dry. "For a long time, being the best was the only part of my life that I felt was *mine*."

I thought of Kivratide, my crown of hawthorn blossoms, my hand in Anton's hand while he spoke to the people and told them how beautiful Riaznin could become. I thought of how large I'd felt when I stood tall in the courtroom, the auras of hundreds of people inside me and submitting to my will. "I understand how secure it feels to have control over your life," I said. "I just don't understand how I threatened your identity at the convent. I was wild and untrained—I never listened during my lessons."

"You were *powerful*," she replied, as if nothing else mattered. "You felt things no one else did. You sensed auras of the deceased. Your aura radiated with boundless energy. That's why you scared the other girls."

My body flushed with a little heat. I didn't know how to respond.

"Anyway, that's all I wanted to say." Nadia settled her head against her arm again, her voice softening with what sounded like sincerity. "I'm sorry for hating you. I hope you can forgive me."

I looked at her for a long moment, then I reached out and clasped her scarred hand. "I hope you can forgive me, too."

A faint smile crossed her mouth. "I think one day I will."

❦ ⚮ ❦

I slept peacefully and awoke to Tosya's cheerful, distant voice. "Is everyone decent?" he called. His words echoed above the dull roar of the waterfall. The sun angled low in the west. It was almost evening. "It's as boring as tombstones up here! I should have bathed with you two!"

Nadia laughed. She was already awake and dressed. She sat on a rock a few feet behind me, lacing up her boots. "Come on down," she shouted back, then flashed a wicked grin at me.

I gasped, cinched the folds of my cloak together, and fumbled to my feet. "You're terrible!" I hissed and raced for my dress. She snorted as I snatched it off the tree branch and shuffled into the forest so my cloak wouldn't flap open.

Tosya's boots clomped onto the pebbled shore just as I vacated the clearing. "Where are you going, Sonya?"

I found a hidden spot behind the thick trunk of a tree, threw off my cloak, and yanked on my dress. I breathed a sigh of relief, grateful he wouldn't see me naked. Once I'd walked in on Tosya while he was changing in a caravan wagon. At first I thought I might throw up, feeling his embarrassment. Then I burst into giggles, and he chased me away.

Tosya's and Nadia's voices wafted from the shore. They sounded light, intimate, happy. I drew my cloak back on and peered around the trunk, thirty feet or so back from the tree line.

Nadia touched Tosya's cheek, and he swept her hair off her face, leaned down, and gave her a deep and drawn-out kiss. My blood lit on fire. Jaw hardened. Fingernails clawed into bark.

Black energy surrounded me. Throbbed through my skull. I rounded the tree, brows pulled low, and strode forward.

Then I ground to a halt. My head hurt as I struggled to understand my own emotions.

Why was I so upset? Nadia had apologized to me this afternoon. I'd taken her hand, and we'd made peace with one another. Tosya wasn't my only friend anymore. I shouldn't be bothered by their shared affection.

Logic crashed into me, followed by dread. This black feeling inside me wasn't mine.

Bartek was here.

CHAPTER THIRTY

I BROKE PAST THE TREES AND RACED ONTO THE SHORE. "TOSYA! Nadia! Get out of the open!"

Their hands were tangled in one another's hair. They pulled apart. Nadia frowned at me in confusion.

"Can't you sense him?" I asked, exasperated. I pointed at the forest behind me as I ran for my dagger. My belt was still at the water's edge. "Bartek is here."

Tosya froze. Nadia's face went white. "Is he alone?" she asked.

"Yes," I snapped. Why was she being so slow? "Wake up and detach yourself from Tosya's energy. I need your help! You're better at tracking people." At least she had an uncanny ability to find me. "We have to run and stay out of Bartek's path. He's bent on killing. I can feel it."

I reached the shoreline and snatched my dagger. Bartek's black energy peaked, stinging my veins with acid. I jerked around.

The bounty hunter stood where I'd just emerged from the forest. His ginger beard hung in two braids, studded with painted beads. He was armed with a bow, and it was drawn, arrow nocked and pointed at Tosya.

"Tosya, watch out!" I cried.

A *whoosh* zinged through the air. Tosya didn't act fast enough. The arrow struck his upper leg. He grunted, clutched the shaft, and fell to his knees. My heart seized as Tosya's pain throbbed through me. Nadia gasped and grabbed his shoulder.

Bartek strung another arrow, this one aimed at Nadia. I shouted her name and unsheathed my dagger. She didn't hesitate. With a panther's grace, she fell into a low crouch. The arrow whizzed near her head, but missed its mark.

"Run!" I said.

She sprang back up, trying to drag Tosya with her.

I locked my gaze on Bartek. Exhaled. Flung my dagger the way Romska knife-throwers did as they practiced for fairs.

Bartek didn't even dodge. The dagger flew wide by six inches. The crystal blade wedged into a tree with a dull *thunk*.

He gave me a greasy smile and stepped onto the shore. "Oh, dear," he said, retrieving another arrow from his quiver. "Looks like everyone except me is unarmed now." He tapped the fletching against his lips.

Tosya grimaced and made a move to stand up. Nadia helped him.

"Uh-uh-uh." Bartek clucked. With his left hand, he whipped out a flintlock pistol. "Don't make me use this. Firearms take out all the fun."

Tosya and Nadia stiffened and lowered to their knees.

Bartek smirked, holstering his pistol again. "Would you like to know what my favorite weapon is?" He looked between us, knowing he had a captive audience.

No one said anything. Tosya's trouser leg bloomed with blood, and he trembled in shock. Nadia held statuesque, her cunning jade eyes on Bartek. My nerves burned as I held my breath.

The bounty hunter lifted a finger, gesturing for us to be patient as he returned his arrow to its quiver. Then he withdrew a weapon strapped to his thigh. "The Abdaran saber knife." He turned it over so we could admire it. "The blade is curved toward the opponent, you see. Much more practical for stabbing than a straight blade."

My legs tensed, mind spun, energy shuddered beneath my skin. For the first time since my confrontation with Terezia, I felt a desperate urge to use my power. But I couldn't make myself. I might kill again. One wrong slip of my emotions and it could be my friends.

Bartek slowly advanced to Tosya and Nadia—not me. "The knife is also heavy enough to cut through muscle and bone. If you twist it upward, you can slit through intestines, liver, lungs, or even the rib cage to the heart."

I swallowed in revulsion. Tosya wobbled like he might faint. Nadia didn't blink.

Bartek's boots crunched onto the pebbles. He was within six feet of my friends. "Would you like to see a demonstration?" He raised the knife.

"Don't touch them!" Adrenaline spiked through my body.

Bartek shifted his weight on one leg and swung sideways to look at me. "You know how this works, Sonya. You either come with me, or I get to perform my theatrics. Honestly, I'm hoping you'll delay awhile longer."

"You won't gain the Duma's respect if you murder innocent people."

"Yes, well, the *Duma*"—Bartek made a face, like the governors were the laughing stock of Torchev—"doesn't interest me anymore."

I exchanged a glance with Nadia. She looked equally nonplussed. "Didn't the Duma hire you?"

He scraped an impatient thumb against the blade. "Did you know the empire used to pay me one-hundred rubles for a bounty—five-hundred for an Auraseer? The Duma offered me fifty." He spat on the ground. "Pinchfist revolutionaries."

"Fifty rubles is better than none," I argued, stalling for time. "You're in no position to bargain unless you're working across borders now."

Bartek cocked an ugly smile. "No need to cross borders, Sonya. You'll fetch the prettiest price here. I know what man to bring you to."

My pulse rocked, unsteady. I fought to discard the ominous feeling. What I feared couldn't be true. I *refused* it to be. "Who could you possibly be talking about?"

The beads in his braids rattled as he jutted up his chin. "Your master before the empire fell."

My body turned to ice. "Valko?" I said on a rasped breath.

Bartek nodded with pride. "His Imperial Majesty has escaped his captors and is raising an army as we speak."

For a moment, all I heard was faint ringing in my ears and the echo of Bartek's words. My stomach creased into a thousand knots. Bile met my tongue. I reached for the pearl in my pocket, but I had no pearl. My shaking fingers hovered over my lips. "H-how did he escape? He was bound. He had four guards."

"Only four?" Bartek's brows lifted with amazement. "What were the Duma thinking?"

I felt blood drain from my face and angled away.

The bounty hunter's aura blackened with pleasure to see me so disturbed. "The emperor's carriage was found overturned a day's ride from Torchev on the trade road to Sanbriel."

I closed my eyes. The soldiers never even arrived at the first military outpost.

"I'm told all the guards and the driver were killed," he went on. "One by a knife to the chest, the others by musket shots. A band of nobles staged the attack to free the emperor."

Terezia Dyomin's followers. I was sure of it. She'd said she had scores of them who were ruthlessly loyal to the empire.

I released a shuddering breath. I thought I'd never have to consider Valko again.

Like me, Nadia's countenance also changed. Her eyes were wide, her gaze lowered. Her body slightly turned from Tosya as she knelt on the shore. I feared she was losing hope.

"What makes you think Valko Ozerov would pay a bounty for me?" I asked Bartek. I doubted Valko had even hired him. I remembered how the bounty hunter had taken matters into his own hands and captured Pia when it was her lover, Yuri, Valko wanted. Now with a band of nobility behind him, Valko had access to money, but for all Bartek knew, Valko hated me. The former emperor had struck me in front of Bartek when I'd pleaded for Pia's life. "I would never serve him again," I said. "He doesn't own the Auraseers of Riaznin anymore."

"But he *will*," Bartek countered. "Have you seen this wartorn nation?" He waved his knife at our surroundings, as if they represented the entire country. "The emperor's army is amassing quickly. People flock to him—nobility, even peasantry. They trust him over the Duma. Already fifty or more soldiers have joined under his banner, and their numbers multiply daily. They're marching toward Ormina, and they'll continue recruiting along the way."

At the mention of Ormina, my heart contracted. Nadia and I shared a pensive glance. Ormina was remote, a safe distance from Torchev, and few people lived at the convent since the fire last winter. Perhaps Valko wished to make it his fortress until his army grew large enough to mount an attack on the capital.

Dread turned my stomach to stone. Valko's actions couldn't be that simple. He could have staked a stronghold in Isker or Illola, but instead he was marching toward a place I was connected to.

This was about me. Spies must have told Valko I'd fled Torchev. He still wanted my power, and he meant to blackmail me by threatening Sestra Mirna and Dasha.

I had to reach the convent before he did.

Bartek flexed his palm around his saber knife. "Now that we've established who I'm going to sell you to, let's get this done with." In three strides, he closed the distance to Tosya and kicked his wounded leg. Tosya cried out. His crippling pain echoed through me. Bartek grabbed Tosya's hair, yanked his head back, and held the knife to his throat.

My muscles caught fire. I tensed to intervene, but kept myself back. Bartek would kill Tosya if I made a wrong move.

"What will it be, Sovereign Auraseer?" Bartek's lips curled against his teeth. He brought the blade a fraction closer to Tosya's neck.

"I'll give you our horses!" I cried. My power prickled along my skin, begging to be used. But did I have the savagery to murder someone outright? "The two mares are a matching white pair. They once belonged to the emperor. That's a fine bargain and far better than losing your life. Valko will kill you if you bring him another bounty he didn't ask for."

"I'm willing to wager you're wrong. Besides, your horses don't tempt me." Bartek's knife grazed Tosya's throat, and a drop of blood trickled down his neck. Tosya winced and turned pleading, shining eyes on me. Bartek snorted at him. "You're just as soft as the Romska children I baited Sonya with last time. Only they didn't cry when I nicked their skin. That took breaking their fingers."

"Step away from him!" I couldn't hear any more of this. I didn't doubt what Bartek would do. "I'll go with you."

My power was unstable. If something went wrong, I couldn't risk my friends being too nearby him. I needed to draw him away first.

The bounty hunter gave me a calculating stare. The copper taste of blood filled my mouth. He still hungered for it. "You *will* come with me," he said. "That was never really the question. So you'll have to indulge me while I satisfy a little compulsion of mine. I'm sure you feel it in me."

My vision flamed with rage. "I also feel your sick lust, your foolish pride, and your weak determination compared to mine."

His brows launched up. "Excuse me?"

"You have no idea what a small threat you pose to me." Heat poured through every space of my body. I trembled with a deadly craving, far more powerful than Bartek's. "You wouldn't have come for me—especially alone—if you knew what I can do."

He barked with scornful laughter. "I can label my emotions on my own, thanks."

"But can you bend them?" I stepped closer. My bare feet clenched the ground. I held my body tight, but my limbs rattled.

Hold yourself in control, Sonya. "Emotions rule a person," I said. "When you manipulate the right feelings, emperors relinquish thrones, countesses slit their own throats, bounty hunters cut out their own hearts."

Bartek adjusted his grip on his knife. His aura emitted a tiny ripple of fear.

Hatred pumped a stream of poison inside me. Bartek was the same man who beat me after I was already his captive. The man who broke Pia's arm and dragged her to Valko's feet. He was bloodthirsty, abusive, cruel, even worse than Valko. At least the former emperor thought his actions were in Riaznin's best interest. Bartek was fueled by money, self-gain. If any man truly deserved to die, he did.

I held my chin high. Pulled in a deep breath. I was justified in using my power. And I would kill him with it.

I had no empathy for him, so I invented lies. His parents never loved him. He ran away from home at a young age. He lived in the wild among beasts, not humans. Good enough.

My aura bridged to his. I found the roots of his sick desires. I turned them inward to self-loathing. Once that was secure, I bloated his dark intent to commit murder.

A deep grimace crossed Bartek's face. I walked to him, speaking slowly. "Lower your knife. It isn't my friend you really want to hurt, is it?"

He shook his head like a boy caught for stealing apples. Hands quaking, he drew his knife away from Tosya's throat.

Nadia's gaze widened. "Sonya, what are you doing?"

I ignored her. Someone had to get us out of this mess. I turned back to the bounty hunter. "Don't you want to step away from us so your blood doesn't fleck our clothes?"

His posture hung like a wet rag. He shuffled a few feet away.

"Good." My veins throbbed with heightening pressure. I wanted more of it. "You'll feel better knowing you died to rid the world of your presence. It will be a generous act."

"Sonya, this is madness," Nadia said.

Anger ripped through me. "I'm saving you right now!"

"Nadia's right," Tosya added. "This is wrong."

I whirled on them. "Let me finish this! Valko is pressing toward the convent every moment you delay me. How much time do you think we have to reach Sestra Mirna and Dasha before he does?"

Tosya's eyes pierced me in earnest. "Listen to me. Terezia's death was a terrible accident. But this will be direct murder."

I remembered last night. Me weeping during the storm, tucked under an overhanging rock with Tosya. Me confessing my regrets to him.

My determination faltered.

"No!" Nadia's gaze shot to Bartek. He made ready to plunge his saber knife into his own chest.

"Stop!" I shouted. My black energy abated. Compassion returned. Leant me mercy. I came back to myself, at least the better half of me. "You don't really want to stab yourself. You're confused." *Just as I am.*

Bartek's hand opened. The blade clattered to the pebbles. I hated that I was letting him go. "Shall I use my pistol?" he asked, reaching for the holstered gun.

"No!" My hands flinched, then I released a steadying breath. "You should set your pistol and quiver of arrows on the ground." Once he was weaponless, I would push his poisonous aura from mine. My stomach lurched and bubbled. His energy was making me sick.

Bartek did as I suggested.

"Go," I said, voice sharp. "You never want to see me again. You're afraid of me. If you turn back to pursue us, I'll cause your horse to run you off a cliff, do you understand?"

With a shamefaced nod, he turned and walked away into the forest. I counted to three hundred, then broke our connection.

The sick feeling oozed out of me. I latched onto Tosya's energy and blocked Bartek's distancing aura. "We have to go at once!" I said. Catching Tosya's gaze, I added, "We'll tend to your wound later."

Wasting no time, I threw Bartek's weapons into the pool, except for his pistol, which I slid under my belt. The gun had only one charge left.

"Grab my dagger from that tree," I told Nadia, as I reached for my boots.

She helped Tosya up, then ran across the shore and began wrestling the crystal blade out of the bark.

I rushed over to assist Tosya. He still felt faint. Just as I reached him, his aura pulsed with dizzying pain. It seized me, and I stumbled into him.

"Well, hello again." Bartek's oily voice rang out once more from the tree line.

I jerked around, severed myself from Tosya's aura, and whipped out my gun.

"Didn't I tell you I had two pistols?" Bartek said, light though malicious. "This one's crafted of Shenglin steel."

My breath came in shallow bursts. We both had our weapons drawn on one another. Maybe Bartek had decided to kill me rather than take my bounty, after all. His energy certainly felt murderous.

"What a fun game we've been playing, little Auraseer. And this is how it will end." One of his eyes closed to square his aim on me.

"Take me!" Nadia shouted abruptly. "I'm an Auraseer, too."

Bartek hesitated. My heartbeat tripped. I cast a shocked glance at my friend.

Nadia stood by the tree with the stuck dagger. She hadn't wrenched it out yet. Her jade eyes were intent upon the bounty hunter. They held a feverish glint. "I'm older than Sonya, more skilled. I was supposed to be sovereign Auraseer, but I was wounded in the fire. I'm healed now. The emperor doesn't hate me like he does her. And I'll accompany you without a struggle."

Tosya struggled to speak past his horror. "No, Nadia!"

"Quiet," she quipped. Her face was as hard as ice, but

sorrow traced her bottom lip, the way she pulled it in tight, like it might quaver otherwise. She wouldn't look at Tosya—or me.

"You don't have to do this," I said to her, my pistol still trained on Bartek's head. I'd never fired a gun, but I would. If I missed, I had other means to kill him. I'd given him a chance to live, but he'd lost it. "I can end him, you know I can."

"No, Sonya." Nadia's voice was solemn. "Tosya's right—your power shouldn't be wielded for death. You have to draw a line." Her heavy gaze flickered to me. "Don't let it change you."

My breath caged inside my aching chest. After all that I'd done to her, Nadia was the last person I'd expected to give me any hope that I could become a good person.

She stood tall, her raven hair feathered around her face, her neck long and erect. "Take me," she said again, returning her stare to Bartek. "Leave my friends unharmed, and the emperor will see you rewarded."

The bounty hunter rapidly scanned over Nadia's burned and tattooed skin. For a brief moment, worry colored his aura. Maybe he wondered if someone so damaged could fetch a fine price. But then his unease lifted. He looked at Nadia like she was a new blade for his sheath, like the fierce and beautiful girl she was. "We have a deal," he said, and his deadly energy withdrew. "Tell your friend to lower her pistol."

Nadia didn't have to ask me. I dropped the gun. I had to let her go. She was a good person, too, and I had to give her the chance to be.

She joined Bartek's side, leaving my dagger in the tree.

The bounty hunter gave me a parting smirk. "I'll be ready for you next time we meet."

I bit my tongue and didn't acknowledge his threat.

He sauntered away, his grip firm on Nadia's arm. She thrust her shoulders back and walked with a queen's grace as they left the shore and entered the forest.

My throat tightened with surprising affection for a girl I'd hated so long.

I took Tosya's trembling hand and held it steady. This wouldn't be the end for Nadia.

I would free her from becoming the next sovereign Auraseer.

CHAPTER THIRTY-ONE

"YOU'RE NOT COMING WITH ME, TOSYA!" I SAID FOR THE hundredth time. We walked our horses out of the darkening forest. I anxiously waited for the trees to thin so we could ride Raina and Hanzi and hurry back to the road, where I planned to part ways with my friend.

"You need to go back and warn the Romska to change direction," I went on, guiding Raina to the other side of the stream and through a tight cluster of trees. "They're traveling toward Ormina, too. The tribes can't be caught in the crossfire of a civil war."

"Their scouts will warn them faster than I can," Tosya replied. He stumbled into the underbrush and hit his hurt leg. I winced, feeling his pain.

Tosya needed to heal. We'd sacrificed precious time removing the arrowhead from his leg, then cleaning and dressing his wound. He hadn't lost too much blood, but he couldn't keep a brisk pace anymore. He certainly wouldn't be able to outrun Valko's soldiers.

"The Romska don't need me." Tosya stiffly moved forward again. "*You* do."

"This is my fight. I don't want you endangered."

"If Valko captures you, he'll find a way to manipulate and use you, and he has a talent for that, even without having a power like yours."

My chest fluttered with panic, but I took a deep and determined breaths. A few days ago, I would have laughed at the idea of Valko trying to imprison my will. But it seemed no matter how I defied the former emperor, I played right into his hand. "It doesn't matter. I have to go. I have to *try*."

Tosya released Hanzi's reins, then limped over and caught my shoulders. "I'm coming with you."

"You're a *poet*. You'll get yourself killed."

"I'm your *friend*. The odds are just as stacked against me as they are against you. Don't deny me my chance to fight." He gave me a fierce look of determination, as if he could take on Valko's men himself. I doubted Tosya had even fired a musket on a target-practice bale of hay.

I was about to tell him so, but then my shoulders fell. I'd allowed Nadia to risk her life by giving herself up to Bartek. It was only fair that I allow Tosya a similar opportunity to fight for the people he cared about. Surely he wanted to do more than protect me and aid the convent; he meant to rescue Nadia, too.

I buried my feelings of misgiving. "Are you well enough

to ride through the night?" He nodded bravely. "Fine, then." I glanced at his leg bandage. We'd made it from strips of my torn-up knapsack. A little blood seeped through it, and my stomach twisted. "We'll rest a short while at dawn. You take the first watch," I said, striving to make him feel important. I understood the fervent desire to be needed.

Tosya nodded, gratitude burgeoning within him. "Of course."

We fell into companionable but tense silence as we led our horses onward through the forest. At last we reached the road. The convent was a two-day journey to the west.

I prayed I wasn't leading my friend to his death.

⁂

We traveled as quickly as we dared press the horses. I cast my awareness wide and felt for the spider crawl of Valko's aura—still absent. I hoped we traveled fast enough to keep him outdistanced. What little Bartek had told us of Valko's advancing army didn't include how close he was to Ormina.

Tosya and I only allowed our horses a few short hours to rest the first night. We tried to sleep ourselves, but we mostly just huddled near a small campfire, well off the road, and struggled to form a plan of action for when we reached the convent.

"We should help Sestra Mirna and Dasha escape," Tosya said, shifting closer to the flames. "Valko's army is a least fifty men. The convent probably only has a handful of guards. They'll be far outnumbered."

Thanks to Anton, the convent had some protection. When

I'd first come to Torchev, I'd asked him to ensure the convent was safe and reinforced. He'd kept his word. He always kept his word.

I took a deep breath and spoke past the ache in my throat. "The size of Valko's army is why we *shouldn't* leave the convent. How far and how long can a small band like us keep running with an old lady, a young girl, and, well . . . ?" I waved a hand at Tosya's leg. "Meanwhile Valko's army will multiply in strength and numbers, and we'll still have to circle back for Nadia at some point. By now, Bartek has probably collected his bounty for her."

I couldn't back down now. I couldn't let Valko hurt people to hurt me. If he didn't win my loyalty and partnership, he would kill me—and he would kill anyone else who stood between us. I had to face what Anton had accepted weeks ago, no matter how terrible.

"Valko's life needs to end," I told Tosya the second night, meeting his gaze above the crackling campfire. Banishment wasn't enough. The former emperor would never depart from his path of destruction. "I have to kill him."

Tosya looked up from the hard cheese he was attempting to melt over a crust of bread, our rations for dinner. The light from the flickering flames didn't reach his eyes. His aura sank with grim acceptance. "I think you're right. I discouraged you from harming Bartek, but that was different. Hundreds of thousands will die if Valko isn't stopped."

I nodded, picking at the hem of the cloak Anton had given

me. It was beginning to fray. The logs in our campfire crackled. A few embers swirled in the path of my downcast stare.

Tosya spoke again, whispering, his voice as quiet as the night breeze. "Can you do it again—kill someone?" I looked up at his grave face. "Not instinctively, not accidentally, not in self-defense. This killing will be premeditated, Sonya. You haven't had to live with that yet." The edge of his bread blackened, and he rotated it. "So I ask you again, can you kill Valko?"

I watched the cheese bubble and drip. The heat from the fire burned my eyes. "Maybe I was given this power for a purpose," I said. "I was the only one who could make Valko abdicate. Maybe I'm destined to kill him, too."

"*Can* you, Sonya?"

Could I? Why had I saved Valko so many times? Why did I identify with his deepest darkness? I wanted to smash the mirror that made me see my reflection in him. "I don't know," I finally admitted.

Tosya withdrew the bread from its perch above the coals and made a study of my face. "You will need to decide before we meet him. If you wait until then, it will be too late. His influence over you is too strong."

I tried to picture killing Valko with Terezia's dagger, passing the crystal blade over to him and commanding him to do it himself.

But it was no use. I couldn't imagine Valko's death at my hands.

Tosya and I stamped out the fire and left before the sun rose. We were in the vast woods outside Ormina. The air grew thick with low-rolling fog and vicious auras. The fog kicked upward as we galloped through it. I imagined pointed teeth and slitted eyes in its curling white clouds.

I'd felt wolves before—the night the convent burned. Thankfully, they didn't rage so desperately now for meat, what with small creatures scampering aplenty in the summer. Still, I felt them prowl at the fringes of my awareness, territorial and violent. I fought to keep my aura separate from theirs and murmured a prayer to Feya that I'd be able to distinguish the wolves' energy from Valko's.

Raina felt ready to topple from exhaustion, which didn't help my own fatigue. But I didn't dare stall for water or rest anymore; instead, I slowed the mare, letting her walk at times when the wolves felt farther away. Tosya kept abreast with us, his stamina failing much more than mine. His wounded leg throbbed past endurance in his effort to stay upright in his saddle. One time his strength gave out, and he slipped sideways.

"Tosya!" I extended my arm, but couldn't reach him. With a grunt, he managed to straighten up again. I nudged Raina even closer to him, my reflexes ready if he fell again. "We should stop for a while. I'm pushing you too hard."

He grimaced, his eyes tightening in the corners. "No. Valko won't rest during the daytime, so neither can we. And he knows you're traveling to the convent; Bartek would have told him. Besides, if we keep a steady pace, we'll arrive there by nightfall."

I struggled to tamp down my concern. "Then I'll sing you songs to take your mind off your pain."

Tosya managed a smile and gripped his hurt thigh, holding his reins with one hand. "I'd like that."

I sang the only songs I knew, the songs he had taught me growing up. At first, my voice came small and shaky, but then it rose in volume, gaining the strength of my emotions.

I sang of soldiers in taverns, children thieving for chocolate, lovers embracing under juniper trees. I sang of the mist over the Azanel River and the dawn rising over Motherland Riaznin. I sang of winter and the endless steppe to the east. I sang of summer and the water trickling from the mountains. I sang of loss and suffering, hope and rebirth.

Hours passed, darkness seeped into the forest. I stopped singing. The wolves grew closer. Tosya and I broke our horses into a quick trot, all that Raina and Hanzi were capable of mustering. The salty tang of the ocean met my nostrils beneath the crisp scent of pine. The convent was only two or three miles away.

An eerie howl split the air. Tosya gave me a sharp glance. My stomach groaned, and my fingernails dug against the lining of my gloves. The wolves' appetites weren't satiated. They wanted more. They wanted us.

We sped to a gallop along the winding road, lined by ancient trees. The howling grew louder. The wolves' auras swarmed inside my breast, nipping and clawing.

Tosya and I bounded onward. On the outskirts of my

awareness, I felt the strains of a separate aura, though it felt just as desperate and frantic as my own.

I ducked low in the saddle and rode faster. I struggled to use the wolves' energy and bloodlust, not fight against it. As it pulsed through me, I latched onto the wolves' single-mindedness, their warrior spirit.

I was the hunter, not the prey.

"Sonya, the convent!" Tosya called.

Past the trees, pale moonlight bit into the clearing ahead. We emerged from the forest, and a whitewashed structure came into view. Our horses raced, plowing up chunks of grass beneath their hooves. I felt the wolves closing in, though they still remained out of sight.

Tosya's back stiffened. Mine went rigid as he startled. "The gates!" he shouted.

I looked to the iron-barred doors between the two stone towers.

Chains and a heavy lock fastened the gates closed.

CHAPTER THIRTY-TWO

"HELP!" I SHOUTED, HOPING SOMEONE WAS STILL AWAKE. I scanned the convent grounds for Basil's hunched walk and bald head, but then my gut clenched in remembrance. The old care-taker was dead. Killed in the convent fire I'd started.

"Hello, out there!" Tosya arrived at the gates first and gave them a violent rattle. "We're surrounded by wolves. Let us in!"

In the reconstructed wing, an upstairs window illuminated.

I reached the gates. They clanged as I shook them. "Sestra Mirna, it's Sonya and Tosya!"

From the woods, more howls shrieked and gained volume. I twitched and growled at them, my frenzied mind losing distinction between us.

A blaze of flame sprang from the convent. Three men ran outside. They carried torches and were in various states of undress. I recognized their soldiers' regimentals from the trousers one wore and the unbuttoned jacket of another. Convent guards.

One of the men turned a key over in a lock that held the gates' chains together. They jangled as the other guards removed them.

Tosya and I squeezed our horses through the opening gates, then the soldiers slammed them shut behind us. Wolves raced into the clearing and leapt at the bars, yipping and howling.

A musket blast ripped through my eardrums. I jolted so hard I nearly fell from my saddle. One of the soldiers had finally loaded his firearm and shot into the night to scare the wolves away. It worked for half of them. The others paced at the gate, like dogs locked outside a kitchen while their master ate supper.

I jumped off Raina, grabbed one of the soldier's torches, and batted it at the wolves. "Go on!" I shouted. They would mask Valko's approach.

They retreated a few feet, but stubbornly refused to leave.

I gathered my focus and fought to dig into the wolves' auras. Theirs resonated on a spiking wave of energy that was difficult to trap.

Just as I began to lose hope, three wolves tipped their heads, as if they'd heard something I hadn't. They spun around and ran off into the forest. Another wolf's ears perked, and he also dashed away. Those remaining in the pack quickly followed suit.

I lowered my torch and released a lungful of air.

"Sonya!" the voice of a young girl called out. I turned

around. Dasha ran to me from the convent porch, fifty yards from the gate, and out of Sestra Mirna's protective hold. Her hair wisped on the breeze. "I told you people were coming!" she snapped at the soldiers, her aura pulsing with frenetic energy.

Dasha charged into me and wrapped bird-boned arms around my waist. Her head burrowed into my side. The poor girl shook like a leaf.

"It's all right." I smoothed the thin strands of her hair. She hadn't broken the habit of ripping it out from her scalp since she'd left Torchev.

"It's not all right." Her voice rang like a tiny silver bell. "You're just as frightened as I am."

"I'm only catching my breath." My pounding heart began to slow. "The wolves are gone now, and I've come back to keep you safe."

"From *who*?" Dasha's large, gray eyes blinked up at me.

Tosya hobbled over to us. He'd passed our horses to one of the soldiers. Raina and Hanzi wearily clopped to the stable. Sweat beaded on Tosya's brow. The spot of blood on his bandage had widened to a large circle. "There are twenty convent guards in total." He pointed to several more who had emerged on the grounds. "That's more than I thought we'd find here. Let's just hope Valko's army hasn't grown much larger."

"Valko Ozerov?" Dasha's voice lifted in wonder and made my pulse quicken. "Is the emperor coming here?"

"He isn't the emperor any more, remember?" I gave her what I hoped was a reassuring smile, as if Valko's lost status meant he was any less dangerous.

Sestra Mirna drew a shawl around her shoulders. "What do you mean, Emperor Ozerov's army is coming?" She advanced with the formidability of a lion. Her wrinkles cut a savage pattern across her face, but, inside her, I felt prevailing fear. It iced through my joints and made them ache and tremble. She glanced from Dasha to me.

I took a steeling breath. "Valko was banished, but he escaped and—" I stopped short, Dasha's aura striking mine like a hammer. She gripped my cloak in her small fist. "What is it?"

I shouldn't have needed to ask. I should have felt the new energy the moment Dasha did. I'd been too focused on Sestra Mirna.

Dasha followed my gaze to the woods. "Is that the emperor?"

My lips parted, but I couldn't utter a sound. I hadn't decided . . . I hadn't decided if I could kill him.

"Reinforce the gate!" Tosya commanded the soldiers. "Someone is coming. He isn't a friend."

The howling wolves raged louder. They'd left the clearing, but hadn't wandered far. My heartbeat aligned with the oncoming intruder's. Had Valko ridden ahead of his army? The sound of galloping hooves came nearer.

One of the soldiers hurriedly reloaded his musket. Several others ran inside the convent, hopefully to fetch more weapons. Two men hauled up the chains to brace the gate.

I stepped forward and wrapped my hands around the iron bars.

"Come inside at once." Sestra Mirna took Dasha's arm and hurried her back to the porch.

"Are you ready, Sonya?" Tosya touched my shoulder.

"I don't— I'm not—" Perspiration traced my spine.

The hooded rider emerged from the forest. He swept into the clearing and charged for the closed gates. As the man reached inside his cloak, a soldier took aim on him.

I gasped, seeing the white horse beneath the rider, the red streaking the stallion's legs—claw marks from the wolves.

The man's familiar aura invaded mine with singular intensity. With it, came his fierce desire to shield me, though *he* was the one outside the gates and I was within.

My heart pounded with the force of a cannon blast. The air purged from my chest. His name came weakly, on my last shreds of breath.

"Anton."

CHAPTER THIRTY-THREE

"WAIT! DON'T FIRE!" I SHOUTED.

The soldier wasn't swayed. He brought the musket to the level of his eye.

"He doesn't mean us any harm!"

Anton's hood fell back, revealing his iron expression of determination. The soldier lowered his musket in astonishment. Anton charged forward, his gaze locked on mine.

A storm of emotions raged through me. Anxiety. Fear. Regret. Shame. Love.

"Open the gates at once!" I commanded the soldiers.

With shaking hands, I yanked the bars as the soldiers flung the latch. Thankfully, they hadn't bound the chains again.

Anton flew toward us. His stallion, Oriel, nearly rammed into the gates, but they opened just in time. The horse ran a few more paces, and then Anton drew him to a sharp halt. As one, horse and rider crashed to the ground, Oriel's stamina giving out.

I raced full-speed and stumbled to kneel beside Anton. I cast off my riding gloves and threw his cloak open to see if the wolves had wounded him like his horse. I was so frantic, I couldn't distinguish if he shared some of Oriel's pain.

"Someone take the horse to the stable and see to his injuries!" I said, as my fingers probed Anton's green kaftan. It was a bit damp, but with sweat, not blood. I couldn't find any slash marks. My scrutiny fell to his trousers—even his boots. Nothing. Unconvinced, I searched his kaftan again.

Anton caught my hand. "Sonya," he whispered, out of breath.

I kissed his knuckles. He held my fingers in a vice grip.

Tosya limped over to us. Sestra Mirna and the soldiers crowded around. Everyone spoke over each other, asking for news. How far away was Valko? How many were in his army? Anton didn't so much as blink at the people hovering over him. He didn't seem to hear them. For several long moments, his eyes held only me.

I wanted to throw myself upon him, weep like a child, tell him how much I'd missed him, how much I loved him, how sorry I was. I brought our joined hands to my chest and placed my other hand on top of his. Warmth rushed through my limbs, and with it came the wrenching pain of my remorse. *Forgive me*, I wanted to say. But I couldn't, not with everyone watching.

He lifted himself up into a sitting position, his nostrils flaring as he labored for breath. Perspiration beaded the dark hair at his temples. "You weren't with the Romska," he said, brows straining together. "Valko . . . he escaped . . . he's coming here."

"We know," I assured him. "We're preparing for him now."

Surrounding us, the soldiers' auras spiked with anxiety. Sestra Mirna crossed her arms and cast a worried glance at the convent porch. The door was shut. Dasha must be inside.

"Valko isn't alone." Anton's breath felt cool against my fingers. He composed himself and gently pushed my hand away so he could freely speak.

My shoulders fell as I sensed a rift form between us. Anton hadn't forgiven me for my betrayal.

"The former emperor has gathered an army," he said, addressing everyone.

Tosya frowned. "How is it you know—?"

"I sent a regiment of soldiers to track Valko's carriage on the trade road to Sanbriel. I needed to be certain he'd arrive." Anton rose to his feet, ran a quick hand through his hair, and brushed the grass from his cloak. The wolves in the forest continued to bay. "Valko's guards were found slaughtered. We suspect a faction of nobles loyal to the empire are responsible."

"Bartek told me," I replied. "Tosya and I came as soon as we heard."

Anton gave me a hard look. "Bartek, the bounty hunter?"

I took a breath to speak, but didn't know where to begin. It was strange that so many weighty things had happened to me, and Anton didn't know. I hurriedly explained about Bartek's attack and Tosya's wounded leg. I left out Nadia's involvement in our escape until last. First, I told the story—to everyone's amazement—of how Nadia had survived the convent fire and came back into my life.

Sestra Mirna's weathered mouth parted in shock. My joints throbbed with her rush of conflicted feelings.

"Valko has Nadia by now," I said gravely. "Tosya came with me to help rescue her."

Anton's gaze searched his friend's face and found understanding in the strong and sure gleam in Tosya's eyes.

"Sonya." Sestra Mirna's pressing voice broke the moment. A terrible chill descended upon me with her ominous aura. "Don't endanger yourself for Nadia. She was a powerful Auraseer. But you must trust me on this, Nadia is *not* your friend."

I fought to shake off a cold rush of dread. Before I had the chance to explain to the sestra that Nadia and I had worked out our differences, the great door of the convent swung open.

Dasha shrieked with delight. "Anton!" She hopped down from the porch and bolted for him.

"Go back inside!" Sestra Mirna said, but the little girl didn't listen. She darted across the convent grounds, dodged the sestra, and plowed into Anton's arms. Despite his tense energy, he couldn't help a small smile as he patted her head and hugged her back.

"Look what I have," Dasha said, pulling three small stones from her pocket. "I throw them every day, just like you taught me."

Before Anton could reply, Sestra Mirna turned on me, as

if Dasha's defiance was my fault. "You have brought war to this convent. You have no idea the power—"

"I came here to defend *you*," I replied, shielding myself from hurt.

"Sonya isn't going anywhere." Anton planted his feet wide.

The sestra's wrinkles webbed in confusion. "You said you came to warn her away."

"It's too late." He gave Dasha's head a final pat and pulled away from her. Something golden flashed to the ground as it fell from his cloak pocket. Anton didn't notice, but Dasha stooped to pick it up. "We must move inside."

"You will do no such thing," the sestra said, watching in dismay as Anton hurried past her, followed by a limping Tosya and me. "The three of you will depart at once!"

The wolves' howling multiplied. "Lock the gate with the chains," Anton commanded two soldiers. "The rest of you, come with us. Gather the weapons and barricade the door once everyone is inside. We need to hold fort until my men arrive. They're several hours behind me. I rode ahead in the night."

I took another step and felt Tosya's strength crumble the moment before his hurt leg buckled. I caught him just as he collapsed. His body was so limp I couldn't hold his weight. Anton came to assist me, and we drew Tosya's arms around our shoulders and kept advancing to the convent.

Sestra Mirna held up her hands as the remaining guards

rushed past her. "Stop! I will not condone bloodshed on these grounds."

"We don't have time to argue," Anton replied.

The wolves yapped and growled in the forest. They sounded nearer—felt nearer—as if they were just beyond the border of trees. I shuddered with the awe radiating from Dasha, a strange reaction to the wolves. I craned my neck at her. Her gaze was trapped on what was in her hands—a gold locket. She had opened it. Delicate lines of confusion formed between her brows.

"I was only ahead of my brother by a few miles," Anton said, as we dragged Tosya forward. Tosya emitted a sickly feeling, like his wound was growing infected. "I rode off the road and circled around his army. He'll be arriving any—"

A volley of distant musket fire rent the air. Sestra Mirna jolted, then grabbed Dasha's hand and ran for the convent. I glanced to the forest, where the blasts came. Each hit tore through my body and choked my breath, though I wasn't bleeding. Another musket shot rang out, followed by a low yelping. "They're killing the wolves," I said. My legs went weak as panic assaulted me. I almost dropped Tosya. "He's here."

There were too many people I loved on these grounds, too many I must somehow protect.

Heart pummeling, I turned to Anton and desperately combed his face, his aura. I hoped he had some ingenious plan. I wasn't ready. I still hadn't decided if I could be what I was born to be—a darkly gifted Auraseer, the person destined to end Valko's life. For me, the two were inextricably linked.

"Hurry!" Anton shouted, his only reply as we stumbled forward with Tosya.

Sestra Mirna and Dasha reached the convent before we did. The Sestra ran inside and slammed the door behind them. We reached the porch moments later. At the gate, two guards hefted the chain and hastened to wrap it around the bars. The men finished. Two more muskets fired, and the men dropped like toy soldiers. I doubled over on the porch steps with the reflected pain of their deaths.

Anton almost fell as I threw him off balance. He set Tosya down on the step and climbed over him to me. "Breathe, Sonya. Focus yourself. That pain isn't yours."

"I'm fine," I said between sharp gasps. The pain slowly abated.

Inside the convent, floorboards pounded as the remaining handful of soldiers ran about to gather weapons. From the forest came the thundering of Valko's advancing army. I froze, watching the trees glow as lanterns and torchlight drew nearer. Any moment now and the army would break through the clearing. The porch was fifty yards from the gate, and the gate was another fifty yards or so from the edge of the forest. Not far enough away.

"You have to get up," Anton said urgently. I snapped out of my paralysis, and we yanked Tosya back to his feet. Together, we took labored steps to the convent doors. They were locked.

I shook the latch. "Let us in!"

More muskets blasted, and we ducked our heads. The wolves' howling faded. My muscles weakened with their waning exertion. The beasts that hadn't been shot must have fled the area.

I pounded the door with my fist. Anton made a move to kick it open.

"Halt where you stand!"

Valko.

His wolf-like aura bled into mine, poison meeting poison. His energy felt several times more vicious than I'd ever sensed it, more savage and unrestrained.

"Don't make another move," he said, "or I'll order my men to kill every one of you, starting with my brother."

I glanced sidelong at Anton. He stiffened and shut his eyes.

Valko's voice carried on the night air again, resonant but relaxed, ever the marauding emperor. "Sonya, turn around—slowly. I wish to speak with you."

"Leave her be," Anton called out, low and deadly.

"Say one more word, dear governor, and I'll shoot her this very moment."

Anton's jaw muscle tensed.

"He won't kill me," I whispered. "He's come too far for that." Drawing a shaky breath, I revolved to face the forest.

Icy fear seized my heart. Our enemies were just beyond the gate. Nearly one hundred soldiers—nobility and a few ragtag peasants—stood in three battle-ready lines. Several men aimed muskets at the convent and its many windows. Others held torches high, prepared to throw them on Valko's command.

The former emperor stationed himself at the head of his army, riding an inky black stallion. Somewhere along the journey, he'd obtained fine clothes: a red kaftan with a sash of gold silk—the colors of Imperial Riaznin. At his side hung a polished saber that gleamed in the torchlight. Everything about Valko looked regal and untouched, except for his dark, windblown hair, which suited the dangerous pulse of his aura.

"Come to the gates, Sonya," he said coolly.

While my legs rooted in the ground, Nadia urged her white horse forward—Danica—bringing the mare abreast to Valko's black stallion, a position reserved for a queen.

Our gazes collided. From the distance, Nadia's scars and tattoos blotted together to form a dark smudge on the side of her face. Her aura, as ever, was void of emotion. Sestra Mirna's warning echoed through my skull, *Nadia is not your friend.* I clutched my cloak at my sides. I wanted to trust Nadia, but my doubts weighed heavy.

"Sonya," Valko beckoned again with a lazy twitch of his hand. His voice rang with false impatience. He knew I would come to him.

I floundered, unable to move. My lungs cramped as I tried to breathe. My legs were made of lead. I glanced at Valko's sheathed saber. A weapon with which he could kill himself. A stab to the gut. A slit to the throat. My stomach gave a sick twist. I couldn't tell if it was from revulsion or bloodlust.

Nadia said if I inflicted more death, it would alter me. She'd sacrificed herself to Bartek to prevent that from happening. I let her go because I knew she was right. My gaze flashed to Valko's army and their weapons. How many of them would I have to kill, too?

I stood arm-to-arm with Anton, though we faced opposite directions. His warm fingers found mine in the overlapping folds of our cloaks. At his touch, steadying calm radiated through my body.

"Listen to me," he murmured without angling his head—nothing to tip off Valko of our hushed conversation. "I didn't come here for revenge against my brother. I came here to protect you. But now I understand I can't. I never could."

My heart contracted. Surprise swept through me and made my skin tingle.

Valko dismounted his horse and passed the reins to Nadia.

"You are stronger than him." Anton squeezed my hand. "You have a power he can never wield, though he's bent on it."

Valko strode toward the gate, his hand casually resting on the hilt of his saber.

"My power is dark," I whispered, my gaze forward and unmoving. "Valko wants it because it is dark."

"You are not evil, Sonya."

Valko opened the gate—the guards had never finished locking it—and stepped over their dead bodies. He didn't deign to lower his eyes. He crossed to the midway point between the gates and the porch. There he came to a standstill and stared at me with unnerving patience. He wouldn't complete the journey to me; I would have to go to him.

I prayed to Feya. Tried to find that spark of the goddess in me that I'd felt the night Valko had abdicated. I needed divine strength.

"Thank you for believing in me," I said to Anton in parting. His hand on mine went rigid. I unwound my fingers from his grasp and descended the steps of the convent porch.

CHAPTER THIRTY-FOUR

VALKO LOOKED MAGNIFICENT AND TERRIBLE, BACKLIT BY THE torch fire of his army. As I came nearer to him down the rut-carved pathway, I saw what I hadn't before—a thin band of gold encircling his head. A crown. He'd reclaimed for himself what he aspired to be.

I determined to do the same.

I halted three feet before him and tunneled inside his aura for the means to control his emotions. Then I resisted the impulse, pressing my lips together in a hard line. I wouldn't so much as make him twitch his smallest finger. If I wished for redemption, I resolved to stifle my gift until absolutely neces-sary. I wouldn't kill Valko and his men unless he gave me no other choice.

He tilted his head. With one sweeping glance, he took in my wild and disheveled appearance—my filthy dress, mat-ted hair, Anton's fine cloak flecked with leaves and brambles.

"Don't you even have a small bow for me, dear Sonya?" His tone belonged to a different time and place, as if we stood together in the gilded ballroom of the palace and he'd just asked me to dance. "I've accomplished quite a feat since last we met."

I locked my spine erect. If this was a dance, I would not let Valko lead. "If by a feat you mean the murder of innocent guards, I won't bequeath you any honor."

He nodded as if he expected my reply, but his aura squirmed for justification. He needed my empathy like an opiate. "When a nation is at war, lives are inevitably lost. It has always been that way. Destruction is the forerunner of peace."

"You've killed your own people. Riaznin is at war with *Shengli*, not among ourselves."

"Aren't we at war? Look at you." He waved a hand up and down at me. "You're the evidence of a country divided. You cannot escape it: Riaznin is in turmoil. It needs one firm ruler—one voice—not a bickering Duma with shifting agendas."

"Riaznin is suffering because they can't reckon with the gift of their freedom, but they *do* need liberty. They've cried out for it for generations. Didn't you learn anything from the night you abdicated?"

"I learned you have a power I never dreamed existed."

I shook my head, amazed by his arrogance. "Is that why you came here, to enlist me as a weapon? You wouldn't be the first. What makes you think I would willingly join your army?"

"Let me see . . ." Valko stroked his chin in mock contemplation.

"You warned me of an assassin and *twice* you defended me in trial—the last time with a mesmerizing display of prowess. The very courtroom was speechless!" His sardonic grin slipped, and his expression softened, the lantern light pooling in his gray irises. "Is the idea that you would aid me again so farfetched?" His voice sounded warm, accepting. It was the voice of the boy in the corner of the palace stables, the same boy who curled into a ball on the cold dungeons' floor. "By your actions, I must believe you see into the reaches of me and feel burdened with heavy regret. You should have never meddled with my abdication. You *know* Riaznin was better off with me as her emperor."

"I regret many things," I replied. "But they do not extend to placing a true crown on your head." I glanced at the gold band around his brow. "Not that trinket of pretense."

"Sonya." Valko frowned, as if what I said hurt me more than him. "I've journeyed far for you. I even killed that bounty hunter you hate so much. He had his chance to bring you to me, and he failed. But no matter. I can reason with you better myself."

"You killed Bartek?" I sucked in a startled breath, then exhaled with undeniable relief.

"With my own saber," Valko replied solemnly. "And I would do the same to anyone who threatened you. Nadia told me Bartek meant to hunt you again, this time for your death, not your bounty."

I looked at Nadia behind the gate on her horse. The breeze whipped through her raven hair. What if the convent fire had triggered more than one rare ability in her? She could block her own aura, but what if she could *manipulate* an aura like I could?

"You have another Auraseer now," I said. If Nadia *did* have power and she'd turned on me, she would have confessed it to Valko in an effort to prove she was the more valuable girl. "You don't need me anymore," I baited him, hoping my suspicions were wrong about Nadia.

Valko's fingers drummed on his saber hilt. "Why can't I have more than one of you? Nadia has proven useful. For one thing, she revealed the latest development of your power, though it was very unfortunate for Countess Dyomin."

My body went rigid. Heavy stones of disappointment dropped in my stomach. Nadia had betrayed me, after all. "That was an accident," I replied. The last thing I wanted was for Valko to know I'd used my power to mete out death.

He shrugged. "Accidents often precede willful acts. I'm confident you can repeat what you did, but on a much larger scale." He shifted nearer, and I flinched. He halted with a frustrated sigh. "I'm on your side, Sonya. Can't you feel that? Together, we can stop this war and defeat Shengli. You want that as much as I do. Look how fast I'm uniting the nation!" He gestured behind him. "I have an army now. It will grow, day by day. With your power, we can do better than manipulate General Jin Pao. We can slaughter the Shenglin and ensure they never set foot in Riaznin again. Our empire will be safe, and it will be safe because of you."

My breaths quickened. My chest ached with need. I wanted to protect my homeland and those I loved within it. I longed for a great purpose equal to the great power I was given. This could be my chance to make a lasting difference.

Valko eased nearer, slower this time so I wouldn't startle. "You could *save Riaznin*, Sonya. My abdication wasn't the way to do that. *This* is—you and me, working as a team, as we always should have been."

The heady pulse of his aura merged with mine. I swayed a little on my feet, laboring to think clearly. "How can I trust you after everything you've done?"

"We've both committed terrible deeds. Who understands you better than me? Won't that understanding forge trust over time?" His eyes were so earnest, so pleading. "When I learned you had left Torchev, I asked myself, why would my brother let you go? Now it makes perfect sense. Anton is afraid of you and what your destiny could be. But I accept you for who you really are, and I need you. Riaznin needs you."

His words rang with such truth, preyed upon all my doubts and yearnings. I pictured myself at the head of Valko's army, banners waving behind us as we marched against the Shenglin. I saw thousands upon thousands falling to their deaths as I turned their bloodlust back upon themselves. My heart pounded and Valko's conviction bled into me. I believed I could be that powerful. I could spare the lives of so many of our people.

"Come, Sonya," he whispered. "Come and no one else has to die tonight."

Invisible threads pulled at my limbs, compelling me to move, follow him. I dug in my heels. Struggled to claim my own feelings and what I really believed in.

Valko was right: Riaznin *had* known more peace under the empire. Perhaps this first attempt at a democracy was a failure. But that didn't mean that Anton, Tosya, and I should stop fighting for it. Freedom and equality were rights everyone deserved. They were gifts I'd always wanted for myself. Valko's vision was the very opposite.

"No," I said, my voice breathy, just a wisp on the wind, though I'd tried to speak loudly as I fought to detach myself from his aura.

His overconfident gaze loomed down on me. He hadn't heard my word of defiance.

I clenched my shaking hands. I was so tired of him thinking he owned me. My self-belief was stronger than his pretended faith. The only part of me Valko believed in was my power. But it wasn't his. None of me was.

"No," I repeated. My voice reverberated with a growl on the night air. "Your dream is not mine. And I'd rather die fighting for a lost cause than subject myself to you ever again."

The light went hot in Valko's pale gray eyes. They smoldered like ashy coals, mirrors of the blistering rage within him. "Very well, Sonya." He sauntered back a step. "We'll do this my way." He turned to the convent porch. "Are you ready?" he called to Anton and Tosya. "I want you to pay close attention to how I win this battle."

Panic gripped me. I stole a glance over my shoulder.

Anton and Tosya stood side by side. They appeared as they had when they'd been locked together in a prison cell: two revolutionary friends, their bright dreams defeated.

"Soldiers, take aim on my brother," Valko commanded. Three men lifted their muskets.

My heart shot up my throat. "No! Stop!" I struggled to use my power, but I was too frantic to concentrate. "Kill him, and I'll march your army into the ocean, Valko. I'll compel every man to hold still while he drowns."

His brow arched. "Now there's a battle strategy I never thought of. You see what wonders we could do together?" He inched closer, flourishing a hand at himself. "What I find most fascinating is whom you said you *wouldn't* harm."

Acid flooded my body, so pure and corrosive, it could have eaten through glass. "You are not exempt from my wrath. I'll kill you first!" I trembled to control myself. Dark energy swept along my nerves, raging for release.

Valko gave a careless smirk. "Can you?" He raised his hand high and shouted to his army, "At my signal, fire!"

Time slowed. My heart crashed in percussive beats. Blood rushed through my head. I whipped around to see Anton. His eyes captured mine, his head tipped in a subtle nod. It spoke volumes. Surrender. Love.

Focus, Sonya. Save him. I gathered my emotions into a fine beam of concentration. I pulled in more energy. Felt Valko's hundred men. Their auras racked me. Despair choked my breath, fear cramped my muscles, resolve pushed my shoulders back. These men served Valko, not out of respect, but because they felt they had no better alternative for survival. I'd worn the robes of sovereign Auraseer and dedicated my life to protect him for the same reason, even when he hurt me.

As my understanding perfected, the men's auras latched to mine, bones to my bones.

With one thought, I could bend them, break them, force devastating emotions upon them.

My breath rattled in my chest. My skin flushed with fire and ice.

Now was the moment to act, now before Valko lowered his hand and decided my fate for me.

Twenty yards behind Valko, Nadia's eyes lifted to the convent. Her brows drew together with intensity and focus. Her mouth contorted, and she cast me a hard glance.

I jerked around to follow her gaze. In an upper-story window, Sestra Mirna stood frozen, hands pressed against the panes. Her eyes were wide with terror, her lips parted as if she'd meant to scream. She held her position unnaturally, as if she were sculpted in marble.

I turned back to Nadia. She *did* have power like mine. But why attack the sestra?

Valko waited until he'd reclaimed my attention. With a decisive sweep of his hand, he gave the signal to fire.

My voice ripped from my throat. "No!" I spun on my heel and raced for Anton. At the same time, I wielded my power to overtake the soldiers' auras. My arms spread wide as I threw myself into the line of fire. The door of the convent flung open. Shots rang out from behind me. I didn't duck my head. I leapt to shield Anton. A small figure darted out from the porch and launched forward.

Dasha.

I moved to throw my arms around her, but she blazed past me, her gray eyes large and wild, her aura tremendous, far surpassing her tiny frame.

I looked to the army, worried they might shoot at her. But their muskets weren't pointed at us; they were trained upward. They must have fired into the night sky.

What game was Valko playing?

Shots fired again, this time from the convent. Panic flaring, I rushed toward Dasha. Anton was safer against the convent's walls, but Dasha was out in the open.

Valko's face was a mess of confusion. "What are you doing?" he raged at his men. "I commanded you to fire—at the prince!"

The soldiers looked dumbly at their self-proclaimed monarch, but Nadia's gaze fixed on me, unrelenting and impenetrable. Had she intervened and prevented the soldiers from killing us?

"Leave us alone!" Dasha ground to a halt once she reached Valko. Her legs shook like quivering branches beneath her flapping nightgown.

Valko's eyes slowly narrowed on her. My mouth watered with his fierce hunger. His lips curved. "Well, hello, little one. I was hoping you'd sneak out to see me."

"Dasha." I grabbed the girl's hand. I had to take her to safety before guessing at Nadia's loyalties. "You must go inside. Hurry!"

A roar sprang from the forest. The underbrush crunched with trampling feet. At least a dozen shadowy figures emerged from the trees. Their arms rose with a flash of knives, nocked bows, muskets, and sabers. The convent guards.

My heart leapt. The majority of the men must have crept out of the rear gardens, then circled around to surprise Valko's army. I hadn't felt them close in—I'd been fixated on the terror at hand.

Another volley of shots rang out from the convent, and a whistling arrow struck its target. Pain radiated through me as three of Valko's men dropped in succession. Dasha gasped, also feeling their agony. Nadia's horse bucked and flung her off her saddle to the ground.

Dasha fought to wrench away from me. "Let me go!"

"They'll kill you out here!" I said. "Do you understand?"

Her eyes bulged in fright, and her resistance caved.

Nadia screamed as her horse bucked again. She rolled over in the grass, scrambling to get out of the way, but Danica's forelegs crashed down and knocked the side of Nadia's head.

Valko's army refocused. Some men rushed to reload muskets, while others turned to fight the convent guards with drawn-forth sabers, knives, and daggers.

As the battle intensified, I latched onto Dasha's aura and

instructed her to do the same. "Only let yourself feel me," I said, as we raced toward the porch. "Align your heartbeat to mine. Can you do that? Then you won't feel the pain."

She bit her lip and darted a glance up at the convent, her stomach tightening with guilt.

"Sonya!" Anton shouted. He and Tosya had obtained muskets. They aimed their barrels just a fraction behind me. "Move out of the way!"

Dasha looked over her shoulder and shrieked. I spun around, nearly colliding with the curved blade of Valko's saber. I jumped back just in time as he swiped it at me.

"You made your choice, and this is what follows." He raised his saber for another strike.

I lurched out of his reach again, throwing my arms up to shield my face.

"STOP!" Dasha railed at the top of her lungs.

The command flooded through me with such force that I felt compelled to obey. My muscles seized. My boot caught on a stone. I fell over, my limbs immobile. Unable to catch myself, I landed hard on my backside. My arms were still cast above my head, frozen in a self-protective stance. I didn't dare move. I wouldn't. Couldn't.

An eerie silence descended.

I peered through the gaps of my arms, only to find the battle as arrested as I was. The soldiers and convent guards were locked in motionless combat. If the war had continued, it was clear the guards would have been defeated. Valko's men surrounded them, ten to one, like leaden figurines on a game board. Among them, Nadia still lay unconscious on the ground.

Quiet weeping sounded from beside me, a delicate noise. The feeling behind it was powerful, shaken. Dasha's bell-tone voice trembled. "Look what you all have made me do."

Shock blazed through my statuesque body. My mind reeled to make sense of the obvious and terrible truth.

Nadia hadn't commanded anyone's will.

Dasha had.

CHAPTER THIRTY-FIVE

"Sonya." Dasha hiccupped as she wept harder.

My mouth couldn't move to speak. I desperately needed to warn her. If Dasha didn't control herself, every one of these people could die. All it would take was a careless turn of her emotions. I knew from experience.

"I feel sick," she said. "I feel everyone. But . . . they're not in me. I'm in *them*." Her voice lifted in wonder. "I don't know what to do inside them, Sonya. They're going to keep killing each other."

The soldiers and guards looked frozen in time, but their minds and auras felt pliable. They whirred and pulsed, still coherent. I'd never achieved anything on this scale.

Dasha's power was stronger than mine.

"Sonya . . ." Her small hand lighted upon my shoulder, weighing no more than a sparrow. "Say something."

Warmth rushed through my muscles, and they became

flexible. She'd set me free. I pulled my arms from my face and stared into Dasha's grief-stricken eyes. Tears clumped her dark lashes together, and her chin quivered. She trembled with abundant energy, the mass of auras bubbling within her. I should have felt pity. Instead, dark jealousy rushed through me. I craved what she felt. I could taste it through her, but I wanted it for my own.

"Don't do anything just yet," I said in what I hoped was a soothing, motherly tone. "Just breathe and focus on me."

"I can't hold them still much longer. Their bones feel like eggshell. I'm afraid I'll break them. But—" Dasha's eyes turned to Valko, standing before us, his saber caught where it had swept through the air for me, as if carved in ice.

"Look." I wrested the saber out of Valko's grasp, ignoring his shifting eyes and spidery aura. He'd overheard everything we'd said. "He can't harm us anymore." Dasha's doubt fed my own misgiving, so I guided her a few feet away from him. Anton and Tosya now had a clear shot at Valko, assuming their fingers could flinch to pull triggers again.

I gripped Dasha's arm to reclaim her attention. She winced, and I immediately eased my hold. I hadn't meant to be rough. My heartbeat stuttered. The auras she held reverberated through me, escalating my desire to seize power over them. I could end this madness, make Valko's men kill themselves.

No. I caught my dark thoughts in their tracks. I'd hesitated to use my power to begin with because I wanted to be merciful.

I had to stay true to my ideals and not surrender to hate and bloodshed. That was Valko's approach.

I inhaled a long breath, gathering my focus, and touched Dasha's shoulder. "I'm going to take control of the auras now, all right? Then you can let them go, and I'll save us."

Dasha jerked a step back. "I don't trust you. You can't have them!" Her nightgown fluttered around her shaking legs. "Your feelings keep changing, Sonya. You want to do bad things." She clutched something to her chest. The locket belonging to Anton. Its gold chain dangled from her fist.

My teeth were on edge. Dasha was beyond reasoning with. *Fine.* I'd take the auras from her by force. I stretched my awareness wide, feeling to the depths of everyone surrounding us. But when I tried to bridge a connection, I hit a wall— Dasha's unrelenting grip on their energy. I whirled on her. "Let them go."

"No." She shook her head stubbornly.

I tried to overpower her, but a pang of shock jolted through my body as she shoved me out. Flexing my jaw with impatience, I knelt beside the little girl. As soon as we were face-to-face, my heart softened. Tears filled her eyes. Her skin flushed with exertion as her brows spasmed.

A small sob escaped her. "It hurts to hold them, Sonya. But I can't give them to you."

"Dasha . . ." I felt ashamed she'd sensed my dark feelings. I felt more ashamed for having them at all. "Do you think you can make Valko's soldiers throw down their weapons? Then when you release the auras, the good people will win, and the convent will be safe."

She cast a fearful glance at the frozen battle. "I don't know how to tell everyone apart. Can't I make them *all* drop their weapons?"

"No, we must help our side." I tucked a thin strand of hair behind her ear. "If something goes wrong, we must allow our guards the ability to defend us."

"But they're killing people, too." Her lower lip jutted out. "Killing is wrong. They should be punished." Energy swelled within her into euphoric and deadly righteousness.

"Dasha—Dasha, look at me." I turned her face. "Sometimes wars need to happen and bad people must die so the good people can be safe." I inwardly cringed. How I sounded like Valko. "Now concentrate and command the former emperor's men to cast aside their weapons."

Her face reddened with anger. "I told you"—she choked on more tears—"I can't feel the difference between them. I just want them to go and leave us alone!"

"Calm yourself!" I blew out a shaky breath, fighting to take my own advice. "You must be careful where you direct your thoughts." I blinked away the image of Terezia Dyomin slitting her throat.

"Why is this happening?" Dasha pulled her hair at the scalp. "How can I do any of this?" She snuck a glance at Sestra Mirna against the upper-story window. The sestra must have been trying to prevent Dasha from coming outside. "I'm an Auraseer," she added defiantly. "I shouldn't be able to hurt people."

"You're not hurting anyone."

"But I *can* hurt them . . . I feel it."

"Don't." My voice rang too harsh. I took another deep breath. "I miss Kira." Dasha sobbed.

I dropped Valko's saber and wrapped my arms around her. She cried into the crook of my neck, her tiny body vibrating with all the trapped auras. "You're not alone. I understand you."

"You understand *everyone*. You have no choice."

"This is different . . . I'm special, like you. We're the only two people who have this gift."

Dasha stopped weeping. Her body went still, her aura suspicious. She pulled away, her gray eyes rimmed with red. "You're afraid of me."

She sounded like my long-delayed echo. I'd accused Anton of same thing to dismiss his feelings for me. "I fear for many things at this moment," I confessed. *Losing Anton, failing to defeat Valko, being unable to protect Dasha, accidentally killing a hundred men.* "But I do care for you, and I trust we can work through this together. Will you let me help?"

She deliberated. "As long as I can keep the emperor's aura. Your feelings go black whenever you look at him."

"You can sense his aura separately from those inside you?" Tonight was the second time Dasha had ever even seen Valko.

She sprang open the clasp of Anton's locket. Together, we stared at the miniature portrait of the dowager empress.

Katerina Ozerov was beautiful with Valko's gray eyes and Anton's mouth and brown hair. Her portrait exuded an air of mystery and sadness. Dasha traced the crown on her head. "Why does the emperor hate his brother?"

I released a pensive sigh. "That's a very long story. Come, Dasha. We must hurry. Give me your hands."

At last, she consented. Her wide sleeves fell back as she lifted the locket around her neck, then extended her hands to me. Our fingers touched. Nervous energy shot through my palms. I offered up a silent prayer. I had no idea what I was doing.

"Now, then," I said, adrenaline pumping, stomach knotted, "release the auras—slowly—one by one."

Dasha's trembling voice grew weary. "But I *can't* feel the difference between them!"

"That's all right. *Relax.* Just let them go, one at a time, and I'll catch them from you." I tried to make it sound like a fun game, like no lives were at stake if I lost control and the battle raged again. "I'll hold some auras and you hold some, and together we'll change the soldiers' bad feelings to good ones."

Her brows knitted in determination. Striving to bury my anxiety, I looked down at our clasped hands and knelt with her on the ground.

She summoned the first aura.

A trickle of energy shimmered through her. We were so attuned I felt it collect in her chest before she sent it away. It traveled down her arm to her hand, like a boat on a river.

Before the aura slipped to the ground, I sucked it into me. Warmth rushed up my fingertips to my shoulder, then showered energy over my body. Now freed from Dasha, the aura surged inside me with vicious intent. I wrestled with it and delved deeper to find its roots. There I found the bright pulse of righteous desire.

"These soldiers are just people like us," I told Dasha. "Some of them have loved ones they're trying to protect. Let's help them remember the goodness inside them. We'll find those feelings and make them bigger, all right? Then we can make the soldiers leave."

"I can't do that and hold everyone still!" Dasha's hands shook and made my body quiver. "They're fighting to break free." A tear rolled down her cheek. "It hurts."

"That's because you're struggling against them. Work *with* them, Dasha. And if any auras are too difficult to bear, send them to me. I'll carry them for you."

She blew out a shaky breath and sniffed, her mouth pinching in concentration. She released three more auras. As I snatched them up, I felt her wrestle with another one inside her. A few seconds later, she gasped with amazement. "I did it! He's happy now."

"Good. Don't let him go yet. Tuck his aura away and move on to more. We have to make them all happy."

We managed to bend the emotions of ten more people in the next two minutes. I could only work as fast as Dasha passed the auras to me. I tried to keep focus and not be distracted by the unnerving silence surrounding us. The soldiers and guards watched us kneeling together, though they couldn't move or say a word. Anton's gun pointed on Valko, thirty yards away, but both brothers' gazes strained in our direction. Tosya's bandaged leg dripped blood. His eyes were the only pair locked somewhere else—Nadia's unconscious body.

Another minute passed. Five more auras. Dasha's skin was pale. I felt her weakening, the heat of a fever brewing inside her, her cramping nausea and lightheadedness as her breaths went shallow. I tried not to panic. If she fainted, I'd have to catch all of her trapped auras at once.

I turned her hands over in mine, brushing my thumbs across her palms. "Stay with me, Dasha. You're a strong girl. You're doing wonderfully."

My gaze fell on the space between her wrist and elbow. My focus shattered. I didn't catch the freed aura she released. I could do nothing except stare in shock at the pinkish-brown mark on Dasha's inner forearm.

A birthmark.

Shaped like a lynx in profile, its mouth open in a snarl.

A mark matching Anton's.

The fortune he'd received from the Romska woman slammed into mind. She'd told him he would meet a girl who would change his life forever. Their two souls were fitted for each other.

Anton and I had wanted that person to be me. But the girl

in the fortune was never me, never a soul mate. She couldn't be. Dasha was a *child*.

More auras flicked down to my hands and bounced off, liberated. The grass whispered under the feet of rousing men. My heart thundered. I couldn't think past the all-encompassing thought that Dasha was a match to Anton. How?

"Sonya, I can't hold them anymore!"

I scarcely heard her. Barely felt the flood of energy rushing off my palms. Numbness overcame me. I felt senseless to even my own heartbeat. I scoured every detail of the little girl's face—things I'd neglected to see before. The aristocratic slant of her nose and her delicate upper lip, her ruler-straight brows and wolf-gray eyes, the waving texture of her sparse, dark hair.

Impossible.

The grass whispered again, this time with the intoning ring of a blade. A voice spoke, fierce and rattled. "She has your power," Valko declared.

With a start, I looked up. The gleaming end of his saber hovered between Dasha and me.

Dasha had inadvertently released Valko's aura, and I'd failed to catch it.

I couldn't process what was happening. Even as I stared down Valko's blade, my mind raced to piece together the mystery of Dasha. Who was the family she believed was her own all these years? Sestra Mirna had said they died of the ague. Was that a lie?

I didn't have all the answers, but I felt in my gut the reverberating truth—the familial strains of Dasha's aura and what people they tied to.

My mouth could only shape three words. I summoned the strength to utter them. They were my last defense against Valko.

"She's your sister."

CHAPTER THIRTY-SIX

VALKO AND DASHA TURNED WIDE EYES ON EACH OTHER. HIS gaze dropped to the birthmark she shared with Anton, the locket she wore with the empress's portrait in it.

Anton's wonder peaked, his energy catapulting toward them. Shocked, Dasha jerked her hands out of mine. The rest of the auras avalanched out of her. She crashed to her knees as her power gave way. The battle resumed. Muskets blasted. Men roared, shouting in agony. They thudded to the ground. I felt none of their pain. I was too latched onto Dasha and Valko and Anton.

Siblings, the three of them.

Anton unfroze and pulled the trigger. The musket shot whizzed past Valko's head.

Valko yanked up Dasha by her nightgown and set his saber to her neck. "Hold your fire!" he yelled at Anton. "Unless you want to see our sister die." My heart drummed with Valko's, though he didn't feel my same astonishment. I was still grappling to believe the truth.

Fear and helplessness chased through Anton. He lowered his musket. Tosya did the same. Dasha whimpered. She'd spent her strength and hung like a rag doll.

"I'm doing this to protect you," Valko told her. "We're leaving together." He slowly backed her toward the gate, his words spilling in a feverish rush. "You're a princess, Dasha. I suspected it the moment I saw you in the courtroom. You seemed the right age. It corresponds to a time my mother—our mother—went missing in my life, too ill to visit." He gave a wry laugh. "Our parents were known to keep marvelous secrets. This one of Mother's tops them all. You look so much like her, you know. But your skin . . . well, clearly Emperor Izia wasn't your father."

I held utterly still, paralyzed by a spell of my own making. *Valko already knew.* He hadn't only come to the convent seeking me. Maybe I'd never been his ultimate target.

"You should have never been in this place," Valko said to his sister, steadily dragging her backward. "You're royalty. Who would have guessed the Ozerovs would share blood with an Auraseer? I always knew we deserved such power."

"My parents are dead," Dasha croaked, scarcely breathing with the blade against her neck. "Their whole village is dead." I felt her struggling to overpower Valko's will, but she was too weak, too undecided, too torn with the possibility that she had a living family—brothers.

"Are your parents *really* dead?" Valko's gaze flicked between me, Anton, and the gate. "What if that is a lie? Why don't we travel to your village and find out? Would you like that?"

Valko's offer was sincere, and Dasha felt it. She leapt at the desperate hope he dangled before her like a starved pup. "Yes," she answered, her voice ringing clear.

I didn't dare move with her life at stake, but, past my shock, I finally found my voice. "He's not your friend or your master, Dasha. We aren't meant to serve him any longer. He's the emperor of nothing!"

Dasha's eyes shone, though they were heavy with weariness. "He can help me find my family. Maybe he *is* my family."

"Anton is also your brother."

She looked to Anton, her mouth twisting in indecision—a gesture that was so distinctly *him*.

Turning to him, I swallowed. "She bears your mark." My pain eased as I watched his face fill with radiant hope. His aura expanded to make room for it. What he'd wanted from childhood—a loving and secure family—was finally within reach.

"Dasha." He trembled over her name, like it was new to him, precious. But his dilemma was the same as mine: what could he do to keep her here? "Valko, let her go," he demanded. "Don't drag an innocent child into war."

"War?" Valko repeated lightly, his saber fast on Dasha's neck. He reached the gate and threw it open. His army rampaged behind him. Men fell in bloody heaps upon the ground. "Why, I'm taking her from it, far away from here." He chose his words carefully so they resonated with truth. Dasha couldn't decipher his honesty from his deception.

"Sonya." Anton's eyes cut across the convent grounds to me. My breath hitched with the force of his grave and dire emotions. "Stop my brother," he pleaded, his voice pitched low and deadly. "Don't let him take her away."

I understood what he was really saying: *Finish what I tried to do. Use your power and kill him.*

My muscles tensed. I felt ever strung taut between the two brothers. If I let Valko take Dasha, he would use her to win his war. She was young and moldable. He would poison her mind and pit her against Anton and me.

I couldn't let Valko steal her away.

My heart pounded as I made a choice. I prayed I wouldn't lose myself to the darkness of my power if I channeled it to exact death.

Valko's grip tightened around his saber hilt. His gaze seared to mine as he yanked Dasha backward. He was ready for me.

He whistled for his black stallion. The horse bounded forward, dodging the mayhem of the battle.

I aligned myself with Dasha's aura and absorbed it inside me. I couldn't let her interfere with what I was about to do, and she didn't have the strength to resist me this time.

I opened my arms wide, feeling our combined energy pulse along my veins. My body thrummed and vibrated. Our hearts beat the same rhythm.

Breathing deeply, I turned my fiery gaze on Valko. His aura

collided against mine in challenge. He still believed I'd do what I'd always done—spare his life. He placed one foot in the stirrup of his stallion. His saber never lowered from Dasha's neck. He watched me, unsure how to make his next move.

I burrowed into his energy. Matched myself to its dark, impassioned fluctuations. I'd always understood Valko. He never measured up to his father or was loved by him, just like I could never be good enough for Sestra Mirna. Valko cared for his mother, but she abandoned him as a child, while my parents gave me up to the Romska.

Just when I feared the hollow feeling in my chest would eat through me, I quivered with burning anger. We had even more in common. Valko had learned not to trust his family, while I learned never to depend on a home. Valko loathed Anton, Anton threatened Valko's claim to the throne, more people admired Anton than Valko. I was more like the brother I hated than the brother I loved. Anton possessed qualities Valko lacked—calm poise under pressure, prevailing intellect, compassion, and an unrivaled sense of duty. Valko detested his own shortcomings—a hot temper, being ruled by emotions, and his cowardice masked by arrogance.

I grasped that hate in him and held it in the tight fist of my power. I inflated the loathing and turned it into formidable self-hatred.

Valko's eyes flashed wide. He realized what I was doing a second before I'd sealed the feeling inside him. He flung his saber several yards away. He knew how I'd killed Terezia.

The battle continued to rage in mayhem. Valko leapt onto his horse and pulled Dasha up with him. His movements slowed as abhorrence overcame him. His face drew heavy, bitterly sad. With great effort, he took up the reins. Dasha sat limply in his lap, flopped back against him. Clammy perspiration coated her brow.

I panicked, rethinking my plan. I hadn't fully seized control of Valko.

Anton's aura snapped with urgency. He jumped off the convent porch, hurriedly reloading his musket as he bolted for his brother.

Valko's eyes were accepting. *Do it*, he seemed to say.

One of Valko's soldiers attacked Anton, knocking the musket out of his hands. The soldier kicked him to the ground and lifted his dagger to stab him.

"Anton!" I cried.

My fragile hold on Valko's aura slipped as I redirected my power. I captured the soldier's energy and turned his wrath into pity. He dropped his dagger. Anton grabbed the man by the legs, sending him toppling, then scrambled over the soldier and punched him hard in the jaw. "I'm fine, Sonya!" He struck the man again. "Stop Valko!"

My heart hammered. Valko had turned his horse about-face to ride away.

"Wait!" I ran nearer so only twelve yards separated us. As I reclaimed Valko's aura, he pulled back his reins. "Turn around," I commanded, breathing heavily. "You came all this way. This might be the last time we ever meet. Do you really want to leave without saying good-bye?"

I found the strings of Valko's obsession with me. I yanked them, forcing the feeling to grow larger. For once, I would use his lust against him. "We've shared so much together. I was so much more than your sovereign Auraseer. You confided in me. You gave up alliances for me."

Valko's shoulders rose and fell with a shudder. He pulled his stallion around and beheld my face. All the tenderness he'd ever felt for me, all the ownership, all his oppressive desire collected in his hungry but lamenting gray eyes. "Good-bye, Sonya," he said.

"Yes, this is good-bye." I stepped closer, chin lifted. "Soon I will never have to taste your foul aura again."

He flinched. Musket fire railed on my ears. Cries and shouts surged together like a roaring waterfall. Deathblows ricocheted off of my awareness. I was impenetrable to anyone else's pain. Every last ounce of my strength targeted on the boy looking down at me, his possessive grip on his newfound, powerful sister.

"Do you know why you really hate yourself?" I asked, twisting the ravenous pulse in his aura back to self-loathing. "Because you can never fully overpower me. You failed to kill me the same night I persuaded you to cast off your crown. I bent your verdict in your favor, but I also banished you. I didn't join you in your clever plan to manipulate the Shenglin general. And now, after you've tried to demonstrate you can unite Riaznin, I still didn't commit."

Valko's emotions spiraled downward in terrible disillusionment. A vein throbbed on his forehead, and betrayal and hurt glistened in his eyes.

"You must feel so defeated," I said. "If you can't win over the one person you thought understood you, how can you win over all of Riaznin? Give up the fight, Valko. It's over."

He blinked twice at me, eyes wide and distraught, his aura riding every wave of dark emotion I fed him. I turned the waters darker, more tumultuous. I made them deadly, as well—too powerful to overcome.

I looked to the nearest soldier, a young man with blond hair slicked into a ponytail. "You," I called, "with the flintlock pistol." He took cover behind his horse as he prepared to fire upon a convent guard. I captured his fear and twisted it into docility. "Your master is in need of a weapon." I could have passed him my crystal dagger, but I wanted this quick and clean.

The soldier bowed his head and crossed the few yards to Valko. He lifted the pistol like a goblet on a serving tray.

"Go on." I told Valko calmly. "You'll feel steadier with it in your hand."

He wrapped his fingers around the grip of the gun.

Clear purpose filled my breast. My lips twitched into a righteous smile. I felt godlike. Justified. Valko would pay for his crimes here and now, and I would not weep with regret.

"Your father was brave enough to slay himself to spare his empire. Are you strong enough to be your father's son?"

He set the pistol against the side of his skull. Tears surfaced in his eyes. He didn't look away from me.

All the sounds of the battle seemed to silence on my ears. My vision narrowed as I blocked out everyone else, only Valko. My heart rocked with heavy thuds. I heard the intake and purging of my breath. My knees rattled, hands flexed. I felt miserable, vile. I desperately wanted all of this to be over. For Valko to be over. All I had to do was make him feel the same, send him one last vicious feeling, and then he would fire on himself. Without a leader, his soldiers would retreat. Dasha would be free.

My mouth opened to speak, but then my gaze dropped to the little girl in Valko's arms.

Dasha's face was tearstained, her large eyes round with terror. She was staring at me—afraid of *me*. I was the only other person with her gift, and I was showing her how to kill with it.

My brow twitched. Knees shook harder. I wavered in indecision.

When I couldn't lift my voice, Valko raised his own. "I guess this is where you and I end, Sonya." Something about his gaze wrenched through my heart.

He cocked the pistol hammer.

Flipped his wrist toward me.

Fired.

Pain burst through my gut. My mouth gaped open. I stumbled backward from the blow.

"Sonya!" My name skittered around my skull. Anton's terrified voice.

I pressed a hand to my stomach. It throbbed like pulsing fire. Every beat of my heart made it worse. My fingers drenched with warmth. I looked down. A rush of blood soaked the cloth of my violet dress.

This wasn't someone else's pain. This wasn't another person's radiating deathblow.

This was mine.

I understood. Valko didn't need me anymore. He had Dasha.

I heard her cry as I crumpled to my knees. I couldn't look at her. My gaze fastened to my bloody hands.

Thundering hooves sounded as Valko rode away, followed by his army.

My gut convulsed. Crimson pooled the earth beneath me. Dizziness seized me, and I keeled over to the ground. My head slammed against a hard rock. My vision blackened, bursting with stars.

"Sonya!"

Anton raced over and crashed to his knees beside me. He pulled me into his arms. I blinked up at his desperate, terror-stricken eyes.

I heard my name again. A woman's voice this time. It clanged against my fading hearing. Sestra Mirna swam into view. Shocked wrinkles splayed across her brow.

She wrested my hands away from my stomach, gasped, and placed her own hands on my wound. A terrible pressure bore down on my gut. I cried out with agonizing pain. More stars showered across my vision.

My eyes fluttered closed to the picture of Valko's army scattering into the dark forest. I had failed.

CHAPTER THIRTY-SEVEN

HORRIFYING PAIN. A DARK ROOM. THE BOUNCING LIGHT OF a candle. Shadowy figures hovering over me. My gut on fire as I thrashed in bed and screamed. A cup pressed to my mouth. Choking on a bitter drink. My agony abating. Numbness. Blackness. Dreams. Nightmares.

A little girl with gray eyes. Dark and wispy hair. A princess's crown. Another crown for the woman beside her. No ability to move. "Your power is magnificent, Dasha. Look how you hold Sonya captive." Hands pulling out hair. "I can kill her, too, Mother. She taught me."

Blackness. Daylight. Nakedness. A forest pool by a waterfall. Paddling to stay afloat. Another girl with me. Her tattooed, burned face. "I am not your friend." My head pushed underwater. Screaming a spray of bubbles. A flood of crimson. My stomach bleeding uncontrolled.

The convent infirmary. Inconceivable pain. Anton. Tosya.

Sestra Mirna. Blurred vision. Another press of a cup. More bitterness burning down my throat. An opiate?

Valko. The edge of a cliff. Wind whipping through our hair. An abyss of nothingness below. My voice. "I can make you jump." His voice. "I can make *you*." His hand on my hand. A pull. A leap. Falling together. Into the black.

The pulse of nothingness like a living thing. Only my feelings here. No others inside me. Trying to hide. Being found. By me. Only my feelings, only my feelings. *You lost Dasha. Valko will ruin her. He'll destroy Riaznin with her power.*

"You tried your best, Sonya. It isn't your fault. Please know I don't blame you."

Anton. Hearing but not seeing him in the dark. A warm hand on my cheek. His scent, musk and pine. "I wish I could bear your suffering." His baritone voice attempting to whisper. "You're always forced to hold everyone else's."

A growing light, but still blind.

"Sestra Mirna says you will live. Please understand why I have to go."

His scent fading. His touch gone. Blackness. Only my feelings.

❦

Something pried against my lips. Not a cup, a spoon. Warmth poured into my mouth. It wasn't bitter. I liked the taste. I opened my eyes.

The infirmary was the same as I remembered. Tiled floor, a hearth, three beds, stone walls like the rest of the convent. From the yellowy light spilling into the windows, it must be morning. The last time I'd been in this room, Yuliya had just died.

My chest fell heavy, and I drew back my gaze. Someone shifted at my bedside. Nadia.

I startled and jerked upright. Splitting pain racked my stomach. I sucked in a harsh breath.

"Calm down, Sonya." Nadia forced me back against my pillows. "You've been in and out of consciousness for nine days. You're in no state to try to run away from me."

Eyes wild and wide-awake, I stared at her. Nadia's hair fell in raven waves, catching hues of red in the sunlight from the infirmary window. She had an easy expression about her face, as if we were the best of friends. We weren't. I remembered everything from the night Valko shot me. Nadia had betrayed me to him. Apparently, he'd left her behind. That gave me a small measure of satisfaction.

"Don't look at me like that." She fed me another spoonful of vegetable broth. I drank it begrudgingly, starved for food. "I suppose you think I should apologize because you almost died. I won't." She gave a light shrug. "I tried to warn the emperor about you. Your power could have gotten him killed. *I* would have been a better servant. But Valko only wanted your power more than ever. And now he doesn't need either of us. How perfect is that?" Her smile thinned as she brought the spoon to my mouth a third time.

"He never needed you." I shoved the spoon away. The broth spilled onto my blanket, but I didn't care. "You *lied* to me."

Nadia hadn't felt Bartek creep up on us at the forest pool. I'd sensed every danger in our travels before she had—she'd just been echoing *my* reactions. "The trauma from the convent fire did more than cause your aura to stop emitting; your ability to *sense* aura is also gone."

Nadia stiffened, eyes narrowing. A sneer pulled her mouth taut. "Finally," she said, falsely pleased. "It's taken you ages to put two and two together."

"Did you really think you could become Sovereign Auraseer in a reborn empire?" My voice was weak and hoarse, but I packed all my scorn into it.

"My gift will come back. I'm not done healing."

"You're delusional."

"I'm determined. It's better than being careless and changeable like you."

I couldn't bear to look at her anymore. I angled slightly away and pressed a hand to my stomach. Beneath the bed sheet, I felt a tight bandage wrapped around me. "What does Tosya think of you now that you've turned on us?"

"I wouldn't describe it as turning on you." Another spoonful of broth met my lips. I swallowed, too tired to fight her any longer. "Tosya and I haven't spoken, but his actions speak stronger than words. He protected me from being trampled when the emperor's army retreated. I owe him my life." Nadia absently stirred the broth, her gaze downcast. "Now that he's mended and had a taste for being a hero, he wants more adventure, I suppose."

My head prickled with a rush of numbness. For a moment, I forgot what we were talking about. The bitter opiate I'd been given earlier must not have fully worn off.

The door to the infirmary opened. Sestra Mirna stepped inside. I blinked hazily at her. I already felt myself on the verge of falling back to sleep under the spell of the drugs.

"What are you doing in here?" she snapped at Nadia. "Sonya needs to rest."

Nadia turned to me and rolled her eyes. "I better be off." She tipped another spoonful of broth into my mouth. "But I did mean to tell you"—her voice lowered to a faint whisper as she leaned closer—"I picked the lock of the chest of records in the library."

My vision went fuzzier. Half of Nadia's face was a dark, swirling blur of tattoos and scars.

"I discovered the name of my mother."

Past my dulling senses, my heart gave a pang of dread.

"Leave now, Nadia," Sestra Mirna commanded. Her shoes clipped against the tiles as she advanced.

Nadia's mouth moved to my ear. "Terezia Dyomin."

I stopped breathing. My wounded stomach quivered as all my muscles cramped.

Nadia pulled back and observed my reaction. Her expression changed infinitesimally—a sliver of a lifted brow, a razor-fine sharpening of her eyes, a tickle of a curling lip. I couldn't sense her aura to be certain, but I felt viciously threatened, hated— more than I'd ever been in my life, even by her.

"Don't go looking for your crystal dagger," she whispered. "It belongs in the family, wouldn't you agree?" She stood, collecting her bowl and spoon, and raised her voice. "I can't wait to visit you again."

"You will do so with my permission next time." Sestra Mirna's brow creased in a rash of hard lines.

Nadia gave a little curtsy and glided out of the room, ever swanlike and elegant.

My gut spasmed as I exhaled. I winced, holding my stomach tight. Nadia was gone, but I still wasn't safe. Not at the convent. Not with her under the same roof. Dizziness racked my head.

"Relax, child." Sestra Mirna sat beside me. "Breathe and try not to tear your stitches."

I curled my legs beneath me, frantically trying to get up without using my stomach muscles. I had to run. Leave here. "Nadia wants to hurt me."

Sestra Mirna held me still. "There, there. Nadia's spitefulness has been a plague to us all, but she can't do you any real harm."

"You don't know what she's capable of!" Nadia wanted me dead. She'd practically said as much by stealing by dagger. *Feya, forgive me. I really did kill her mother.*

"Did you see what Anton left for you?" Sestra Mirna's voice was kind, like she was trying to distract me. She stood and walked around my bed to a small table beside it. "You should admire this before it wilts."

She placed a delicate crown of red poppies on my lap. I stopped squirming. My heart thudded slower. My mind felt sluggish and muddled. I couldn't remember why I'd been so panicked just seconds ago. I gazed at the wreath. No white hawthorns were woven in with the flowers; those only bloomed at Kivratide. But this crown was even more beautiful.

"He's gone, isn't he?" I asked sadly, touching one of the petals with shaking fingers.

"Anton left this morning with Tosya and a company of soldiers. He commanded the other half of his army to stay here and guard the convent." Sestra Mirna paused when I didn't say anything. "He came to say good-bye, don't you remember?"

I gave a little nod, pressing my lips together. My chest grew tight and heavy. I didn't know if Anton and I would ever meet again, or if he'd truly forgiven me for all I'd done. I hadn't only betrayed him in Torchev; I'd also failed to save his sister from his brother.

I glanced up at Sestra Mirna. Tears fell down my cheeks. I'd failed her, too. "I'm so sorry about Dasha."

She sat beside me once more. "You should rest now. Your face is flushed. You've overexerted yourself."

"Please forgive me."

She looked at me with helpless eyes. "I'm to blame, child, not you. I should have given Dasha to the tribes after the empire fell. I had no right to be her guardian when her . . ." She shook her head.

I stared blankly at her.

"But the Romska only take—" I thought of Dasha's coloring, a lighter shade of the nomads' brown skin. I thought of her enhanced ability that marked her as an Auraseer descended from the tribes, like me. Then there was the Romska chief, Motshan, a king of his own people. I couldn't think of another tribesman who would have the boldness to act on his feelings for an empress. "Motshan is Dasha's father."

Sestra Mirna frowned. "I never told a soul."

I shook my head. "I know he helped the empress travel in secret to visit her sons."

The sestra released a sigh that seemed years in the making. "Motshan doesn't know he has a child, and Katerina wanted to keep it that way. The empress wouldn't tell me her reasons, not even when she came back from time to time to visit her daughter."

I recalled how captivated Dasha had been by the miniature portrait in Anton's locket.

"Dasha never knew, of course, that Katerina was her mother or the *empress*."

I was too weak to be surprised by these revelations. After being shot by Valko, not much else had the power to shock me anymore. Dasha being half Romska and half royalty made perfect sense. I only wished I had discovered both secrets much sooner. Anton or Motshan could have helped protect Dasha. *I* could have.

A forceful wave of fatigue hit me. My head slumped sideways on my pillow. I struggled to stay awake. I had so many questions for Sestra Mirna. Did she know Dasha would be powerful when she was born? Why had the empress given her daughter to the convent instead of taking her to some hidden manor, like her sons? Was Dasha's illegitimacy the only reason?

My eyelids fell closed. My mind was going black with sleep. "Sestra Mirna?" I mumbled.

She took my hand. I'd never felt such gentleness in her touch. "Yes, child?"

My tongue felt thick. I tripped over my words. "I know you . . . you're only letting me stay here because I'm injured."

She rubbed my hand, not denying it.

"Once I'm better, I promise to . . ."

The sestra gently jostled me awake. "You promise to what?"

I struggled to focus. "I'll save Dasha. I'm the only person who can. I'll save Kira, too. I promise to save all of us."

I'd also find a way to save Riaznin. *Without* Valko. I'd join Anton and redeem myself.

The sestra's wrinkled face blurred before me. My heartbeat slowed, along with my breathing. The opiates in my bloodstream kept dragging me downward. I couldn't fight sleep much longer.

"Look at me, Sonya." Sestra Mirna squeezed my hand. "I want to tell you something before you rest."

The earnestness in her voice forced my eyes to crack open. Motes of shimmering dust floated like golden embers above her head. She looked like an ancient goddess, or at least the last stalwart protector of Riaznin's Auraseers, which she was.

"I prayed for you, Sonya, after you left the convent and were taken to the palace. I prayed for you even after I buried what was left of your sister Auraseers. You were obstinate and wild, but I never gave up hope that you might find yourself."

I studied the drooping slant of her eyes, wondering if her gaze held sorrow. "I *did* find myself," I assured her. "I know what my purpose is now." At least I had a start.

She touched my cheek in the way a mother might do, the way mine might have. "That is all I wished for, child. I do care for you. I always have, even if you haven't had the skill to decipher it."

I blinked, unsure I understood her. I never expected the sestra to utter words of affection, far less so words that hinted at forgiveness.

Past my bleary senses, I reached to grasp the depths of her feelings. I searched for the strength of familial love, the grief of painful memories, the hope of a peaceful relationship, the sympathy for my good intentions despite my tragic failings. I waited for my heart to quicken or my blood to warm, for my lungs to ease open or my nerves to prick with the resonating pulse of Sestra Mirna's aura.

I frowned, trying harder, but I still wrestled to decipher her emotions. My brain felt heavy. "How many doses of opiates did you give me? They're dulling my senses."

Her wrinkles lifted in an arching pattern of concern. "I haven't given you any since yesterday. The opiates were worsening the effects of your head injury. You hit that rock hard after you were shot. I was afraid you might never wake up."

Panic set in. My fingers tightened on my flower crown. Some of the red petals broke off onto my lap. "What did Nadia put in my broth?" I asked sharply.

The sestra's wrinkles crisscrossed in confusion. "Nothing. I prepared the broth myself and brought it to your bedside. Nadia stole in here while I went to speak with the soldiers about keeping quiet below your window. If you're sleepy, it's because of your head. Between your concussion and your musket shot, it's a miracle you're alive."

My fingers curled tighter. More petals dotted my blanket with red. I gasped for breath. I couldn't find it. I panted, clawed at my chest, fighting to inhale, exhale.

"Sonya!" She stood and gripped my shoulders. "What's wrong? Is your wound hurting? I'll give you the opiate if you need it."

I gazed up at her, completely ungrounded. The world fell off its axis. I had no bearings. Felt no radiating pulse from Sestra Mirna's aura.

I thrashed in my bed. My poppy crown knocked to the floor. The stitches in my stomach pulled. The pain was nothing next to the horror pressing down on me.

I fought to concentrate. Stretch myself. It was no use. There was only blindness. Suffocation. Numbness. Of feeling. Of all I knew.

A void surrounded the sestra. Impenetrable. And it was widespread. I knew it. I felt it in the deafness of the convent. The soldiers' clatter rang up to my window, but I sensed none of their flickering energy. This was a thousand times worse than being unable to sense Nadia's aura. She was just one person.

"Sonya, you must tell me what is the matter!" Sestra Mirna grasped my chin and forced my gaze on her. She was a beacon in a storm-tossed sea. I couldn't feel her, but she was here, she was trying to help me.

I found breath. It filled my lungs. I used it to support my shaking voice.

"I can't sense you." Tears streaked down my cheeks. "I—I sense no one."

My throat ached with despair. My chest collapsed, bearing down weight on my heart.

My identity shattered, a mirror broken in a thousand pieces.

"I'm no longer an Auraseer."

ACKNOWLEDGMENTS

My deep gratitude goes to:

My publisher, Katherine Tegen, and her team at Harper-Collins, including my publicist, Ro Romanello, and book designer, Amy Ryan. They make me feel so at home, especially my "emperor editor," Maria Barbo, and her assistant, Rebecca Aronson, who worked tirelessly to help me unravel the story I wanted to write.

My agent, Josh Adams, and his wife, Tracey, at Adams Literary, for compassion and endless support.

Jason, whose perseverance inspires me to write true heroes. My children, Isabelle, Aidan, and Ivy. You are my #1 dream.

My besties, Sara B. Larson, Emily R. King, and Erin Summerill, for a safe place to cry, whine, laugh, celebrate—and get this story right! Ilima K. Todd, Robin Hall, and Emily Prusso. You are my second family. Kate Coursey, Amie Kaufman, Michelle Argyle, Jenny Cole, and Amanda Davis, for being true friends.

My readers. Your love for my reckless empath is a gift to me.

My mother. The world's best cheerleader and pure in heart.

My father. I dedicated this book to you the day after you passed away. Your life wasn't long enough, but it was filled with charity and purpose. You poignantly understood my struggle to write this story, so your encouragement was what I needed most. I love you, Daddy, and I miss you terribly. Until we meet again.

And to God for His grace. Prayers work, even for novelists.